Intuitive Digital
Computer Basics

McGraw-Hill
Series in Intuitive IC Electronics

This series will help the reader gain an intuitive understanding of electronics and computers. Mathematics is kept to a minimum, as the reader gets "inside" the devices and circuits to grasp, from the electron level up, the workings of integrated circuits, digital computers, operational amplifiers, and other electronics-related topics. The following volumes are planned for the series, and each one is written by Thomas M. Frederiksen, whose Intuitive IC Electronics *(McGraw-Hill, 1982) has proved popular with engineers, managers, students, and hobbyists worldwide.*

INTUITIVE DIGITAL COMPUTER BASICS: An Introduction to the Digital World (1988)

INTUITIVE ANALOG ELECTRONICS: From Electron to Op Amp (1988)

INTUITIVE OPERATIONAL AMPLIFIERS: From Basics to Useful Applications (1988)

INTUITIVE CMOS ELECTRONICS: The Revolution in VLSI, Processing, Packaging, and Design (1989)

INTUITIVE IC ELECTRONICS, Second Edition (1989)

Intuitive Digital Computer Basics

An Introduction to the Digital World

Thomas M. Frederiksen

McGraw-Hill Book Company

New York St. Louis San Francisco Auckland
Bogotá Hamburg London Madrid Mexico
Milan Montreal New Delhi Panama
Paris São Paulo Singapore
Sydney Tokyo Toronto

Library of Congress Cataloging-in-Publication Data

Frederiksen, Thomas M.
   Intuitive digital computer basics: an introduction to the
digital world/Thomas M. Frederiksen.
       p. cm. – (The McGraw-Hill series in intuitive IC
electronics)
   Includes index.
   ISBN 0-07-021964-8   ISBN 0-07-021965-6 (pbk.)
   1. Electronic digital computers.   I. Title.   II. Series.
TK7885.F74 1988
621.39–dc19   87-26471
                                                             CIP

Copyright © 1988 by McGraw-Hill, Inc. All rights reserved.
Printed in the United States of America. Except as permitted
under the United States Copyright Act of 1976, no part of this
publication may be reproduced or distributed in any form or by
any means, or stored in a data base or retrieval system, without
the prior written permission of the publisher.

1234567890 DOC/DOC 8921098

ISBN 0-07-021964-8 {HC}

ISBN 0-07-021965-6 {SC}

*The editors for this book were Daniel A. Gonneau and Nancy
Young, the designer was Naomi Auerbach, and the production
supervisor was Richard A. Ausburn. It was set in Century
Schoolbook. It was composed by the McGraw-Hill Book Company
Professional & Reference Division Composition Unit.*

Printed and bound by R. R. Donnelley & Sons Company

> Information contained in this work has been obtained by
> McGraw-Hill, Inc. from sources believed to be reliable.
> However, neither McGraw-Hill nor its authors guarantees
> the accuracy or completeness of any information published
> herein and neither McGraw-Hill nor its authors shall be
> responsible for any errors, omissions, or damages arising out
> of use of this information. This work is published with the
> understanding that McGraw-Hill and its authors are supply-
> ing information but are not attempting to render engineer-
> ing or other professional services. If such services are re-
> quired, the assistance of an appropriate professional should
> be sought.

This book is dedicated to the memory of Emily Frederickson, formerly of Advanced Micro Devices and Signetics.

Contents

Preface ix
Acknowledgments xiii

Chapter 1. Some Preliminary Topics — 1

What Makes Up the World? — 1
Dealing with Very Large and Very Small Numbers — 10
Handling the Calculations that Aid Understanding — 12
The Displays of Three-, Three-and-a-Half, and Four-Digit Voltmeters — 15
What Is an Electronic Circuit? — 16
Getting Familiar with the Lab Kit — 17

Chapter 2. Voltage: The Pressure of the Electrons — 21

Cells and Batteries — 22
Ways to Pump Up Electrons: The Generation of Electricity — 25
Measuring DC Voltages — 29
Determining the Voltage Needed to Operate a Relay — 34

Chapter 3. Circuit Components Operating with Direct Current — 39

Resistors: To Resist Current Flow — 39
Current: The Intensity of the Electron Flow — 56
Power: Whenever a Current Flows — 64
Capacitors: The Capacity to Store Electrons — 67
Piezoelectric Quartz Crystals: The Frequency References — 89
Diodes: The Two-Terminal One-Way Devices — 91
Transistors: The Three-Terminal On-Off Amplifying Devices — 99
The Silicon-Controlled Rectifier — 110

Chapter 4. Learning to Think Digital — 113

Fitting Things into a Two-State World — 113
Doing It with Logic — 120
Codes that Aren't Secret — 137
Some Logic Circuits — 146
Flip-Flops: The Circuits that Remember — 161

Communicating in Digitalese	177
Thanks for the Memory	182
Looking at the Output of a Computer	189
A Computer for All Reasons	193

Chapter 5. The Techniques of Digital Computers   197

How to Make Logic Circuits Compute	197
A Basic Computer	207
Computer Architectures	228
Programming: The Software Some Find Hard	231

Chapter 6. A Look into the Future   241

Gate Arrays and Beyond	241
Interconnecting Computers	242
The Electronic Office	243
The Electronic Home	244
Artificial Intelligence	245
Here Come the Robots	246

Index   247

Preface

We are in the midst of the computer age. Everyone is aware of it: Some like it, many detest it, and a few think it is necessary to enhance productivity to allow the survival of western culture. The revolution in computer costs, from extremely high to almost free within a short span of approximately 20 years, has caught many by surprise. What is this all about? Why now, and what does the future look like? While many are speculating, even more cannot comprehend all of this technology and are almost completely without an understanding or an appreciation of what is happening. A new vocabulary has appeared. Businesses and jobs are rapidly changing. There are even new electronic computer games for your leisure time. Handling data is suddenly important. The need for communication is increasing. Home computers and even hand-held computers are common. But still, what is it all about—and why now?

The purpose of this book is to provide an intuitive insight for the nonelectronic reader into this explosive computer revolution. No prior training is assumed in digital electronics. The new words, including those used in this preface, will be defined and examples will be given. The lack of this vocabulary can cause intimidation for those who must interact with engineers.

To assist the learning process, a lab experience is included that incorporates a commercially available electronic projects kit and a digital multimeter. These provide a hands-on experience with electronic components and digital circuits and make a major contribution to the understanding of each chapter of this book.

The early chapters provide background material on electronic components and electronic measurements. Some preliminary topics are presented in Chapter 1 to introduce things like elements, basic atomic structure, chemical reactions, and the solid state of a silicon crystal— the key to semiconductors. In addition, the scientific way to work with both very large and very small numbers is presented, along with the common metric system prefixes, to aid in understanding calculations (that can be made on the simplest four-function calculators). This chapter ends with an overall description of the electronic projects kit which serves as the lab kit for the experiments in the book.

Chapter 2 considers voltage, the basic ways to generate electricity, and how to set up the digital multimeter to measure voltages. An experiment is then described to determine the voltage necessary to actuate the relay that is available in the lab kit.

Circuit components, such as resistors, capacitors, diodes, and transistors, along with current flow, power, and Ohm's law, are presented in Chapter 3. To better understand resistors, an experiment shows how to make a carbon film resistor and a potentiometer using a pencil line on a piece of paper. This resistor is then measured and the operation of a potentiometer is also demonstrated using the multimeter.

Digital concepts are introduced and nibbles, bytes, words, and long words are defined in Chapter 4. The binary number system is introduced as "counting, using only your thumbs." Many of the standard digital codes, such as two's complement, binary-coded decimal, hexadecimal, and the American Standard Code for Information Interchange (ASCII), are explained. Analog-to-digital and digital-to-analog convertors are introduced as encoding and decoding devices.

The operation of logic gates is presented, an example of the use of logic circuits is given, and both bipolar and simulated CMOS logic circuits are constructed using the components of the lab kit. This demonstrates the reasons for the low-power benefits of CMOS logic circuits. Flip-flops are described and a 2-bit ripple counter, complete with a display of the count, is then made with the lab kit.

Both serial and parallel digital communication are described, output devices (displays, printers, and plotters) are discussed, and the many basic types of computers are presented.

All of the useful types of memory devices are covered, from the bulk memories to the read-only memories (ROM), programmable read-only memories (PROM), the random access memories (RAM), and the new electrically erasable and reprogrammable (E^2PROM) memories. Finally, the concept of a register is introduced both as a part of, and as a form of, memory.

The techniques used in digital computers are the subject of Chapter 5. How logic circuits can be used to add two binary numbers and an algorithmic way to multiply are described. The function of the internal "calculator" for the computer, the arithmetic and logic unit (ALU), is then introduced. Microcodes, internal buses, and internal clocks are described so a "feeling" can be obtained for all of the simple internal steps that a computer must go through to execute a single instruction of a program.

A basic computer is then discussed and the internal operation is indicated using simplified examples that illustrate the basic concepts of such things as instruction decoding and register transfers on the internal buses. The way data gets into and out of a computer and the basic way a computer fetches and then executes the instructions that are provided in a program are then explained.

Computer architectures are described and the idea of programming, including the concept and the requirement for computer languages, is then introduced. This discussion extends from machine code to several popular high-level languages. The meanings and reasons for assemblers, compilers, interpreters, and translators are also discussed.

The book ends with Chapter 6, a look into the future. The benefits of gate arrays and cell arrays, the networking (interconnection) of computers, the electronic office and home, artificial intelligence, and the modern robots are presented. It is noted that computers are rapidly moving into the new role manipulation.

Acknowledgments

The author would like to acknowledge the support of the group of Marketing, Mask Designers, Advertising, Personnel, and other support people at National Semiconductor who have braved my seminars that used this manuscript as the handout. Their appreciation of the seminar content and the use of both the lab kit and the digital multimeter as a way to assist their understanding of basic concepts has greatly helped this book.

Chapter

1

Some Preliminary Topics

This chapter provides a basic background in many areas that are necessary to aid the understanding of digital electronics. The word "electronics" is built around the magic "electron." So we will start by taking a look at the electron.

Much is missed in the study of electronics without the ability to do some simple mathematical calculations. The new thing in electronic circuits is the wide range of the numbers that are involved in the calculations. These numbers range from extremely small numbers (such as a millionth part of a millionth part of 1) to very large numbers (such as 10 million), so a way of working with this wide range of numbers in a manageable form will be presented. Finally, an electronic-project lab kit, which is a major support for this book, will be introduced. This kit provides the hands-on familiarity that is necessary to make many of the concepts in electronics seem real to a student.

What Makes Up the World?

Today everybody is hearing about electronics. Electronics implies things that make use of electrons. The natural question is, "What are electrons, and why are they so useful in electronics?" Let's start by considering electrons and how they are involved in the composition of the objects that comprise our physical world.

Things more elemental than the elements

There are many different types of elements, ranging from the common metals such as iron, copper, zinc, and aluminum to elements that are gases in their natural state, such as oxygen. Each element contains a specific number of electrons; carbon has 12, oxygen has 16, and hydrogen has only 1. The important thing is that the number of electrons that is associated with each element controls the formation of chemical compounds.

Water is a chemical compound that is composed of elements, and each element in turn is composed of protons, neutrons, and electrons. The protons and neutrons contain most of the mass of the elements but occupy only a relatively small total volume. The small spot in which the mass of an element is concentrated, the "nucleus" of the atom, is comprised of these protons and neutrons. Surrounding this nucleus, at relatively large spacings, are layers, or "shells," of electrons. These electrons exist in "cloud-like" formations surrounding the nucleus. The outer layer of electrons affects the way elements react with each other.

Figure 1.1 shows a model of one of the simplest elements: the hydrogen atom. At the center of this atom is the nucleus which has one proton with a positive charge of +1. The nucleus of all atoms is where the mass, the fundamental thing that provides the weight of the atom (and all material things), is concentrated. It is interesting that the diameter of this relatively heavy nucleus is very, very small, and it is also an extremely small percentage of the total atomic diameter. The atomic diameter is established by the shells or layers of the electrons that are in orbit surrounding the central nucleus. This is very similar to our

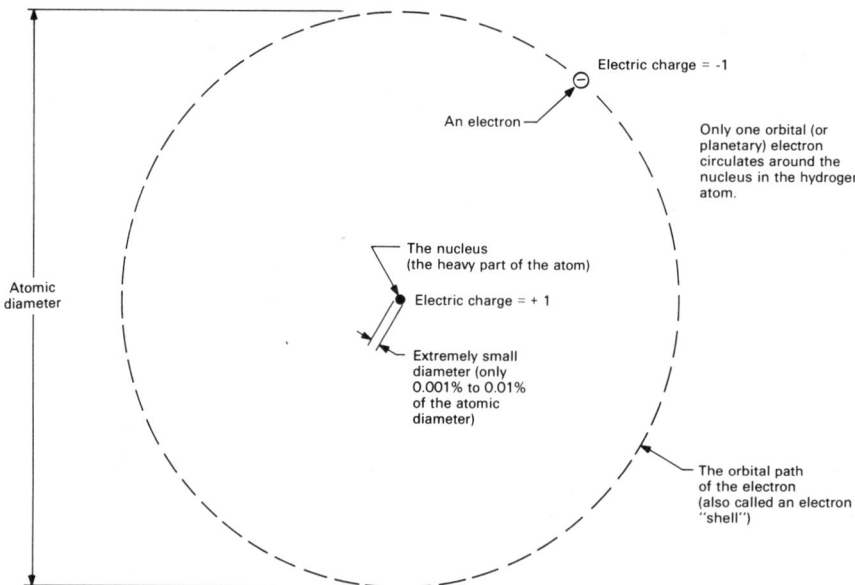

Figure 1.1 The hydrogen atom.

solar system in which the planets are in orbit circling about the center of this system, our sun. In the hydrogen atom, there is only a single electron in orbit around the nucleus.

The hydrogen atom is the simplest atom: it has only one electron. For the other elements, additional orbital electrons (and also an equal number of additional positive charges, the protons) are added. As the complexity of the atom increases, only two electrons are allowed in the innermost layer, the electrons closest to the nucleus. After these two electrons exist in the first shell, a second shell starts building. This second shell can contain a maximum of only eight electrons, and then a third shell starts. In general, the basic idea is to add to the innermost electron shells and then add to the next outermost layer of electrons as the elements continue to increase in complexity (although it is actually more complex than this). Outer shells of all elements contain at most eight electrons, and those elements that contain exactly eight are chemically inactive.

Chemical reactions

Chemical reactions are governed by the outermost electrons of an atom. Figure 1.2 indicates the electron shells that move out from the nucleus of an atom. As electrons are added to make the more complicated or larger atoms of the elements, there are a varying total number of electrons that occupy the outermost shells of each atom. It is these electrons in the outermost shell of an atom that give the element the characteristics that are needed to form chemical compounds and also the characteristics that are needed to provide the useful semiconductor crystals that are responsible for the present electronic age.

To provide stable chemical compounds, atoms of various elements group together and share their outermost electrons in what chemists call a "covalent" bond. This sharing of electrons between two or more atoms in a chemical compound has a maximum total of eight electrons in the outermost shell around each atom. This magic number of eight is the basis for the various ways that elements combine to form chemical compounds and also is involved in forming crystal structures.

The basic diagram of a more complex atom, an atom of oxygen, is shown in Figure 1.3. A total of eight electrons is associated with this atom. This implies that the innermost shell is filled with two electrons and that the next, outermost, shell contains six electrons. The six electrons in the outermost shell give rise to the chemical characteristics of oxygen.

The chemical symbol for the very familiar molecule of water, H_2O, indicates that a molecule of water is composed of two atoms of hydrogen and one atom of oxygen. The oxygen atom supplies six electrons in its outermost shell, and each hydrogen atom supplies one electron, as

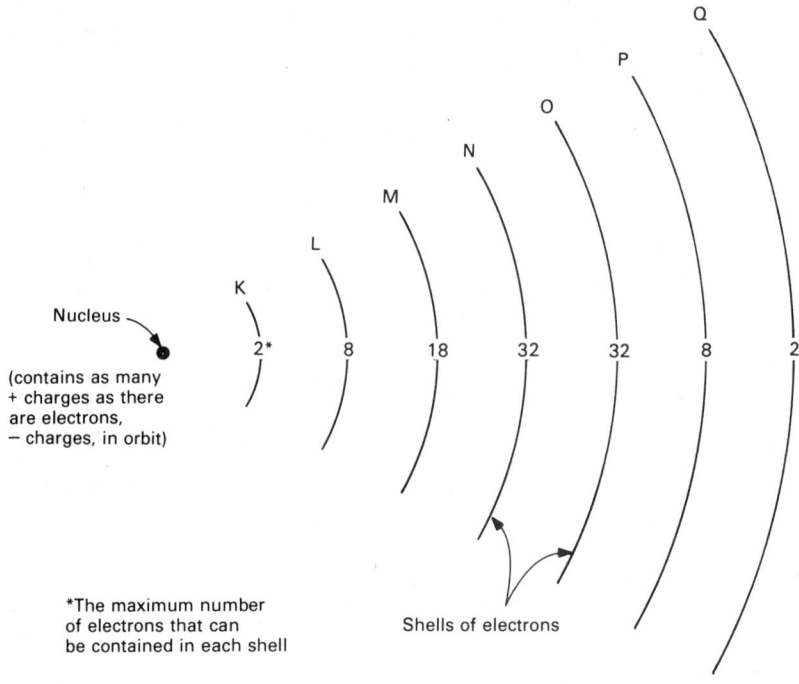

Figure 1.2 The shells can each contain a maximum number of electrons.

shown in Figure 1.4. Adding two hydrogen atoms provides a total of eight shared electrons in one molecule of water. The oxygen atom is shown in the center of this figure. There is a hydrogen atom to the left and to the right, providing the stable system of eight shared electrons. Chemists diagram the sharing of these electrons as H—O—H. The H represents a hydrogen atom and the O, an oxygen atom. The line or bar between these letter symbols indicates the covalent bonding of the electrons.

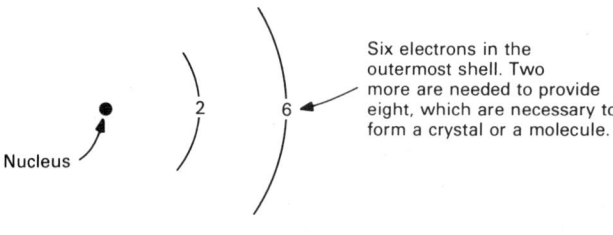

Figure 1.3 The element oxygen.

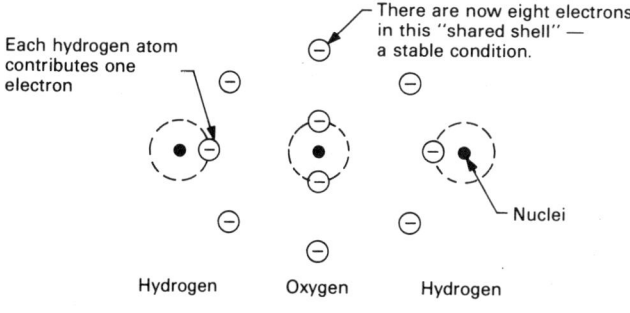

Figure 1.4 A molecule of water, H_2O.

The elements that have four electrons in their outermost shells are right at the balance point. They neither have too few, like hydrogen with only one electron, or too many, like oxygen with six valence electrons. In fact, these can be called the "hermaphrodite" elements because they are perfectly happy to combine with themselves.

One of the first elements that has four electrons in its outermost shell is carbon, shown in Figure 1.5. Four is half of the magic number of eight, and this allows carbon to have a lot of different possibilities in forming chemical compounds. As shown in Figure 1.6, carbon can bond with itself. This is a unique thing. The example is the gas ethane which has a single covalent bond between two carbon atoms. The six hydrogen atoms each supply an additional electron to form the stable shell of eight electrons around each one of the carbon atoms. So a molecule of ethane can be represented as two atoms of carbon and six atoms of hydrogen. The chemical formula would be C_2H_6, where the numerical subscripts indicate the total number of each of the atoms that are contained in the molecule.

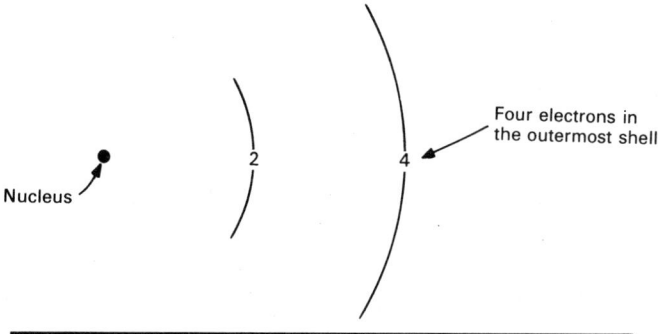

Figure 1.5 The element carbon.

6 Chapter One

The gas, ethane

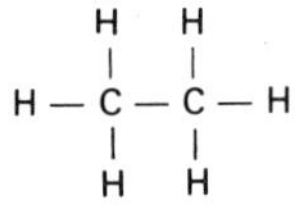

```
       H   H
       |   |
   H — C — C — H
       |   |
       H   H
```

C_2H_6

Figure 1.6 Carbon can bond with itself and also other atoms.

An interesting thing about carbon is that it can completely bond with itself, as shown in Figure 1.7. There are no atoms involved here other than carbon. Each carbon atom is completely linked up, sharing electrons with other carbon atoms. This now forms a very strong and stable crystal structure. These so-called "valence" crystals (crystals that are formed out of only one element) are extremely tough structures. Very strong electrical forces are involved in this bonding, so these atoms, and even the associated electrons, are very difficult to break loose. This lack of free electrons makes these crystals rather poor conductors of electric current; therefore they are "insulators."

The crystal form of carbon is the high-cost diamond. Because carbon has a small atomic size, diamonds are extremely hard materials. Diamonds, for example, can scratch all other materials because the stronger electrical bonding between the atoms of a diamond allows it to break up the atomic bonding of other materials.

With these outermost electrons completely tied up in covalent bonding, a diamond will not conduct an electric current and therefore forms a solid insulator. In fact, a diamond remains an insulator even at relatively high temperatures.

The semiconductors

Most of the good conductors, such as the metals copper, silver, and gold, form solids in which the individual atoms of these metals are sur-

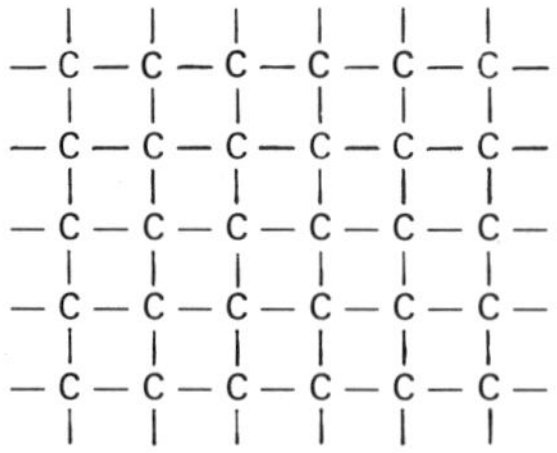

```
  |   |   |   |   |   |
— C — C — C — C — C — C —
  |   |   |   |   |   |
— C — C — C — C — C — C —
  |   |   |   |   |   |
— C — C — C — C — C — C —
  |   |   |   |   |   |
— C — C — C — C — C — C —
  |   |   |   |   |   |
— C — C — C — C — C — C —
  |   |   |   |   |   |
```

Figure 1.7 Carbon bonding with itself.

rounded by a loosely held "sea" of their accompanying electrons. When a voltage is applied across a metal, this large number of available (free or mobile) electrons is responsible for the large current that flows.

The elements germanium and silicon are very similar to carbon. They bond with themselves and form relatively strong crystal structures. Germanium and silicon are not good insulators, like diamonds, and yet they do not have the large supply of free electrons that exist with metals. This causes germanium and silicon to be neither good insulators nor good conductors. Therefore, they are called "semiconductors." Today, the emphasis is on silicon; so we will restrict our discussions to this popular semiconductor.

Silicon forms a valence crystal that has a crystalline structure like a diamond. Most of the electrons within silicon are relatively tightly held in position; therefore they are not free to move around within the crystal structure. When a voltage is applied across a piece of silicon, there are only a relatively few electrons available to carry a current. These free electrons are provided by the thermal energy that exists at room temperature which causes a few covalent bonds to be randomly broken within the crystal structure. As temperature is increased, the resistance of silicon decreases.

The electron shells for an atom of silicon are shown in Figure 1.8. Notice that the first shell is filled up with two electrons, the second shell with eight, and four electrons remain in the outermost shell, for a total of fourteen electrons.

Figure 1.9 illustrates the sharing of electrons in the covalent bonding of silicon atoms. The circle with the silicon symbol (Si) in the middle represents the nucleus of a silicon atom. The minus sign with the circle around it represents an electron. The solid line that connects an electron back to an atom indicates that this electron can be thought of as being associated with that particular atom of silicon. A dashed line

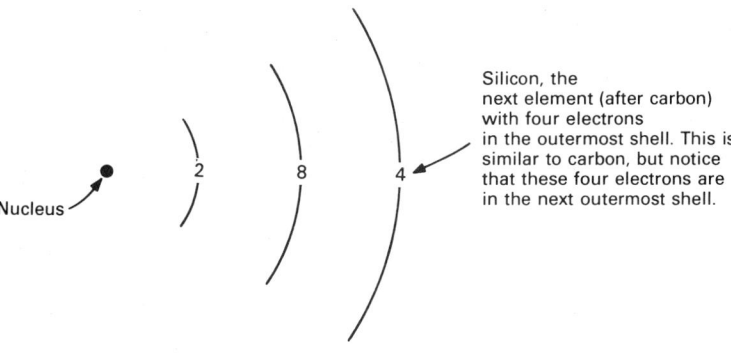

Figure 1.8 The element silicon.

8 Chapter One

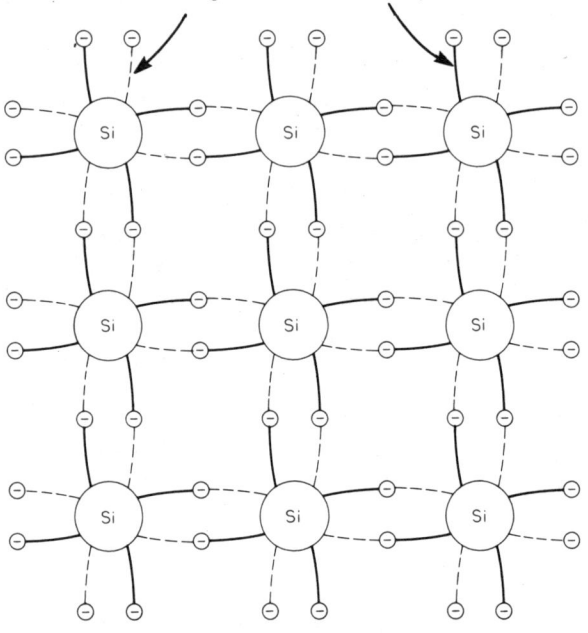

Figure 1.9 A structure formed only with silicon.

indicates the sharing of an electron by a neighboring silicon atom. So, one atom supplies an electron, and an adjacent atom shares this electron. This covalent bonding of the silicon atoms exists in three dimensions to form a solid structure as shown in Figure 1.10. In this way, a stable set of eight electrons surrounds each of the silicon atoms, and a very stable, well-ordered crystal structure results.

Silicon is useful in electronics because it can be modified by exchanging a relatively small number of the atoms within the crystal structure with atoms of a different element. This modified or contaminated silicon is called "doped silicon." The process of doping is the occasional substitution of a different atom for a silicon atom in the solid structure of a silicon crystal.

There are two very useful possibilities when doping atoms are substituted into the crystal structure of silicon. A doping atom with only three electrons in its outermost shell will create a place for an additional electron, a "hole." This hole is then available to conduct an electrical current. Or, alternatively, a doping atom with five electrons in its outermost shell will provide *a spare electron* within the crystal structure of silicon that can be easily stripped away: a free electron. This free electron is then available to conduct an electrical current. The conductivity of silicon will increase with either P-type or N-type doping.

This gives rise to what is known as P type for those doping elements that have less than four valence electrons because they will provide a place for an electron, a hole. These holes act essentially the same as if they were positive charges, and therefore the P-type designation is used.

A designation of N type is used for those doping elements that introduce a spare electron (a negative charge) in the crystal structure of silicon.

A bar of pure silicon material, in a nice crystal order, would not be a very good conductor. This means that if a voltage were applied between two wires that are attached to the silicon, not much current would flow. But, if this semiconductor material were doped with either P-type or N-type dopants, current would flow. Holes would provide temporary resting places for conducting electrons as they moved through a P-type-doped crystal, or the free electrons would allow current to flow

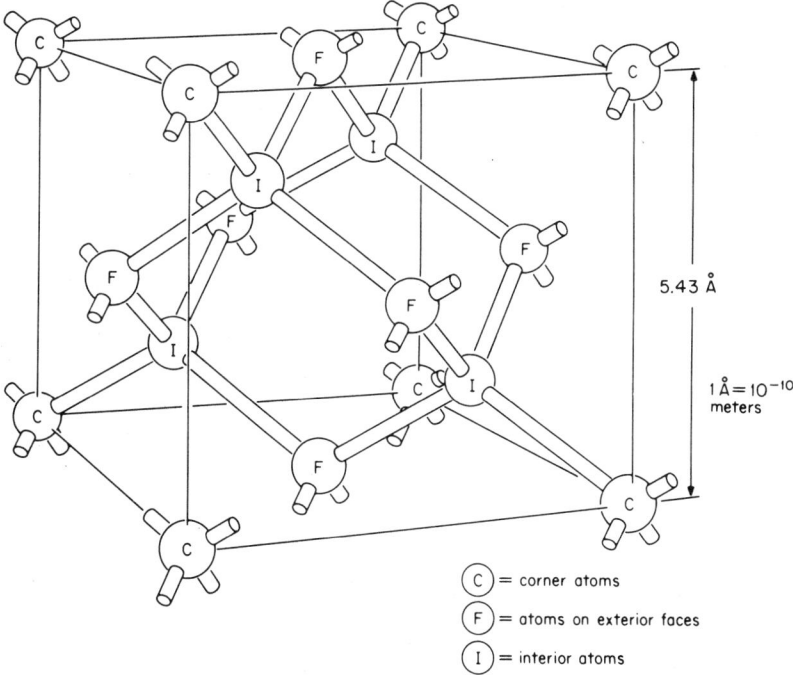

Figure 1.10 Three-dimensional bonding of silicon to form a solid crystal.

for an N-type-doped crystal. A bar of doped silicon therefore becomes a resistor, an electrical component that conducts more current than an insulator but less current than a conductor. Doped regions of silicon are used to form resistors within integrated circuits.

When a region that has been doped P type is bordering a region that has been doped N type, the very useful PN junction (a diode) is formed (diodes are discussed in Chapter 3). Diodes are also basic to the operation of bipolar transistors (the solid-state amplifying devices also discussed in Chapter 3) that are used in electronics.

These basic physical concepts of material structure are necessary in order to understand how a solid piece of single-crystal silicon can be converted into many useful electronic things such as diodes, transistors, and resistors.

Dealing with Very Large and Very Small Numbers

In the calculations that are used in electronics, numbers are both extremely large and extremely small. Very large numbers, like 1000, 10,000, 100,000, or 1,000,000, require writing down a large number of digits. The notation technique that scientists use to handle very large numbers is shown in Figure 1.11. This simplifies the problem of excessive writing, makes calculations easier to handle, and reduces errors that are often made in calculations.

In scientific notation, large numbers are expressed as a small number ranging between 1 and 9 (like 2.98 or 4.53) and then a separate

Numbers from 1 to 9 are easily handled in calculations. To make calculations easier, a very large number can be expressed as a number from 1 to 9, followed by 10, 10^2, 10^3, etc., because:

$10^0 = 1$
$10^1 = 10$
$10^2 = 100$
$10^3 = 1000$

Therefore:

120. V = 1.2×10^2 V (Check: $1.2 \times 100 = 120$)

First, move the decimal point two places to the left to express the number in the range 1 to 9. The number of places moved to the left (2) then becomes the exponent of 10.

And,

490000. V = 4.0×10^5 V
54321

Figure 1.11 The scientific way to write very large numbers.

"scaling factor" is used to show how big the number is. Powers (exponents) of 10 handle the scaling factor, as shown in Figure 1.11. A scaling factor of 10 to the first power, 10^1, is 10. A scaling factor of 10^2 (10 × 10) indicates 100 times, and 10^3 (10 × 10 × 10) indicates 1000 times. (10^0 has been defined to be equal to 1.)

For example, 120 volts (V) can be expressed in scientific notation as 1.2×10^2 as shown in Figure 1.11. This can be thought of as moving the decimal point from 120.0 to 1.20. The decimal point was moved to the left two places; therefore 2 is the exponent on 10.

The second example in this figure shows a much larger number: 490,000 V, a very large voltage. Rather than writing this as 49 with four trailing zeros, it is certainly easier (and less prone to errors) to write 4.9 (that is the number between 1 and 9) and then indicate how big the number is as an exponent on 10. In this example the decimal point had to be moved five places to the left, so the exponent is 5. The notation 4.9×10^5 is an easier way of writing 490,000.

Figure 1.12 shows how this same concept is used to express very small numbers. Many small numbers that may be only a millionth or a millionth millionth part of 1 must be written down and handled in calculations. Again, exponents of 10 are used, but these are negative exponents. The expression 10^0 is 1, 10^{-1} is 0.1, 10^{-2} is 0.01, and 10^{-3} is 0.001. For example, 0.028 V is written as 2.8×10^{-2}. In this example the decimal point was moved to the right two places in the original expression to arrive at the number to place the numerical part of the number in the range of 1 to 9; the exponent is -2. In scientific notation, moving the exponent of a number to the left creates a positive exponent; moving the exponent to the right creates a negative exponent. This can be remembered because moving the exponent to the right

---

Use the same idea, express the number in the range 1 to 9, but now follow with 10^{-1}, 10^{-2}, 10^{-3}, etc., because:

$10^0 = 1.0$
$10^{-1} = 0.1$
$10^{-2} = 0.01$
$10^{-3} = 0.001$

Therefore:

0.028 V = 2.8×10^{-2} V
   1 2

You now move the decimal point to the right to express the number in the range 1 to 9. This number of places moved now becomes a negative exponent of 10.

And:

0.000 056 V = 5.6×10^{-5} V
  123 45

Figure 1.12 The scientific way to write very small numbers.

is making the number larger. Therefore a negative exponent of 10 must be used to bring it back down to where it started.

Another example, 0.000056, is shown in Figure 1.12. This number is difficult to write down. In this case, the decimal point must be moved to the right five places. It is much easier to refer to this number as 5.6×10^{-5} rather than to write down all of those zeros.

In electronics there are very large values of resistance, very low values of capacitance, and very low values of current flow. This shorthand way to write down these wide ranging numbers is very convenient.

Handling the Calculations that Aid Understanding

When doing calculations with numbers that are very large and very small, you can quickly see the benefit of using scientific notation. For example, the problem of multiplying a couple of the numbers from the previous figures is shown in Figure 1.13, 490,000 V multiplied by 0.000056 V.

Both of these numbers are first expressed in scientific form as 4.9×10^5 V and 5.6×10^{-5} V. The numerical parts, 4.9 and 5.6, are multiplied, and then the scaling factors are multiplied. The numerical part of this product (4.9×5.6) can be handled on a standard four-function calculator.

To multiply the scaling factors, simply add the exponents of 10. Adding the exponents +5 and −5 results in 0, and 10^0 is the same as 1. Multiplying any number by 1 does not change the number; so 10^0 can be simply dropped. The answer therefore is 27.4.

Both of these numbers are voltages. Volts times volts provides (volts)^2, or V^2. It is very important to carry the units in all calculations. When the units properly cancel or combine, it indicates that you are using the correct equation. In this particular case, the product is expressed as 27.4 V^2, or 2.74×10 V^2.

Multiplying the number from the previous figures:

(490,000V) (0.000,056 V) = ?

First, express both numbers in scientific form:

(4.9×10^5 V) (5.6×10^{-5} V)

or (4.9) (5.6) × [(10^5) (10^{-5})] V^2 *

or 27.4 × 10^0 V^2

27.4 V^2

When multiplying the powers of 10, algebraically add.
Here: + 5 − 5 = 0 and 10^0 = 1

*Note: V × V = V^2 because the units also multiply.

Figure 1.13 Multiplying very large and very small numbers.

Instead of multiplying numbers, let's take a look at an example in which these numbers are divided, as shown in Figure 1.14. For simplicity, the same numbers will be used, 490,000 V ÷ 0.000056 V. After these numbers are written in scientific form, the numerical part of the number is separated from the scaling part to give 4.9 ÷ 5.6.

To divide these scaling factors of 10, *the exponent of 10 that is in the denominator is moved up into the numerator by simply changing the sign on the exponent of that factor of 10.* This provides $10^5 \times 10^5$. The exponents are simply added to accomplish the multiplication. So, the power (or the scaling factor) of this quotient will be 10^{10}, a very large number (this is approximately the number of stars that exist in the observable sky when the best telescope is used).

When the numerical parts are divided (4.9 ÷ 5.6), the quotient is a little less than 1 (0.88). The scaling factor of this quotient is 10^{10}. Again, this quotient will be expressed in scientific form, so the decimal point is moved one place to the right. This makes the numerical part of the quotient larger; therefore the scaling exponent of 10 (also 10) must be reduced by 1 to bring it down to 9. So, the answer for this indicated division is 8.8×10^9. Notice that volts were divided by volts, so the volts cancel. This quotient is now a dimensionless ratio. One voltage is compared with another voltage.

With modern calculators, multiplications and divisions are easily done. Usually, the scaling factor powers of 10 can be handled in your head because this involves adding and subtracting relatively small numbers. Therefore, a four-function calculator can be used to handle these calculations. If you do happen to have a scientific calculator, you can make use of the ability to directly enter the exponent along with

Dividing the numbers from the previous figure:

$$\frac{490{,}000 \text{ V}}{0.000{,}056 \text{ V}} = ?$$

First, express each number in scientific form:

$$\frac{490{,}000 \text{ V}}{0.000{,}056 \text{ V}} = \frac{4.9 \times 10^5 \text{ V}}{5.6 \times 10^{-5} \text{ V}}$$

Note: The sign of the exponent is changed when it is moved up into the numerator.

or $\left(\dfrac{4.9}{5.6}\right) \times \left(\dfrac{10^5}{10^{-5}}\right) = \left(\dfrac{4.9}{5.6}\right) \times [(10^5)(10^5)]$

Exponents add when multiplying.

$\left(\dfrac{4.9}{5.6}\right) \times 10^{10} = 0.88 \times 10^{10} = 8.8 \times 10^9$ (a dimensionless ratio)*

*Note: V/V = 1; The units cancel.

Figure 1.14 Dividing very large and very small numbers.

each number. Then you won't have to handle the exponents by hand calculations. If you would like to pursue the study of electronics, the investment in a scientific calculator is certainly worthwhile.

In electronic engineering, the "metric prefixes" are used as scaling factors. This then provides a word description for the scaling factor. It is much easier to use a word description than to say, "Three point one five times ten to the seventh" (3.15×10^7). The standard metric prefixes are used, whether the numbers refer to lengths or weights or (in the electronic case) ohms, volts, or amperes.

For example, as shown in Figure 1.15, the metric prefix for 10^3 is "kilo" (k). You probably have heard of kilograms (kg) or kilometers (km); that is a thousand grams or a thousand meters. In engineering, 1×10^3 V would be called 1 kilovolt (kV).

The metric prefix for 10^6 is "mega" (M); that is a million. As an example, 3.2×10^6 V would be referred to as 3.2 megavolts (MV) (3,200,000 V).

The last example in Figure 1.15 is 4.95×10^5 V, but 10^5 is not one of the standard metric prefixes. If this scaling factor were brought down to 10^3, it would be kilo. This can be done by expressing 10^5 as $10^2 \times 10^3$. The 10^2 is moved into the numerical part (4.95) as 495. Therefore, 4.95×10^5 V becomes 495 kV. The next larger metric prefix could also be used as 0.495 MV. This designation would be used if the other units that are being discussed happened to be megavolts.

Small numbers use the metric prefixes shown in Figure 1.16. In electronics, there are usually more small numbers than large numbers. Whereas kilo and mega are generally all that are needed for the large numbers, many more metric prefixes are used for small numbers. Therefore, metric prefixes are used for 10^{-3}, 10^{-6}, 10^{-9}, and 10^{-12} (metric prefixes only exist for each factor of one thousand). So, 10^{-3} in metric is "milli" and is abbreviated as m (you have probably heard of millimeters in cigarette ads). Milliamperes and millivolts are used in elec-

The metric prefixes for the positive exponents of 10 are:

10^3 = kilo (k)
10^6 = mega (M)

Therefore:

1×10^3 V = 1 kV

and
3.2×10^6 V = 3.2 MV   The sum of these exponents is still 5.

and
4.95×10^5 V = $4.95 \times 10^2 \times 10^3$ = 495 kV   rather than 0.495 MV

Figure 1.15 The engineering way to write very large numbers.

Use metric prefixes for the negative exponents of 10 as:

10^{-3} = milli (m)
10^{-6} = micro (μ)
10^{-9} = nano (n)
10^{-12} = pico (p)

Therefore:

2.8×10^{-2} V = $\underline{2.8 \times 10}$ ($\times 10^{-3}$) = 28 mV

5.6×10^{-5} V = $\underline{5.6 \times 10}$ ($\times 10^{-6}$) = 56 μV

9.3×10^{-7} V = $\underline{9.3 \times 10^2}$ ($\times 10^{-9}$) = 930 nV

Figure 1.16 The engineering way to write very small numbers.

---

tronics. A millionth part, 10^{-6}, is called "micro," and the abbreviation is the Greek letter μ. Even smaller factors are 10^{-9}, "nano" (n) and 10^{-12}, "pico" (p).

For example, the scientific number 2.8×10^{-2} V would be expressed as 28 mV. Similarly, 5.6×10^{-5} V would be called 56 μV. These are certainly easier to say than if these numbers were expressed in scientific form. This metric format is a way to more easily talk about small and large numbers.

With this background on calculations, the strangeness of the numbers that are encountered in electronics can be eliminated. These scientific and metric number representations will be used in calculations throughout the discussions in this book so that you can get a feeling for how this game is played. Unfortunately, there is a lot of mathematics associated with electronic design, but if you are not going to become a circuit designer, all you need is a speaking acquaintance, a recognition of what the words mean so you can understand what is going on.

The Displays of Three-, Three-and-a-half-, and Four-Digit Voltmeters

Display devices make use of a strange sounding way to describe the number of digits of numerical data that they can indicate. For example, the digital multimeter that is recommended to accompany this book is called a "three-and-a-half-digit meter." The obvious question is, "What is this half digit?" This sounds confusing, and the answer lies in the way that the electronics for each digit is provided.

As in counting, an overflow or carry out of a lower digit to the next-most-significant digit is provided. The trick of the half digit is to make use of this overflow out of the most significant digit to increase the range of numbers that are displayed. All of the expense of the next-higher-digit electronics is not needed. This low-cost, easily added extra digit displays either nothing (representing zero) or a 1. As shown in Figure 1.17, this relatively simple half-digit feature extends the range of the three-digit display of Figure 1.17a from 1000 steps (000 through 999) to 2000 steps (0000 to 1999) that are realized when the half digit is added, as shown in the three-and-a-half-digit display of Figure 1.17b. If all of the electronics for the extra digit were provided, the four-digit display of Figure 1.17c would result, and this would increase the display range to 10,000 steps (0000 to 9999).

Another confusing thing about displays is the full-scale range. For example, the digital multimeter used with this book makes use of full-scale ranges that are 2, 20, 200, etc.; yet the maximum display indication is only 1.999, 19.99, 199.9, respectively. The display range of the meter indicates how to interpret the scaling factor of the displayed digits; the display will not provide the actual full scale numbers of 2, 20, 200, etc.

What Is an Electronic Circuit?

An "electronic circuit" uses an energy source, such as a battery or a power supply, and some wire to hook up various circuit components that include active devices (transistors) in such a way that a useful electronic function will be obtained. There are many different types of electronic circuit components. These range from the passive components (which are also used in electric circuits), such as resistors, capacitors, and inductors, to the active components, such as transistors (that are unique to electronic circuits and provide voltage gain). Chapter 3 will describe some of the passive components that are used in electronic circuits.

Whenever there are no transistors or other amplifying devices in a circuit, it is called an "electric circuit," not an electronic circuit. In homes, the lighting system and the control of the heating system are electric circuits in contrast with radios, calculators, and home computers, which use electronic circuits.

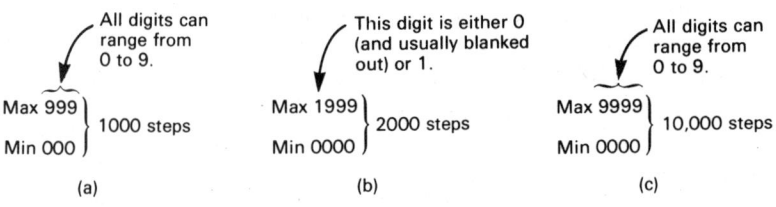

Figure 1.17 The resolution of (a) 3-, (b) 3½-, and (c) 4-digit voltmeters.

Getting Familiar with the Lab Kit

You will find that the 200-in-One Electronic Project Kit (Radio Shack Cat. No. 28-265) is a very convenient way to learn about electronics. Within this kit are a lot of the basic circuit components that are used in making electronic circuits. The springs associated with each one of these components make it very easy to use the wires provided to hook up these components with each other to make circuits.

This lab kit, Figure 1.18, provides a neat assemblage of basic electronic components that will assist your learning. In the upper left-hand corner are 20 resistors. Adjacent to this are two silicon diodes. Batteries are in the upper right-hand corner. There is also a relay. Two digital integrated circuits (a dual *JK* flip-flop and a quad two-input NAND gate) are along the center right. Both of these will be used for experiments in Chapter 4.

This lab kit uses an easy way to interconnect the electronic components that consist of a number of wires of various lengths. Contact springs are provided for all of the components, as shown in Figure 1.19a. To connect a wire to a contact spring, the top of the spring is pushed sideways, as shown in Figure 1.19b, and then the end of the wire is slipped between the opened spring coils. When the spring is released, it will return to its normal position, and the end of the wire will be firmly contacted, as shown in Figure 1.19c (a slight tug on the wire is recommended to verify that a good electrical contact is provided by the spring).

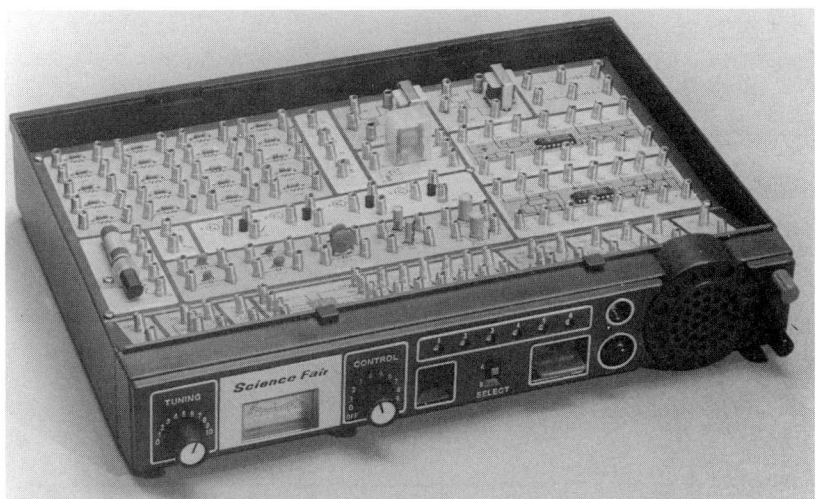

Figure 1.18 The 200-in-One electronic project lab kit. Radio Shack cat. no. 28-265.

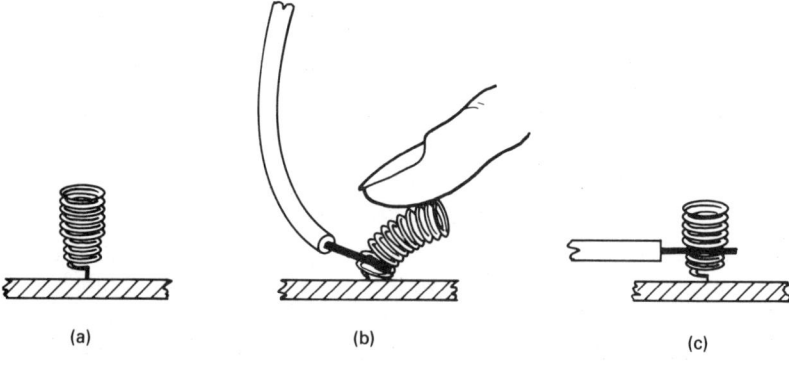

Figure 1.19 Connecting wires between kit components. (*a*) Contacting springs used in lab kit, (*b*) bend spring over just enough to allow slipping the end of a wire between the coils of the spring, and (*c*) let spring return with wire stuck in the coils of the spring. (Pull gently on the wire to check the contact.)

Multiple wires can be attached to the same contact spring, as shown in Figure 1.20. Up to three wires are easily contacted if the wires are spaced around the spring so that previous wires don't drop out as the next one is added.

A problem can exist. The wire ends, which are attached to closely spaced springs, can inadvertently touch or short out, as shown in Figure 1.21. Always check to insure that this undesired connection is not happening as a circuit is being hooked up.

As you go through this book and study each component, you'll use this lab kit and make some basic measurements and observations about each component as you are learning about it. You will therefore have a hands-on opportunity to see many electronic components, hook them

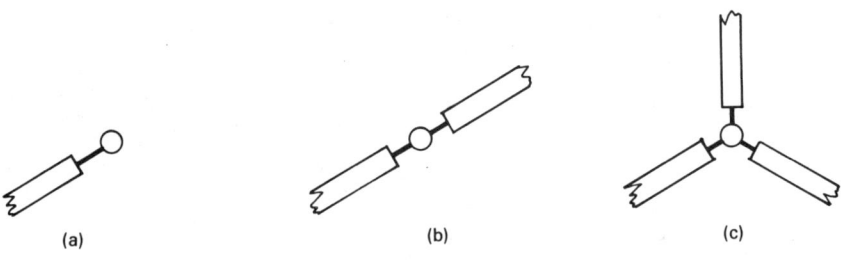

Figure 1.20 Connecting more than one wire to a spring terminal. (*a*) One wire, (*b*) two wires, (*c*) three wires.

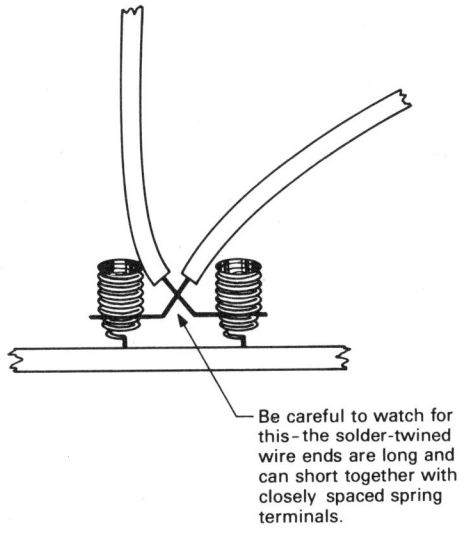

Be careful to watch for this- the solder-twined wire ends are long and can short together with closely spaced spring terminals.

Figure 1.21 Don't let hookup wires short out.

up, make useful circuits, make meaningful measurements, and in this way greatly increase your understanding of electronics.

Now, with these preliminaries out of the way, we'll start our investigation of electronics by first considering voltage.

Chapter 2

Voltage: The Pressure of the Electrons

Voltages are most commonly associated with batteries. For example, many people are familiar with the standard 1.5 V that is provided by flashlight cells or the 12 V supplied by the battery in an automobile. In addition, there is the 110 V that is supplied to homes. So, most people are somewhat familiar with a number of voltages, ranging from relatively small voltages (1.5 V) to larger voltages (110 V).

In electronic circuits, *voltage provides the electric force* (the equivalent of water pressure in a hydraulic system) *that causes the electrons to move around, to flow through a circuit.* The movement of these electrons constitutes the current that flows. So, a source of voltage is necessary to make any circuit "come to life."

Voltage sources are provided in many ways. For example, homes have electrical outlets on the walls, and various appliances can be plugged into these outlets to obtain 110 V. Electronic systems are basically designed to be either plugged into an outlet where power is provided or to operate from batteries or cells, as in a portable system like an electronic wristwatch.

What is considered a large voltage? If the voltage is large enough to kill someone, it is generally considered a large voltage. In electronics, up to about 30 V is considered low voltage. Many linear electronic systems make use of +15-V and −15-V power supplies. Digital systems typically operate from a single +5-V power supply.

In this course, a battery-powered meter and a battery-powered laboratory kit are used. We are not encouraging use of the meter anywhere around the 110-V wall outlets. The intention is to teach something about electronics without risking lives.

In general, everyone considers voltages of 200 V and larger to be high voltages. But under the right conditions, electrocution can take place with only 40 V (generally, this is when your body is moist, because this reduces the resistance and allows more current to flow).

Voltages are also the "signals" that contain the information in electronic systems. Very small voltages (1 to 100 μV) are provided by the antenna of a radio receiver. In contrast, signals in digital systems are relatively large voltage swings between 0 and +5 V. These voltages can represent various things in a digital system as will be discussed in Chapter 4.

Cells and Batteries

Cells and batteries (a collection of two or more cells and therefore a "battery" of cells) provide the voltage sources for portable electronic equipment. Batteries can be classified as being either made up of "primary cells," which provide electrical energy from an internal chemical reaction, or "secondary cells," which are storage elements for electrical energy. Storage batteries use secondary cells, which have to be periodically recharged (and also initially charged) to provide a source of electrical energy. Examples of storage batteries are the battery in your car (it is recharged by the alternator on the engine), and the nickel-cadmium (Ni-Cad) batteries that are being used in all types of portable equipment, even power tools.

In contrast to this are the primary cells, like the flashlight battery (which actually is a flashlight cell), in which an internal chemical reaction provides the electrical energy. Once the internal chemicals become depleted, the battery or cell is discarded. A single flashlight cell is shown in Figure 2.1. Also, this figure shows the symbol for a single cell. A lot of symbols are used in electronics instead of drawing an actual picture of what each electronic component really looks like.

Figure 2.2 shows that the two cells in a flashlight have to be properly installed so that the individual voltages of each cell will add up. In Figure 2.2a, the button in the center on one end of the cell (the positive terminal) typically contacts with the backside of the other cell (the negative terminal). In this way the 1.5 V that is provided by each cell will add to provide 3 V for the flashlight.

If the cells are placed in a flashlight in the way shown in Figure 2.2b, the two center buttons are in contact. The voltages of each cell therefore do not add up; they subtract to provide 0 V. If a flashlight is to be stored, put the cells in this way. Even if the switch is accidentally turned ON, the cells won't be drained.

Voltage: The Pressure of the Electrons   23

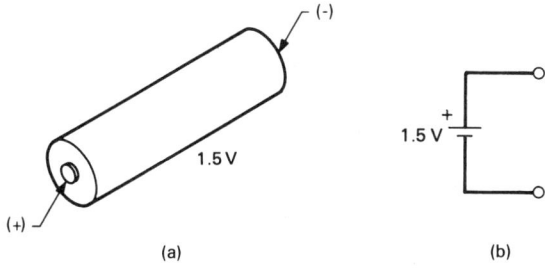

Figure 2.1 An electrical cell. (*a*) a single "flashlight cell" (these are *not* flashlight *batteries*) and (*b*) the symbol for a single cell.

Batteries have a positive (+) side, and a negative (−) side, and it is very important to install a battery correctly to make sure that the voltage that is applied to electronic circuits is not reversed.

Some common batteries are shown in Figure 2.3. Figure 2.3a shows a 12-V automotive battery, a 6-V lantern battery, and a 9-V transistor-radio battery. Internally, these 6- and 9-V batteries are collections of individual cells in which each cell provides 1.5 V. The number of cells that are connected in series determines the voltage of the battery, and the physical size of the individual cells determines the amount of current which can be taken from the battery. Batteries for lights, such as flashlights and lanterns, are relatively large because of the large

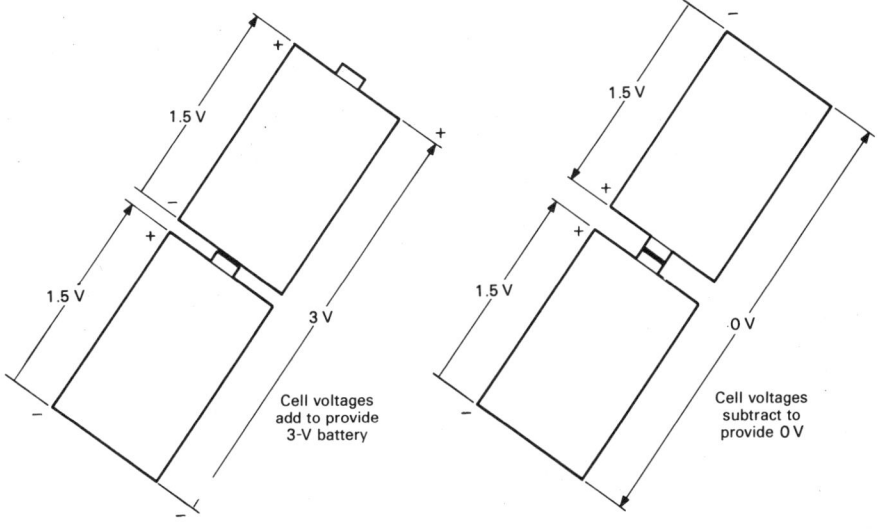

Figure 2.2 Multiple cells have to be properly oriented. (*a*) Stacking cells for a two-cell 3-V flashlight battery and (*b*) improperly stacking cells.

24 Chapter Two

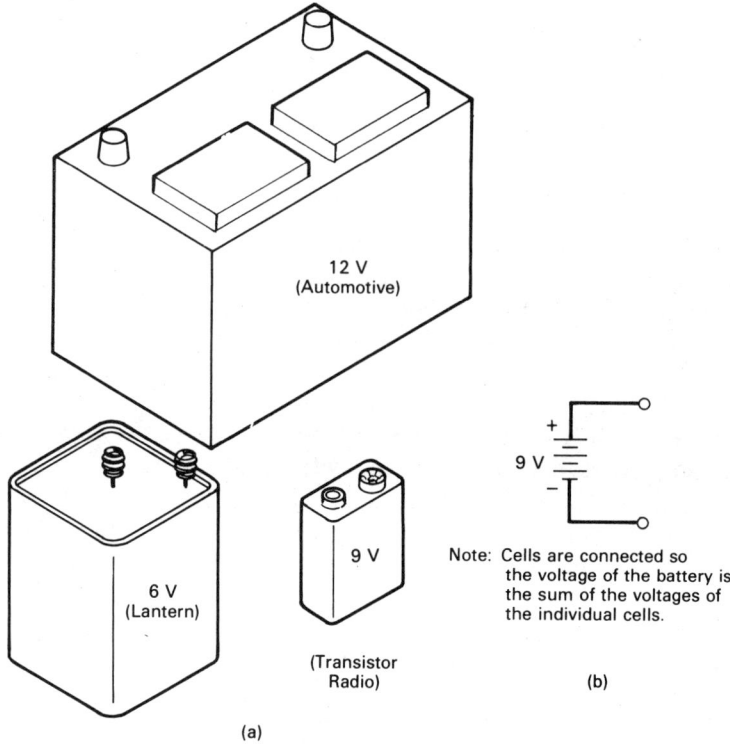

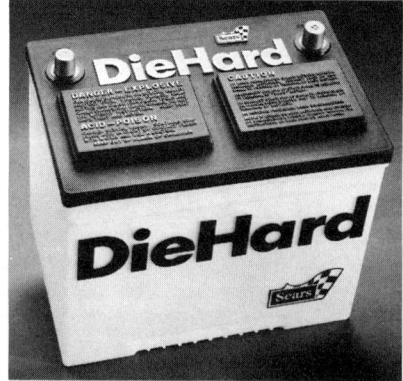

Figure 2.3 Batteries are groupings of more than one cell. (*a*) Some common batteries, (*b*) the symbol for a battery (a number of cells), and (*c*) a typical example of an automotive battery that is needed to start the engine.

amount of current that is required. In contrast, a 9-V transistor-radio battery uses six relatively small-sized cells, all connected in series.

The symbol for a battery is shown in Figure 2.3b. It is seen as simply a stack of cells. The actual number of cells that is used in the battery is not shown. The voltage of the battery is simply written next to the symbol.

Figure 2.4 shows the analogy between a hydraulic circuit and a flashlight, an electric circuit. A hydraulic circuit, Figure 2.4a, makes use of water in an elevated storage tank. The height of this water creates pressure, and it is this water pressure that makes the water flow.

Typically a pipe or a hose is used to carry the water to where it will be used. A relatively large diameter hose will prevent losing much of the water pressure. A spray nozzle is shown on the end of the hose. An ON/OFF valve is used to turn the water flow on or off; this is the ON/OFF switch for the water system.

The nozzle is the main restriction, or "resistance," to the flow of water. The pressure that results from the height of the water tank is pushing the water through this nozzle. The thing that is moving in this hydraulic circuit is water.

With this hydraulic circuit in mind, let's now consider an analogous electric circuit: a flashlight. The two cells in the flashlight example shown in Figure 2.4b add up to provide 3 V. This voltage is the "pressure" in this electric circuit. There is also an ON/OFF switch included in this circuit diagram. The electrical symbol for the lamp used in the flashlight is shown.

When the ON/OFF switch is closed, the thing that will flow through this circuit is "current," and the current flowing through the resistance of the light bulb creates the light. A complete circuit connection is needed, going from the positive terminal of the upper cell, through the switch, through the light bulb, and then back down to the negative side of the lower cell. If this electric circuit is interrupted (by opening the switch), current can't flow. To allow current to flow, a continuous loop is needed, a closed circuit.

In the upper right-hand corner of the lab kit are six AA cells. Contacts to these cells are available through six terminals in the area labeled "batteries," as shown in Figure 2.5. This group of six cells provides the voltage sources for the experiments that use the lab kit.

Ways to Pump Up Electrons: The Generation of Electricity

To generate electricity, ways must be found to take electrons from one place and move them to another place ("pump them up") so a voltage will be established that causes them to return. We'll now take a look at a number of ways to generate electrical energy.

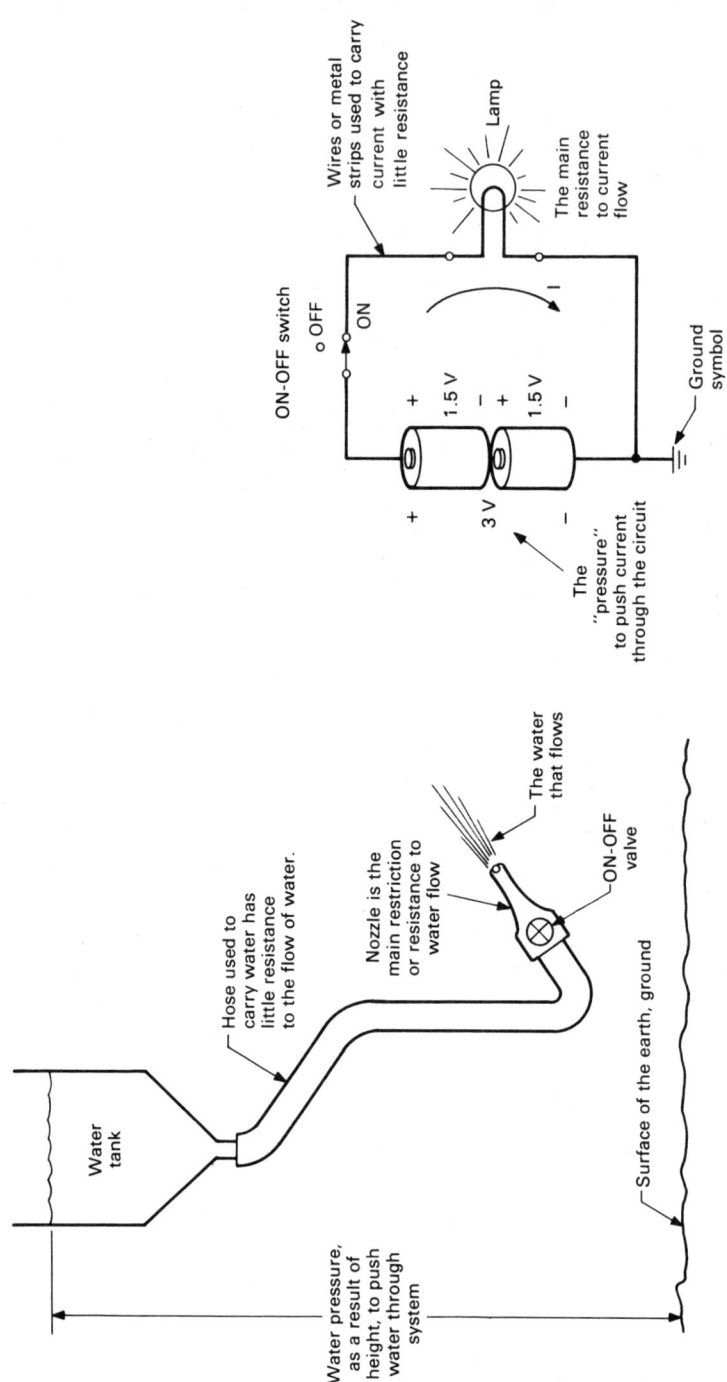

Figure 2.4 The hydraulic analogy of a flashlight. (*a*) A water circuit and (*b*) the electrical circuit of a flashlight.

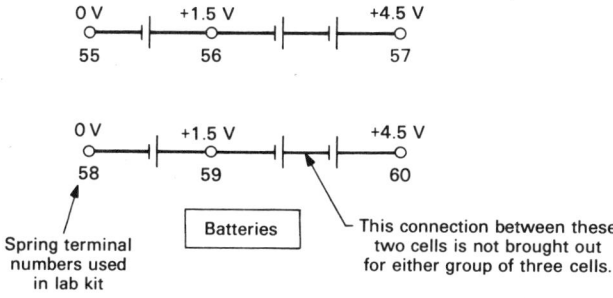

Figure 2.5 Connections to the 6 AA cells of the lab kit.

Stealing electrons: triboelectricity

"Triboelectric voltage generation" takes place when dissimilar materials (one or even both can be insulators) that were once in contact are separated. In this separation, electric charge is transferred. The surprising thing is that two plastics (both of which are good insulators) that are rubbed together and then separated can generate triboelectric voltages.

The simplest example of triboelectric voltage generation occurs when a cat's fur is brushed on a dry day. The cat's fur will stand up and will also respond to the position of the brush. Through a triboelectric generation phenomenon, electrons have been removed from the cat's fur and have been transferred to the comb. A spark discharge can occur as the brush approaches the cat's fur again.

Triboelectric voltage generation has caused many problems for semiconductors because integrated circuits are shipped within plastic carriers. As the integrated circuits slide in and out of these plastic tubes they can generate enough triboelectric voltage to permanently damage the integrated circuits. All of these tubes now have carbon mixed in with the plastic so that they are conductive plastics and will therefore not generate triboelectric voltages.

The new flintless, batteryless cigarette lighters: piezoelectricity

Another way to generate a voltage is to apply a mechanical force to distort a crystal. Voltages are generated within the crystal structure that are trying to restore the crystal to its equilibrium position. This electrical generation phenomenon is "piezoelectricity" and has been used in crystal microphones, earpieces (as in the lab kit), phonograph cartridges, and crystal frequency references.

A phonograph needle, when attached to a piezoelectric crystal, will mechanically stress the crystal as the needle follows the record grooves. This can generate a few volts of electricity.

A more modern application of piezoelectricity has provided a new way to light a cigarette. No longer are flints needed. By mechanically distorting a crystal, a voltage is generated, and the resulting electric spark ignites the flame of the cigarette lighter.

Niagara Falls and rotating machines

Whenever water is moving, or is dammed up and the escape can be controlled, the motion of this water can be made to turn a wheel. At Niagara Falls the water flow over the falls causes large turbines to rotate. Alternators (ac generators) then convert this rotary motion into electrical energy.

These hydroelectric sources of electricity are very important for a lot of America's electrical energy requirements. Hydroelectricity has the benefit of not polluting.

Solar cells: The key to the batteryless calculators

Solar cells on the roofs of homes convert sunlight into electrical energy. Another very common example of the solar cell is the light-powered calculator. No longer are batteries necessary to power a hand-held calculator. If the light is bright enough to allow you to read, there is enough light to operate these light-powered calculators. Both four-function calculators and scientific calculators can be powered from ambient light. This is quite a breakthrough.

The silicon diodes in the lab kit can be used as examples of solar cells. These diodes are packaged in clear glass, and if a flashlight is shone onto these diodes, they will generate a voltage. This is the "photovoltaic effect" that exists with semiconductor diodes.

A resistor can be connected across one of these silicon diodes, as shown in Figure 2.6. The voltmeter measures the voltage across both the diode and the resistor (the use of the voltmeter is discussed in the next section). If light does not shine on the diode, the voltage reading will go to zero. With light, a voltage of approximately 200 mV (0.200 V) can be obtained.

If both diodes were connected in series (and a light was shone on both of these diodes) the 200 mV from each of the solar cells would add up. This is the way higher voltages are obtained from arrays of solar cells.

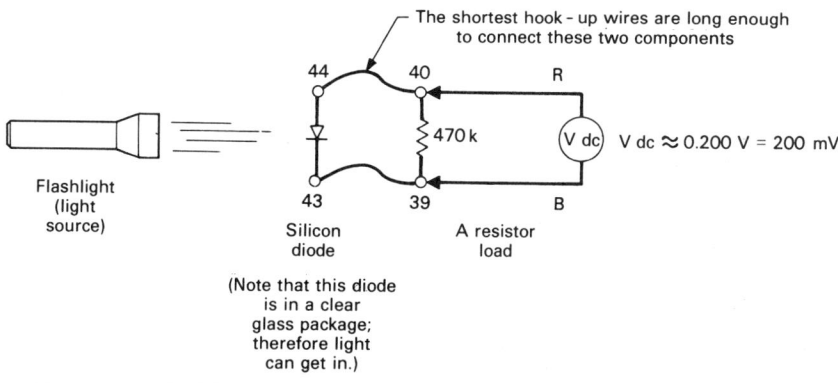

Figure 2.6 Converting light into voltage: The solar cell.

Measuring DC Voltages

While considering voltage, the "digital multimeter" will be introduced, because this can be used to measure the value of a dc voltage. A particular Micronta model (Radio Shack Cat. No. 22-188) is used as an example, but many other voltmeters or multimeters exist and can also be used (the arrangement of the front panel will probably be different, and therefore the owner's manual should be consulted to determine the proper setup to obtain the same measurement function).

The way to set up the digital multimeter to measure dc volts is shown in Figure 2.7. Notice that in the middle of the multimeter is a rotary switch, and there are five different types of measurement functions that are provided by this meter: DC V (the ability to read dc voltages), AC V (the ability to read ac voltages), "diode" CHECK (the ability to test semiconductor diodes), KΩ (the ability to measure the value of resistance of resistors and also the continuity of wires), and DC mA (the ability to measure dc current flow). To measure dc voltages, switch the center selector switch over to the left-most position that is labeled "DC V." The meter is "autoranging" so it will automatically determine the proper range (out of a possibility of five ranges) to use for the voltage that is being measured. For small voltages the range will be 200 mV full scale and "mV" will be displayed in the upper right-hand corner of the display. The four other full-scale ranges that can be automatically selected by the meter are 2 V, 20 V, 200 V, and 2000 V. For these ranges, the decimal point will be automatically located, the "mV" will not appear in the display, and the voltages are directly read in volts. We will be using only the first three ranges, 200 mV, 2 V, and 20 V, in the experiments that are shown in this book.

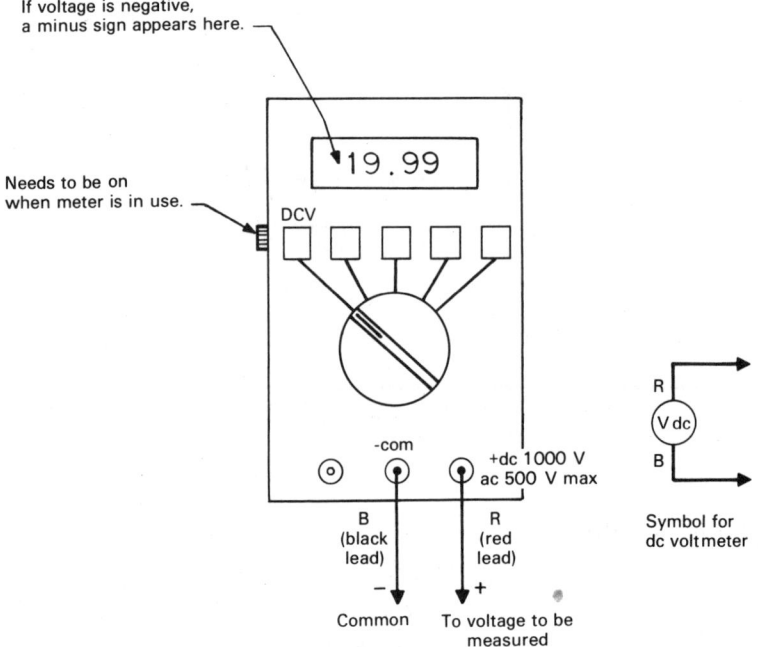

Figure 2.7 Setting up the digital multimeter to read dc volts (V dc). This is a Micronta digital multimeter (Radio Shack Cat. no. 22-188).

To attach the meter probes to the meter, notice that the black meter lead always plugs into the center jack, which is called "−COM" (minus Common). The red lead will go to the right of the black lead to measure both dc and ac volts and, as shown later, it will go to the left of the black lead for reading current (dc milliamps) or resistance.

To set up the multimeter to read dc volts, point the arrow of the selector to the left DC V position. Before a reading can be obtained, the power switch on the upper-left edge of the meter must be turned on. The multimeter is now set up to read dc volts and will automatically provide an easy-to-read display of the voltage value.

A negative sign may appear to the left of the digits in the display. This negative sign simply means that the polarity of the dc voltage being measured is different from what you thought. Typically, the black lead is connected to the negative side or ground side of the measured voltage and the red lead is connected to the positive side. The reading will then be a displayed number; there will be no algebraic sign displayed. This implies that the polarity of the measured voltage is the way you thought it was. In some circuits, both positive and negative voltages exist, and this polarity indication is then a useful feature because the leads don't have to be interchanged between readings.

Voltage: The Pressure of the Electrons 31

When using this meter to measure voltages in the lab kit, notice that the tips of the meter probes nicely fit inside of the contact springs of the lab kit. The probe will just lay sideways making an adequate contact, as shown in Figure 2.8. There is a large mechanical lever arm here, so don't pull sideways on the meter probe because the contact springs of the lab kit can be damaged.

Two different ways to connect the probes of the meter to read the voltage that exists between terminals 58 and 59 of the battery section are shown in Figure 2.9. The meter will indicate the voltage of a single cell, a value of about 1.5 V.

Whenever a voltage reading is mentioned, it is hard to predict the exact value that will be read. Therefore, the approximately equal sign (-) is used. The actual reading should be very close to the value shown. One of the reasons for a difference in the readings is that the voltage of the individual cells that are used in the battery section tends to fall as they are used. You have experienced this with a flashlight. If the batteries are too old, they provide less voltage, and therefore the brightness of the flashlight is reduced (the light also turns yellowish instead of being a bright white). Old batteries in the lab kit will also give lower voltage readings. In fact, this voltmeter can be used to determine if a battery or cell is good or not. It isn't necessary to put a cell into a flashlight or to put a battery into an electronic gadget to determine its condition; simply read the terminal voltage. A low-voltage reading (less than 1.2 V per cell) indicates that the cell or battery should be discarded or recharged.

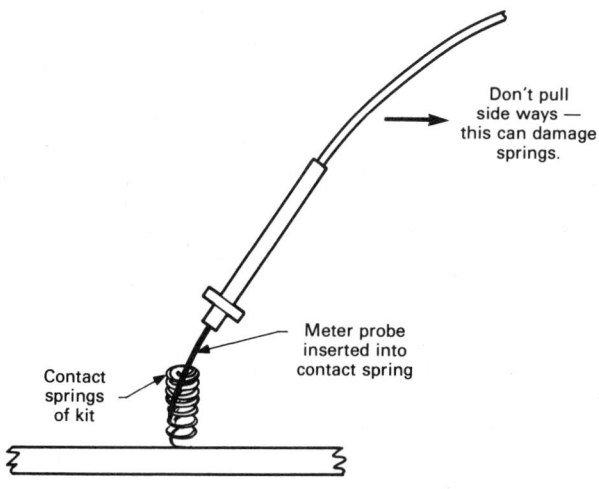

Figure 2.8 Meter probes easily fit into the contact springs of the lab kit.

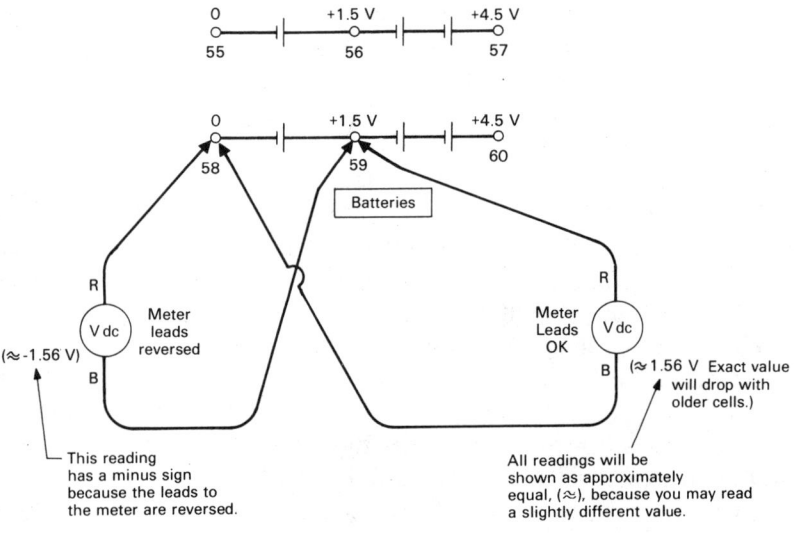

Figure 2.9 Measuring the cell voltages in the battery section of the lab kit.

On the right side of Figure 2.9, notice that the red lead is connected to terminal 59, and the black lead is connected to terminal 58. The meter will indicate a positive voltage very close to 1.56 V with fresh cells. The meter can indicate as low as 0.7 or 0.8 V if the cell is beyond the end of its life.

Now simply reverse the leads, as shown on the left side of Figure 2.9. Connect the red lead to terminal 58 and the black lead to terminal 59. This connects the leads in the reverse order so the meter indication will now be −1.56 V. This shows what the minus sign looks like. If this minus indication is seen, it means that the polarity of the voltage being measured is negative. (Also note that if the red lead is contacted to the negative side of a measured voltage and the black lead is contacted to the positive side, this negative indication will also appear.)

The cells that are available in the lab kit can be used in many ways. In Figure 2.10 a short jumper wire (use the shortest wire available) is shown going from terminal 55 to terminal 60 (always leave this jumper wire in place). If the lower left-hand terminal (58) is used as the common point (or the "ground point", there will be more discussions about ground later) and the black meter lead is contacted to this point, the red lead can be touched to any of the available terminals in the battery area to measure all of the positive voltages that are available. This ground connection allows all of the cells to be added up in series to provide voltages larger than 4.5 V.

Voltage: The Pressure of the Electrons 33

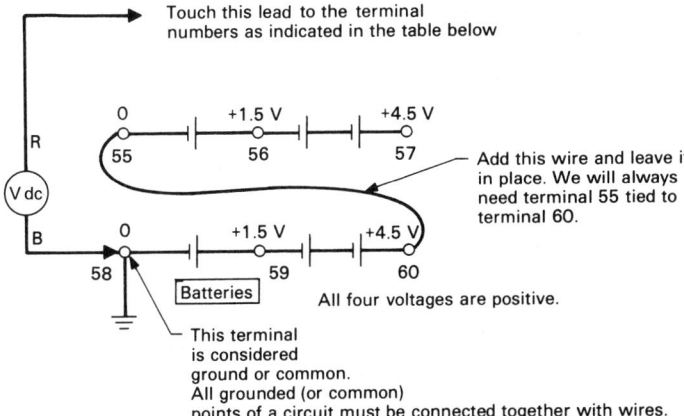

Terminal number	Nominal voltage (V)
58	0
59	1.5
55 & 60	4.5
56	6.0
57	9.0

Figure 2.10 Obtaining multiple positive voltages in the lab kit.

If the red meter lead is contacted to terminals 55 and 60, the meter will indicate 4.5 V. This is the first three cells added together. If the red lead is moved to terminal 56, another 1.5 V are added to provide about 6 V. Touching the red lead to terminal 57 adds up the two 4.5-V sections to provide 9 V. Touching the red lead to terminal 59 will provide an indication of 1.5 V, the voltage of one cell. Write down the actual voltages measured with the cells that are in your kit.

Positive and negative voltages can be simultaneously provided if the jumper wire (the one that ties terminal 55 to 60) is considered to be the common, or ground, point. Connect the black lead of the voltmeter to this terminal. This provides two positive voltages (on terminals 56 and 57) and two negative voltages (on terminals 58 and 59), as shown in Figure 2.11. The nominal voltages that should be read are also shown. Notice that the black lead is tied to the ground point (terminals 55 and 60); therefore, when negative voltages are measured, there will be a negative sign in the display on the meter. This ground connection will be used for the electronic experiments that use both +4.5 and −4.5 V.

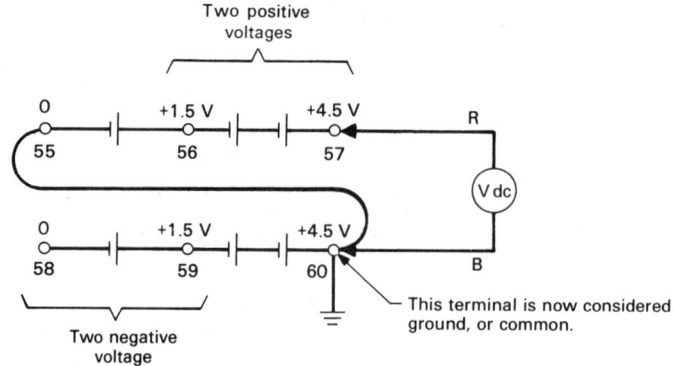

Pin number	Nominal voltage
55 & 60	0
56	+1.5
57	+4.5
58	-4.5
59	-3.0

Figure 2.11 Obtaining multiple positive and negative voltages in the lab kit.

Determining the Voltage Needed to Operate a Relay

Relays are commonly used in both electric and electronic systems. A relay is an electrically actuated switch. The benefit of using a relay is that the large-diameter wires required for a high current load do not have to be run over large distances to get to where the switching control takes place. Also, the high current load can be remotely turned on and off with a low-power control circuit.

When a relay closes or opens, it can perform a switching function on a large current flow. Relays therefore have "power gain"; a low-power circuit is used to control a high-power circuit. For example, every car uses a relay to operate the starter. The starter is an electric motor that is used to turn the engine over in order to get the engine running. When the ignition switch engages the starter, a starter solenoid is energized. This solenoid is a relay that switches the large currents that are needed by the starter motor. This eliminates the cost of long large-diameter battery cables that would otherwise have to be routed into the drivers' area, and it also eliminates a large, high-current manually operated switch that otherwise would also be needed.

There is a relay in the lab kit that is the large component that is located in the upper central area. Figure 2.12 shows connections to the control coil of this relay via terminals 61 and 62. Wires are shown connecting from these terminals over to the batteries. Notice that terminal 62 is connected to terminal 58 with one wire, and another wire is used to contact the other terminal (61) of the relay to different voltages to determine how much voltage is needed to operate this relay.

The relay will produce an audible click when sufficient voltage is applied to the control coil. This control coil sets up a magnetic attraction that moves the armature and thereby switches the mechanically attached relay contacts (terminals 63 and 64 open, and terminals 64 and 65 close).

First, take the wire from terminal 61 and touch it to terminal 59. This applies 1.5 V to the control coil and, as indicated in the table of Figure 2.12, the relay will not operate. Now, move that wire from terminal 59 to terminal 60 (applying 4.5 V to the relay coil). The relay still won't operate. But, when the wire is moved up to terminal 56 (applying 6 V) a clicking noise will be heard, indicating that the relay has operated. Another click will be heard when this wire is removed. This clicking is the noise made by the moving armature as it opens and closes the relay contacts. If the wire is contacted to terminal 57 (applying 9 V) the relay will also operate.

In the symbolic drawing for this relay, the contact between terminals 63 and 64 is shown closed when the control coil is not energized. When 9 V is applied to the control coil of the relay, the center element of the relay (called the "armature") will move down. This movement will close terminals 64 and 65 and open up terminals 63 and 64.

A typical use for a relay is shown in Figure 2.13. Notice that many hook-up wires are needed here. The Key switch (available in the lab kit) is also used. Closing this switch will actuate the relay. The LED lamp (terminals 169 and 170) is also used and is controlled by the normally open set of contacts of the relay (terminals 64 and 65).

Notice that the 3 V for the lamp comes from terminals 56 and 57 of the battery section. Terminal 169 of the lamp goes to a 100-Ω resistor and then to terminal 65 of the relay contacts. Terminal 64 of the relay contacts ties to terminal 56 of the battery section. Terminals 56 and 57 are contacting two cells in series to provide 3 V for the lamp.

The control coil of the relay is powered across all of the cells in series to provide 9 V. Terminal 58 of the battery section goes to terminal 168 of the Key switch. Terminal 167 of the Key switch then goes over to the relay coil (terminal 62). The other relay coil terminal (61) goes up to terminal 57 of the battery section.

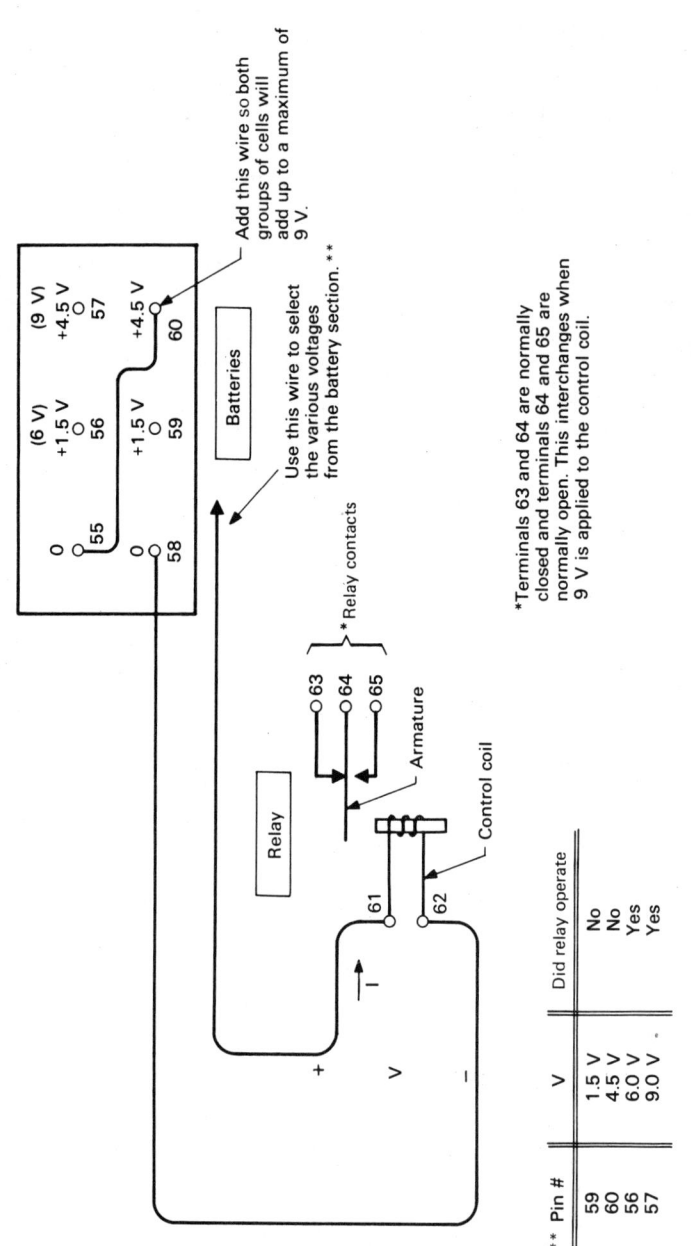

Figure 2.12 Determining the voltage needed to operate the relay in the lab kit.

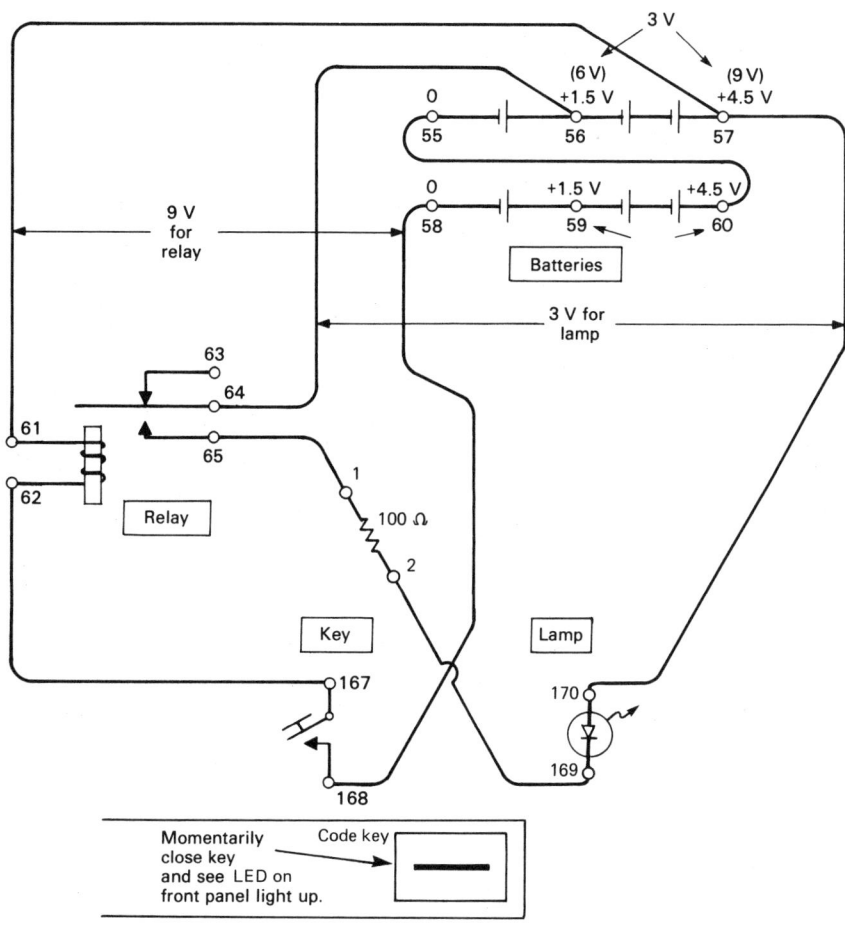

Figure 2.13 Using the relay to operate a lamp.

When the red Key switch is pushed down (closed), voltage is applied to the control coil of the relay. This will cause the resulting armature movement of the relay to connect terminal 64 to terminal 65, which completes the electric circuit to light the lamp. Depress the Key switch to verify that the lamp lights when this switch is closed.

Now that voltages have been discussed, we can move on and take a look at the "passive components" (resistors and capacitors) and also the "active components" (diodes and transistors) that are used to make electronic circuits.

Chapter

3

Circuit Components Operating with Direct Current

In the discussions about circuit components, we will limit our concern to operating with direct current. Direct current (dc) is used to imply voltages that are reasonably constant in magnitude and do not change signs or currents that are reasonably constant and do not change direction. Alternating currents (ac) are currents or voltages that are constantly changing with time. For example, in homes the wall electrical outlets provide 110 V ac. Batteries, on the other hand, provide dc voltages.

There are many electronic components and items of hardware that will not be discussed in detail in this book, such as lamps, switches, connectors, plugs, sockets, jacks, heat sinks, fans, and PC board materials. Many people devote their careers to the understanding, design, and manufacture of electronic components. Another group of people (component engineers) work as specialists within engineering organizations to keep up to date with the latest components, and these component engineers consult with design engineers on component applications.

Resistors: To Resist Current Flow

A very common electronic component is the resistor. Figure 3.1 shows the electronic symbols for various types of resistors. A "fixed resistor" is shown in Figure 3.1a. This is a component that is designed to have a specific amount of resistance. In the center of this drawing is a variable resistor, a "rheostat." A rheostat allows the resistance value to be

40   Chapter Three

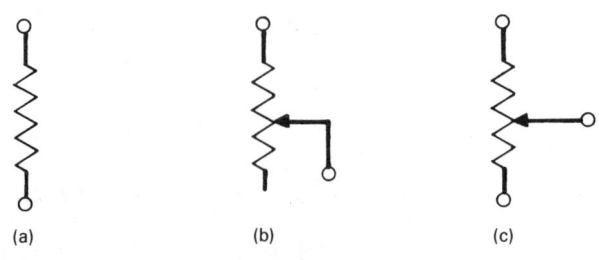

Figure 3-1 Resistor symbols. (*a*) A fixed resistor, (*b*) a variable resistor (a rheostat), and (*c*) a variable tap on a fixed resistor (a potentiometer).

varied, either by turning a screw or a knob or by loosening a clamp and sliding a wiper physically up and down the resistor element.

The last thing shown in this figure is a fixed-resistor element with a sliding wiper, a "potentiometer." This wiper provides a voltage that lies between the voltages that are placed across the main resistor element. The wiper can therefore sample the voltage from one end of the resistor element to the other end. Potentiometers are used as volume controls and tone controls in televisions and radios. To increase the audio level, the wiper is moved toward the higher audio signal voltage that exists at one end of the resistor. To reduce the audio level, the wiper is moved in the opposite direction, to the end that has no signal, the grounded end.

The unit of resistance is the ohm (Ω). Resistors commonly make use of metric prefixes, such as kilo (kilo ohms, or 1000 Ω, sometimes referred to simply as k and also kΩ) and mega (mega ohms, MΩ, 1 million ohms, referred to as meg and also megohm).

Figure 3.2 shows some of the various types of resistors that exist. Even a much wider range of resistors than are shown here are available. Resistors come in many different physical sizes and are also made out of various resistive materials.

Resistors are also very common within the appliances that are in homes. Examples are electric kitchen ranges, electric stoves, electric ovens, bathroom heaters, electric hot water heaters, hair dryers, hair curling irons, electric coffee pots, heat lamps, waffle irons, and electric clothes dryers. All of these, even incandescent light bulbs, are basically resistors. These resistors are used to convert electrical energy into thermal energy, heat.

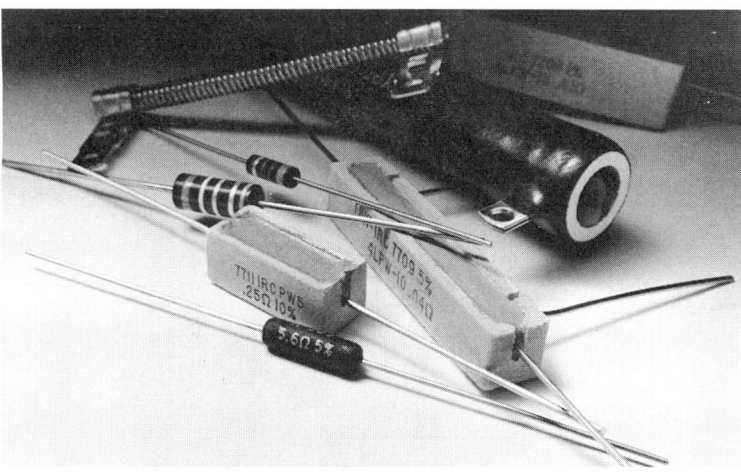

Figure 3-2 Resistors look like this. (*Courtesy of TRW Resistor Products Division.*)

The visible light that comes out of an incandescent light bulb is almost incidental as far as making use of the available electrical energy is concerned. The resistance of the filament wire inside of the glass bulb causes this wire to become extremely hot. When the filament is at about 2000°C, the filament radiates white light. Therefore, this very intensely heated resistor (the filament) serves as a lamp. The problem is that most of the electrical energy that is provided to an incandescent lamp is radiated as heat. The heat is not desired; we want only the light. Fluorescent lights are much more efficient: more of the electrical energy that is provided is converted into usable light.

The electrical line cords that carry electricity to appliances are also resistors. Figure 3.3 shows a number of the different cords that are used in a home. At the top of this illustration is the very thin, small-diameter, electrical cord that is called "lamp cord" or "zip cord." It is used for the small current flow of radios, table lamps, and floor lamps. Zip cord is one of the smallest electrical cords found in homes. Some of the heavier current drain appliances such as hair dryers, toasters, and waffle irons use larger-diameter electrical cords. More strands of copper wire are used to reduce the resistance in the electrical cords of these high-current-consuming appliances. These large currents make the line cords warm and also cause an undesired drop in the voltage that is actually supplied to the appliance.

Resistors come in various tolerances, a way to indicate how precise the value of the resistance is. Common resistors for use in electronic circuits are supplied with a 5 percent tolerance. This means if a resistor is marked 100 Ω, it can actually measure anywhere from 95 Ω (5

42   Chapter Three

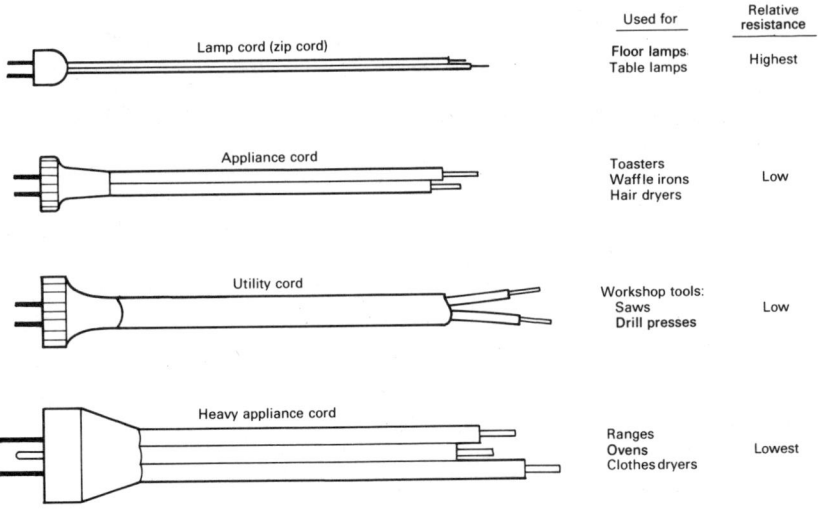

Figure 3-3 Wires have resistance too.

percent low) to 105 Ω (5 percent high). Resistors with a 1 percent tolerance are also available. Therefore, a 100 Ω, 1 percent resistor would measure somewhere between 99 and 101 Ω. In addition, 0.1 and 0.01 percent tolerances are available but are more expensive.

Because of this tolerance, resistors with every possible numerical value of resistance are not made available. There are standard multipliers for 5 percent resistors that are shown in Figure 3.4. This is much like the scientific number system. These standard multipliers are not used to indicate the scale factor. They show what values are available for the numerical part, not the factors of 10. The standard multipliers range from 10 to 91 and they make discrete steps in a sequence such as 36, 39, 43 for 5 percent resistors. This is implying (as shown on the figure) that 10-, 130-, or 240-Ω 5 percent resistors are available but not 3.4 k or 14 or 158 Ω. Lower-cost resistors are also available with a broader tolerance allowance of 10 or even 20 percent. Ten percent resistors use a reduced number of standard multipliers; 20 percent resistors use even fewer. In contrast, the number of 1 percent standard multipliers is much larger, so there is a much broader range of values available with 1 percent tolerance resistors.

What is considered a large value of resistance and what is considered a small value of resistance? As shown in Figure 3.5, this question will be answered differently by different people. For example, electric power people who work with big hydroelectric generators, electric power lines, and electric power distribution stations would consider something

Standard multiples for 5% tolerance	
10	
11	
12	
13	
15	
16	
18	
20	
22	
24	
27	
30	
33	
36	
39	
43	
47	
51	
56	
62	
68	
75	
82	
91	

This list of standard multipliers can have any decimal multiplier over the commonly supplied range of 10 Ω to 10 MΩ.

Therefore 5% resistors have values as:

10 Ω	130 Ω	200 Ω
2.2 kΩ	3 kΩ	3.6 kΩ
39 kΩ	43 kΩ	51 kΩ
620 kΩ	750 kΩ	1 MΩ
1.8 MΩ		

— not 14 Ω, 158 Ω, 660 k, 3.4 k, etc.

Note: A 1-kΩ ±5% tolerance resistor = 950 Ω to 1050 Ω in actual value.

Figure 3-4 The standard resistor values for 5 percent tolerance.

like 0.1 Ω a large resistance value. Large values of current exist so the resistance of the power lines must be kept very small to prevent energy loss as wasted heat.

An electrician who works on the wiring in homes would consider 1 Ω a large value of resistance. A linear circuit designer would say that resistors with values larger than 500 kΩ would be large (on an IC chip 50 kΩ is considered large). Physicists and designers of special measuring equipment would consider 10 MΩ and, in special cases, even greater than 100 MΩ a large value.

Person	Resistance values greater than
The electric power worker	0.1 Ω (one-tenth of an ohm)
Electrician wiring your house	1 Ω
Digital circuit designer	10 kΩ (10,000 ohms)
Linear circuit designer	500 kΩ
Special measuring equipment designer	10 MΩ (10,000,000 ohms)

Figure 3-5 What's considered a large value of resistance?

44   Chapter Three

The color code

Resistors have their values indicated by a color code. As shown in Figure 3.6, there are four color bands (sometimes only the first three are used) painted on the resistor body. By deciphering these bands (converting colors back into the numbers that the colors represent), the resistance value and the tolerance of the resistor can be determined. The bands are usually placed very close to one end of the resistor. The band closest to the end is the first number of the resistor value. The next band is the second number of the resistance value. The numerical value of the resistance is specified by these two numbers. The third band indicates the number of zeros, the scale factor. The fourth band, if used, indicates the tolerance.

An example of how a 100-Ω resistor is color coded is shown in Figure 3.7. The first band is brown (indicating 1) and the second band is black (indicating 0). The number of zeros needed for 100 is one (after the 10 from the first two bands), so the third band is also colored brown. Look at the resistors in the lab kit and make sure that the resistors have been mounted properly. Check to make sure that the resistor color code matches the printed value of resistance that appears next to each resistor on the component board of the lab kit. As an additional aid, remember that 1-kΩ resistors (or resistors in the range of 1 to 9.1 kΩ) have red as the third band. Resistors in the 10- to 91-k range have orange as the third band. Resistors in the 100- to 910-k range have yellow as the third band.

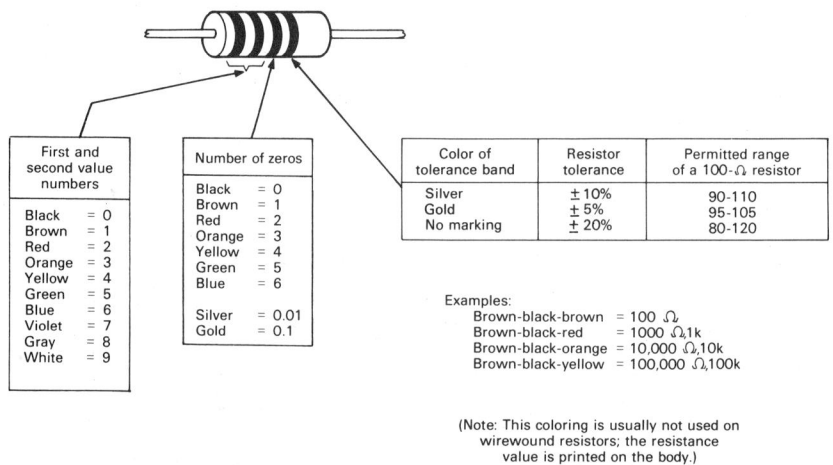

Figure 3-6   Breaking the resistor color code.

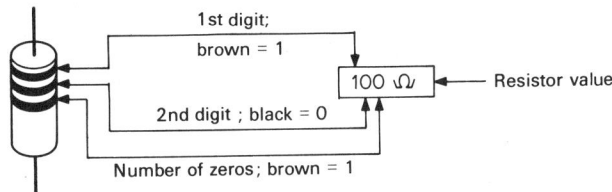

Remember:	1	0	00	
	1k = Brown,	Black,	Red:	Red is the third stripe for resistors from 1k to 9.1k
	1	0	000	
	10k = Brown,	Black,	Orange:	Orange is the third stripe for resistors from 10 k to 91 k
	1	0	0000	
	100k = Brown,	Black,	Yellow:	Yellow is the third stripe for resistors from 100 k to 910 k

Figure 3-7 Deciphering the resistor color code.

Measuring resistance

With this background on resistors, we will now set up the digital multimeter so that it can be used to measure the value of a resistor. This will convert the multimeter into an "ohmmeter." The black test lead stays in the second hole over from the right and the red lead is moved over to the adjacent side, to the jack labeled "+DC mA/kΩ," as shown in Figure 3.8. For ac or dc volts, the red lead is located to the right of the black lead; for ohmmeter functions or milliampmeter functions, the red lead is moved over to the left side. The meter jack on the left end is labeled "200mA MAX." In the experiments that are shown in this book, values of current as large as 200 mA won't be encountered. Therefore, the black lead will always stay in the same meter jack and the red lead will simply move back and forth to change from voltage readings to current or resistance readings. This meter will automatically provide the correct range (autorange) for any of these readings.

There are five full-scale ranges for resistance measurements: 200 Ω and 2, 20, 200, and 2000 KΩ. If a resistor being measured is too large in value for the largest full-scale range, the leading 1 on the display will blink. This overrange indication also is displayed for an open circuit. This feature is made available specifically to check semiconductor diodes to see if they are shorted, open, or okay, but it can't be used to check LEDs because the maximum voltage across the meter leads is maintained at 1.5 V and LEDs require large voltages. The diode check function will not be used. Remember that the left-side power switch must be turned on to power the multimeter before making any of the readings.

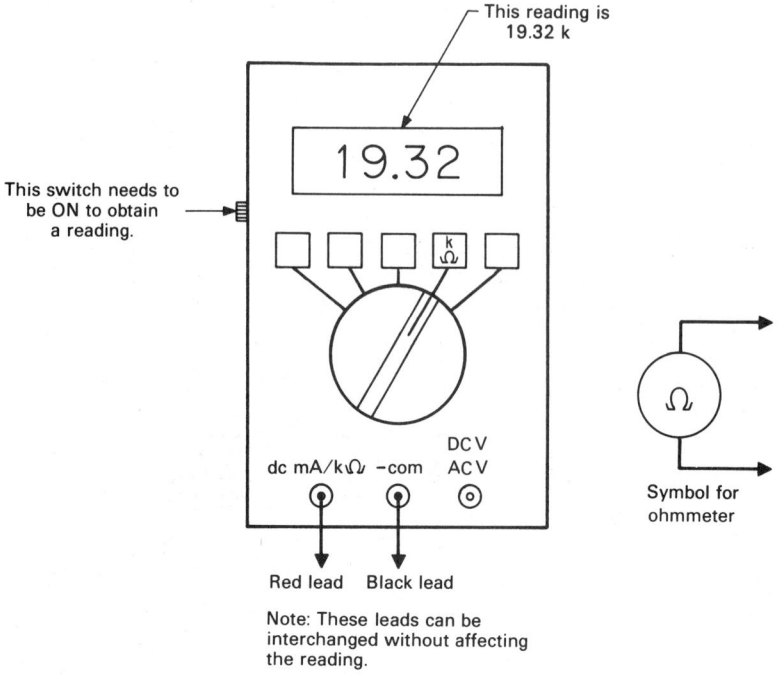

Figure 3-8 Setting up the digital multimeter to measure resistance.

When using the ohmmeter function, the red and black meter leads lose their significance. There is no concern with which end of a resistor goes to the red and which end goes to the black lead because there is no concern about polarity in the measurement of resistance.

The resistors in the lab kit are located in 4 columns of 5 rows each, for a total of 20 resistors, as shown in Figure 3.9. Each one of these resistors has the value printed next to it. It is a good exercise to read the color-coded value, then measure the actual value of that resistor, and write it down somewhere convenient. In some of the later experiments, in which the value of a particular resistor is involved in a calculation, accuracy can be increased by using the actual measured resistance value rather than the marked value.

Read a few of these resistors to get the idea; read as many as needed in order to feel comfortable with the colors of a wide range of resistance values. It might be good to start with the 100-Ω resistor and then read a few kilohm resistors (like 1 k or 4.7 k), then 10 or 33 k, and finally 100 through 470 k. Read a few resistors in each of these relative sizes and use the meter to confirm the values (to also get an idea of how to use the multimeter as an ohmmeter).

When the measured resistance values become small (less than 5 Ω), subtract 0.1 Ω from the reading. If the test leads of the meter are

Circuit Components Operating with Direct Current 47

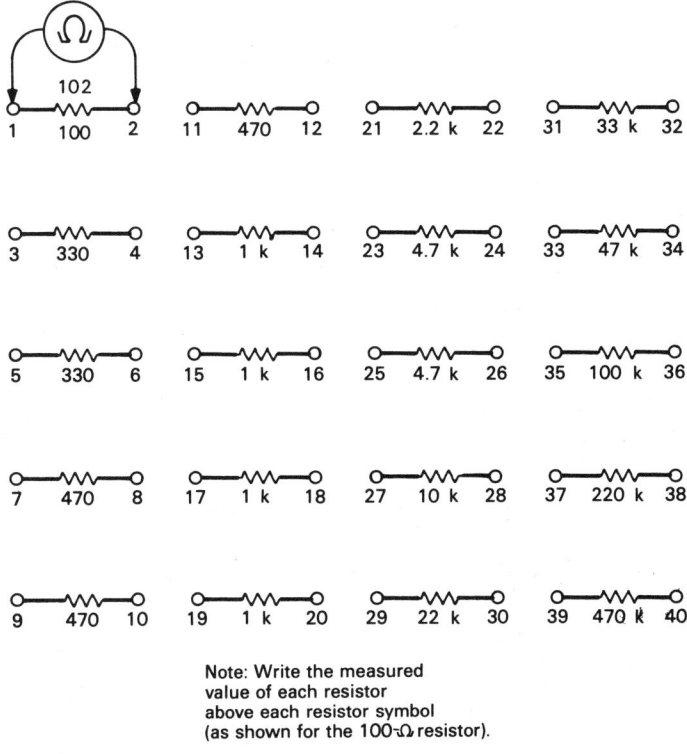

Figure 3-9 Measure and record the resistors in the lab kit.

shorted together, a reading of 0.1 Ω will be obtained. This resistance exists in the wires of (and the contacts to) the test leads. Therefore, to get higher accuracy for lower-valued resistors, subtract this internal 0.1 Ω from the value indicated by the meter.

The resistance of the filament of an incandescent lamp makes large changes from when it is cold to when it is turned on and becomes very hot. Measure the cold resistance of a 100-watt (W) light bulb by applying the terminals of the ohmmeter to the end metal contacts that exist on the light bulb, as shown in Figure 3.10. A typical reading would be about 9 Ω (an overrange indication would indicate a burned-out light bulb). When the lamp is hot, the resistance value increases to about 121 Ω (this value is calculated knowing the applied voltage and the wattage rating, as will be discussed later in this chapter). This is an increase of 13 times in resistance value. This low cold resistance of the filament allows a large in-rush of current when a light is first turned on (this is the reason that light bulbs usually burn out at this time).

On the front panel of the lab kit (just to the left of the loudspeaker, see Figure 3.11) is a cadmium-sulfide (Cd-S) photocell. This cell is

48 Chapter Three

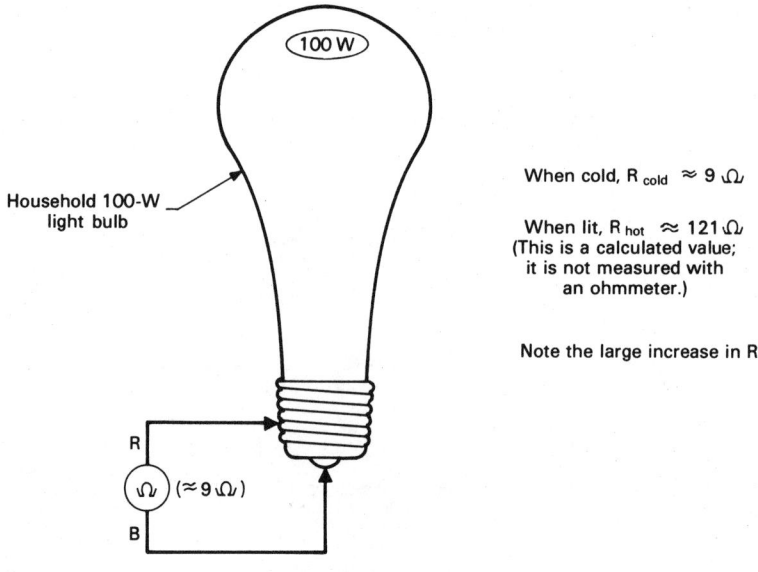

Figure 3-10 Measuring the cold resistance of a 100-W light bulb.

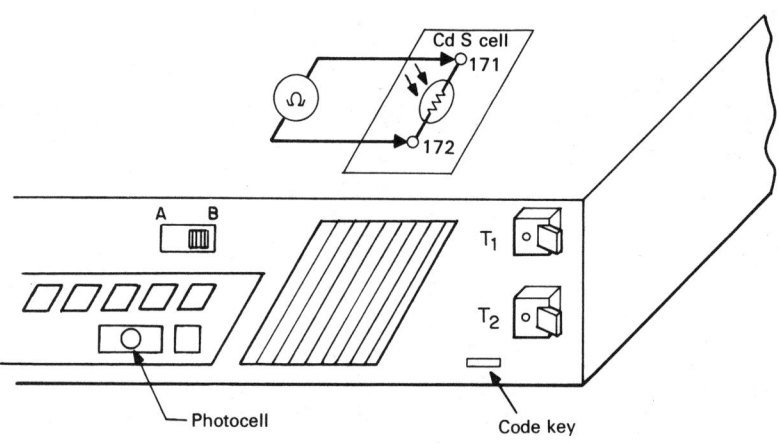

Cover up photocell so no light can fall on it and measure the "dark resistance."

Note the large change in resistance that is caused by light shining on the photocell.

Figure 3-11 A photocell: Resistance depends on light.

exposed on the front panel (to the left of the loudspeaker) just above the large LED panel lamp and is available between terminals 171 and 172.

Cd-S cells are used in photographic light meters because this material drastically changes resistance value in the presence of light. Therefore, the Cd-S cell is a transducer that converts light intensity into a corresponding value of resistance. A circuit can be designed to respond to this variation in resistance and thereby respond to light intensity.

Resistors in series and parallel

Two 1-k resistors can be combined in either series or parallel as shown in Figure 3.12. With the two resistors in series (Figure 3.12a), the total resistance becomes the sum of the individual resistor values.

In Figure 3.12b the resistors are connected in parallel (also called a *shunt* connection). When the resistors are connected in parallel, the resulting total resistance becomes smaller than the value of either of the two resistors (as indicated by the equation shown in Figure 3.12b). This equation indicates that the equivalent resistance is the product of the two resistor values divided by the sum of the resistor values. Two 1-k resistors in parallel therefore have a total value of resistance of 500 Ω. If more than two resistors are connected in parallel, the resistors can be combined (two at a time) into an "equivalent resistor," until the total equivalent resistance is found, as shown in Figure 3.13.

Some uses for resistors

There are many uses for resistors in electronic circuits. A very common application is to use two resistors in what is called a "resistive voltage divider." This is a way to reduce the magnitude of a voltage.

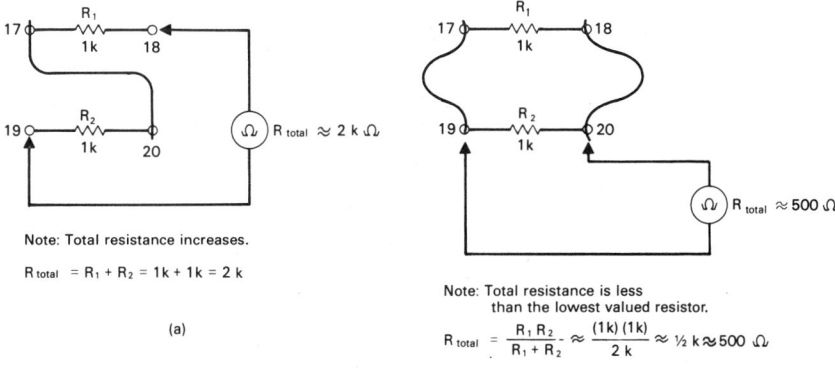

Figure 3-12 Combining resistors. (a) Resistors in series and (b) resistors in parallel.

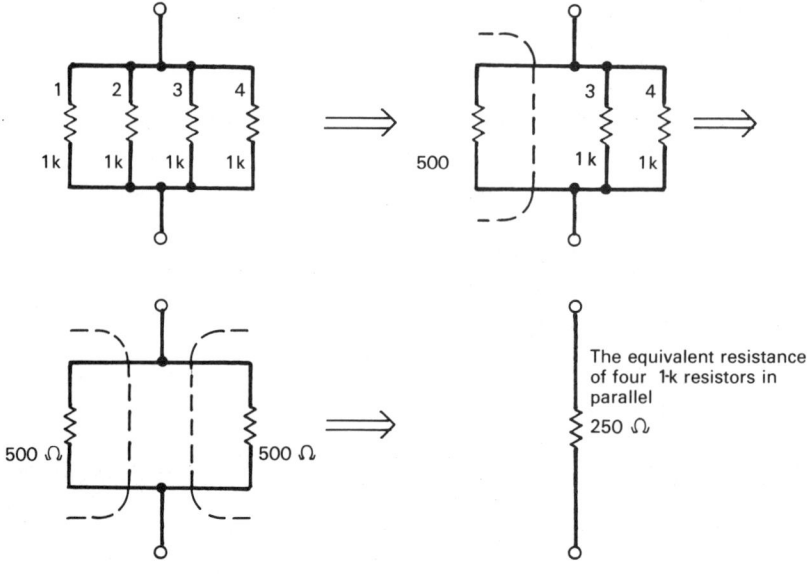

Figure 3-13 Finding the equivalent resistance of paralleled resistors.

For example, the 4.5-V tap from the battery section of the lab kit can be reduced to 0.4 V by using two resistors with values of 100 kΩ and 10 kΩ, as shown in Figure 3.14.

The equation shown in Figure 3.14b indicates how to calculate the voltage that results. Any two resistors that are available in the lab kit can be used and a calculation can be made to predict the resulting voltage. Also, any one of the voltages that are available from the battery pack can be applied to these resistors to gain some experience with this equation. Experiments like this will also provide a better feeling for resistive dividers (also called "resistive attenuators").

The potentiometer in the lab kit is labeled "Control" and has a front panel knob located to the left of center also labeled "Control." The total value of this resistance element can be measured between terminals 137 and 139, a value of about 50 kΩ, as shown in Figure 3.15a. To connect the potentiometer as a rheostat (Figure 3.15b), take a short wire and connect terminal 138 (the wiper) to terminal 139 (one end). The resistance (measured from terminals 137 to 139) will vary from approximately 0 Ω to 50 kΩ as the Control knob is rotated.

Figure 3.15c shows a voltage divider application of a potentiometer. In this case, notice that a 1.5-V cell is connected across the resistive element. Two wires (one going from battery terminal 58 to the potentiometer terminal 139 and a second wire going from battery terminal 59 to the potentiometer terminal 137) are used to connect 1.5 V across the potentiometer. If the multimeter is set up as a dc voltmeter (as

Circuit Components Operating with Direct Current   51

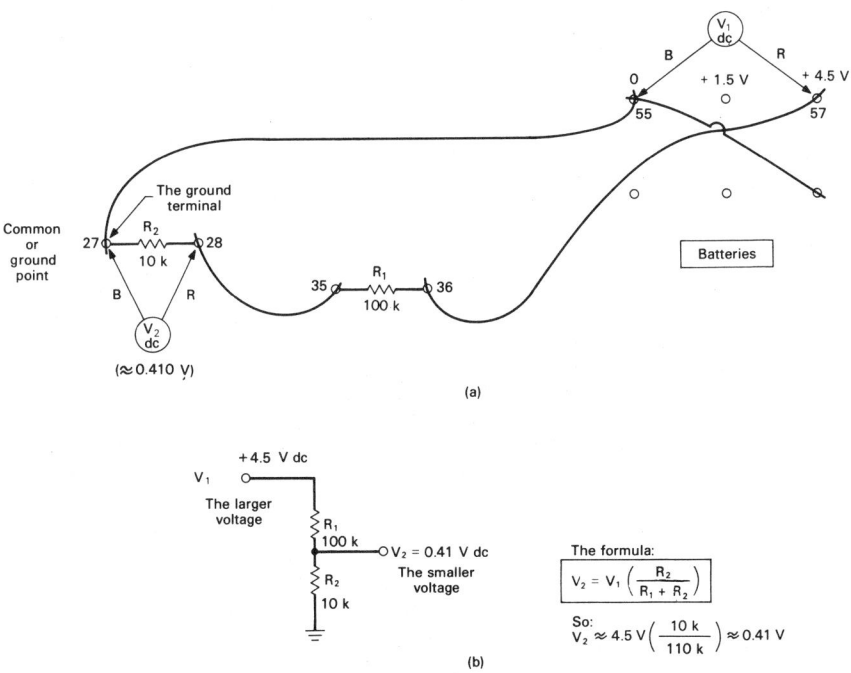

Figure 3-14 Resistors provide small voltages from large voltages. (a) A pictorial diagram and (b) a schematic diagram.

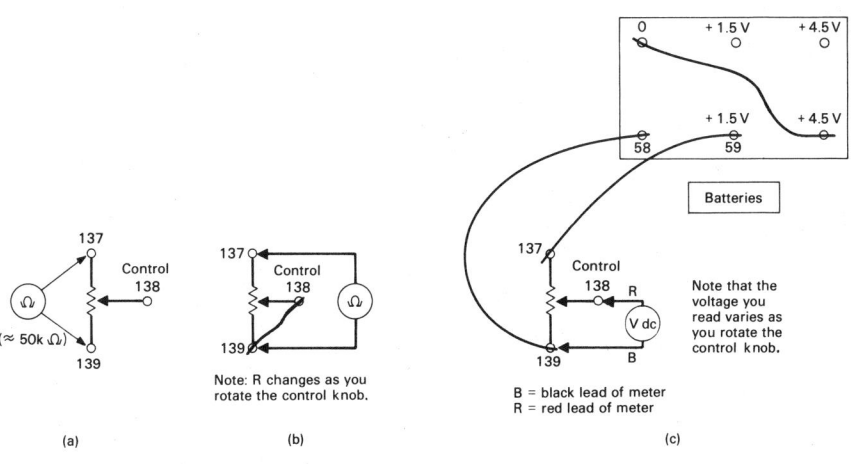

Figure 3-15 The rheostat and the potentiometer. (a) Measuring the total resistance, (b) rheostat connection, and (c) potentiometer connection.

previously used, where the red lead is moved to the right of the black lead to the jack in the lower right-hand corner, and the selector switch is moved to the red "DC V" position), the voltage values that the wiper picks up will be seen to vary from a maximum value of 1.5 V down to essentially 0 V as the Control knob is rotated. Any desired value of voltage can therefore be obtained. As the knob is turned clockwise, a larger voltage will be obtained. If the wires connecting to the resistive element of the potentiometer are reversed, the voltage readings in response to the direction of rotation of the knob will be reversed.

The potentiometer can be modified, as shown in Figure 3.16, by adding resistors at either or both ends. In this figure, a resistor is used at both ends so that the range of the voltage values that can be provided by the potentiometer can be controlled. Both a minimum and a maximum voltage value are established by these resistors. Any voltage that lies between these minimum and maximum values can be selected by the wiper.

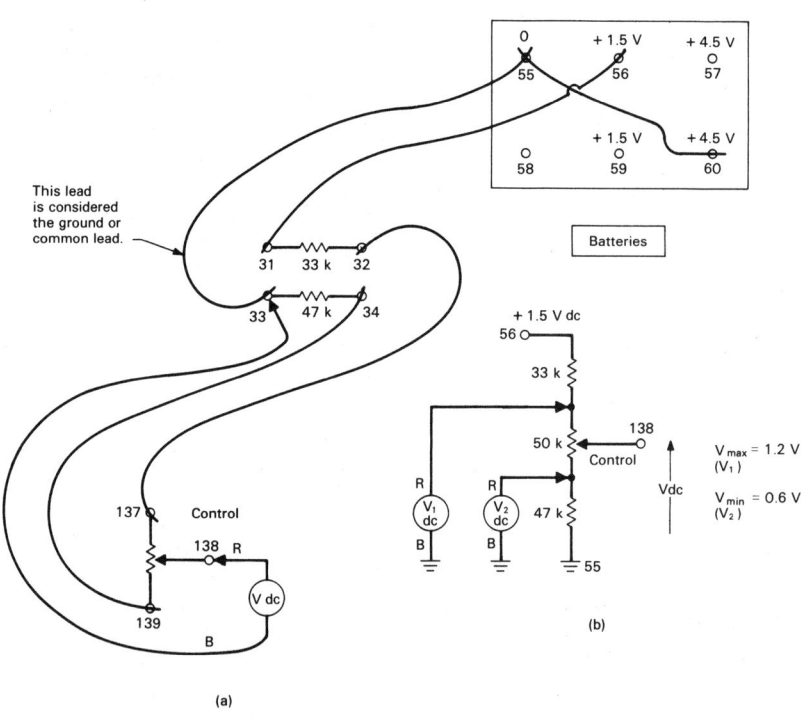

Figure 3-16 Using resistors to establish a limited voltage-adjustment range for a potentiometer. (*a*) Pictorial diagram of the circuit and (*b*) schematic diagram of the circuit.

A resistor and potentiometer made from common materials

To get a better intuitive feeling about resistors, a "carbon-film resistor" will be made. All it takes is a piece of paper and an ordinary lead pencil. In the corner of the piece of paper, draw a line about ¼ inch (in) wide from one edge of the paper to the other, as shown in Figure 3.17. Fill this in by going back and forth with the pencil until the pencil line is a uniform dark color. On either end, where the line comes to the edges of the paper, enlarge the areas somewhat because that is where the wires will be connected to this homemade resistor. This pencil mark on the paper is a carbon-film resistor because pencil "lead" is made out of carbon (graphite).

As shown in Figure 3.18, paper clips are used to attach the ends of the longer wires that are available in the lab kit to the resistor element. These wires then go over to terminal posts T_1 and T_2 that are located on the front corner of the lab kit: the red and black terminal posts. This makes the resistor available via terminals 175 and 176. Set up the multimeter to read resistance and read the value of the resistance of this carbon-film resistor.

Take the resistor just made and apply a voltage of 1.5 V across the total resistance (using terminal posts 175 and 176). Now set up the multimeter as a dc voltmeter and run the red probe up and down the

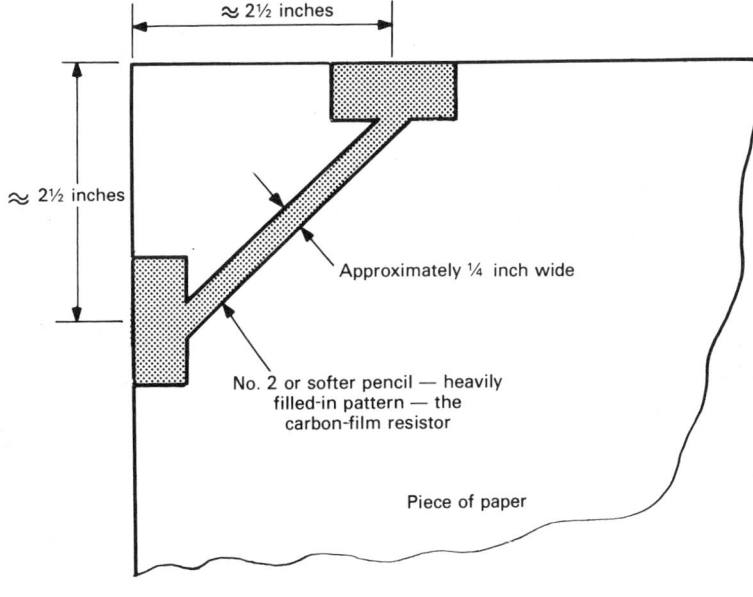

Figure 3-17 Making a carbon film resistor.

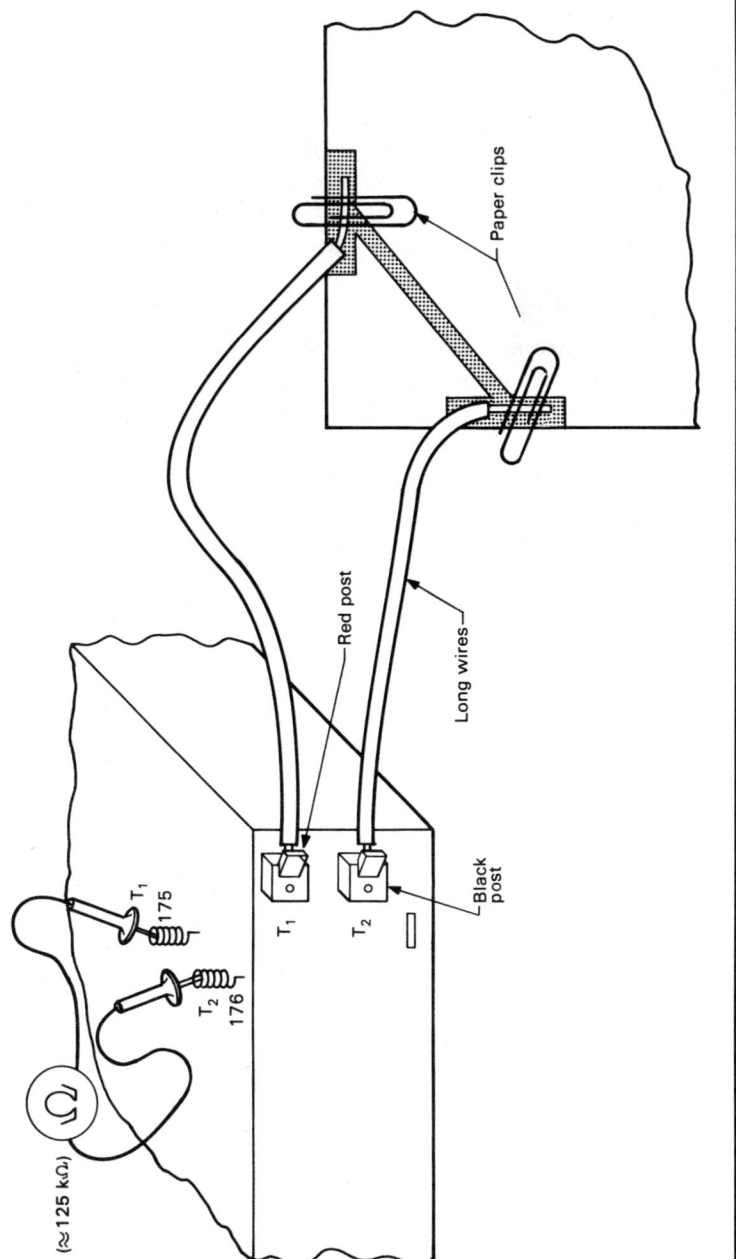

Figure 3-18 Attaching wires and measuring your carbon-film resistor.

pencil trace, as shown in Figure 3.19. This is a potentiometer. The red probe is the wiper and the total resistive element is the carbon-film resistor. In this example, if the red probe is moved down to the lower-left end, the reading will be essentially 0 V. As the red probe is moved up, the voltage will increase smoothly until it reaches a maximum of 1.5 V at the upper end. Any intermediate voltage can be provided by properly locating the red probe.

Temperature effects on resistance

To obtain an idea of how temperature affects a carbon-film resistor, use a hair dryer and direct the heat onto the resistor, as shown in Figure 3.20. While the resistor element heats, watch the change in the resistance value that is indicated on the ohmmeter. The resistance value gets smaller when the resistor is heated. This is implying a negative change in the value of the resistor as the temperature is increased. This is called a "negative temperature coefficient." Carbon film is one of the few resistive materials that has a negative temperature coefficient. Most metals (and even most resistive materials) have a positive temperature coefficient.

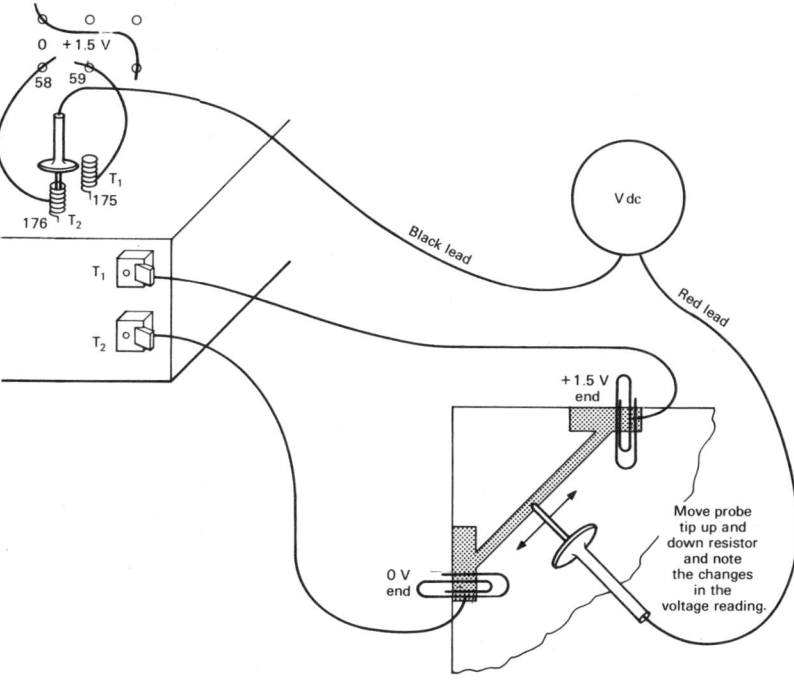

Figure 3-19 Making a potentiometer.

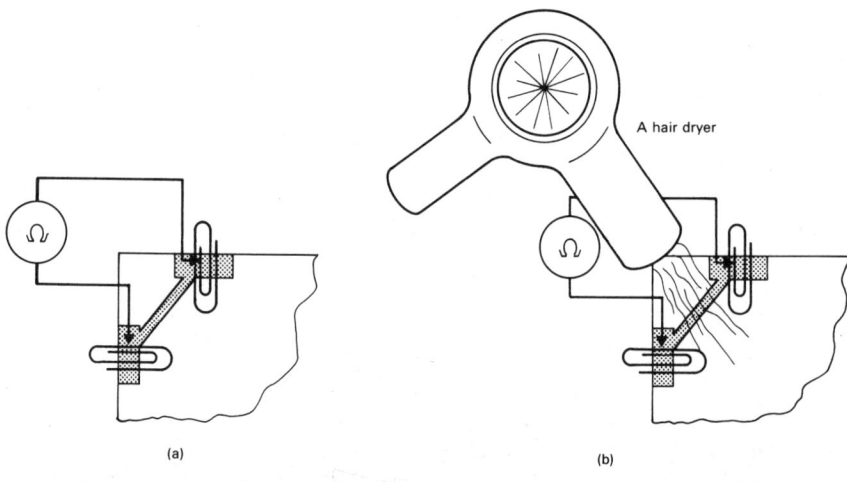

Figure 3-20 Determining the effects of temperature on your resistor. (*a*) Read and record resistance value at room temperature and (*b*) read and record resistance value at high temperature. Did R value increase or decrease?

The temperature effects on the resistors that are available in the lab kit can also be determined. Use the 470-kΩ resistor, as shown in Figure 3.21. Read the resistance value and then bring the hair dryer 2 to 3 in away from the resistor. Heat the resistor and watch the change in resistance that results. The resistance value will most likely decrease as temperature is increased because many of the resistors that are used in electronics are made out of carbon film.

Current: The Intensity of the Electron Flow

So far we have discussed voltage and resistance. The logical next subject to consider is current. The value of current or the amount of current flow is measured in units of amperes. One ampere is defined as 1 coulomb (C) of charge flow per second. This requires 6.24×10^{18} electrons (each electron has a negative charge of 1.602×10^{-19} C, the smallest possible amount of charge) to move by a fixed point every second to carry the charge flow equal to 1 A (ampere is usually abbreviated as A or amp). One picoamp requires a flow of only 6.24×10^6 electrons per second.

The units for electrical and electronic parameters are usually named after famous scientists who, in the past, have made contributions to either the art of electricity or electronics. So resistance is measured in ohms in honor of the German scientist Georg Simon Ohm; voltages are measured in volts in honor of the Italian scientist Volta; current is measured in amperes in honor of the French physicist A. M. Ampere; and

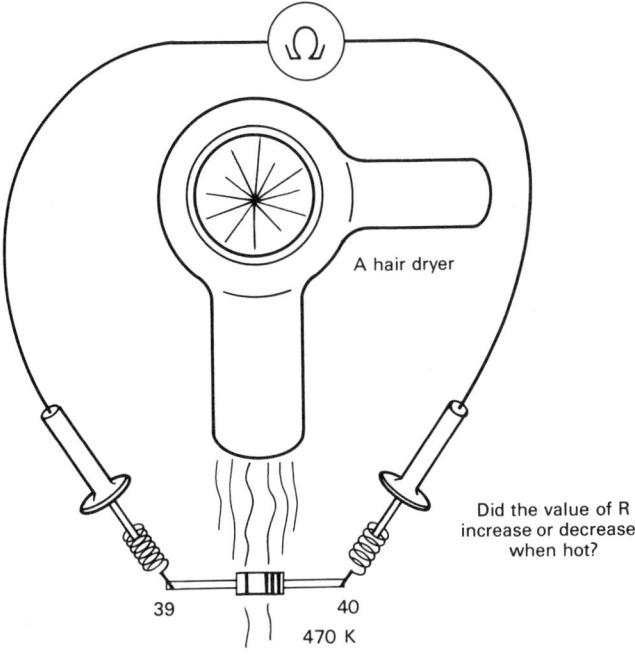

Figure 3-21 Determining the effects of temperature on a resistor from the lab kit.

charge is measured in coulombs in honor of the French physicist Charles Augustin Coulomb.

What are large values of current? As shown in Figure 3.22, this again depends upon who is asked. An industrial electrician working around large factories would consider 500 A or larger high values of current. These currents would be going to the machinery that is used in a factory. Residential electricians, on the other hand, might think that currents larger than 150 A are large. An electronic service technician will think that 10 A is a large current. But, a digital integrated circuit designer would consider a large current to be something like 100 mA

Person	Currents larger than
Industrial electrician	500 A ac
Residential electrician	50 A ac
Electronic service technician	5 A dc
Digital IC designer	0.1 A (100 mA) dc
Linear IC designer	10 mA dc

Figure 3-22 What is considered a large value of current?

58 Chapter Three

(one-tenth of an amp). Linear IC designers many times consider 10 mA a large current, especially if this is the current drain of a single IC circuit.

Today, everyone tries to make electronic systems and electronic circuits that will operate with very small currents. This creates many advantages. If an electronic system is battery operated, long battery life results if only small current flow exists in the circuitry. Even if the electronic device plugs into a wall outlet, it is a benefit to only draw small currents. Then the electronic system doesn't get hot and therefore fans or other ways to cool the electronics are not needed.

Measuring current flow

The multimeter can be set up to read dc current, as shown in Figure 3.23. The red lead stays in the same jack that was used for measuring resistance. The only change needed is to move the selector switch to point to the box labeled "DC mA." There is only one range from dc current, and this is 200 mA full scale.

The currents that flow in the seven-segment display (located in the front center of the lab kit) can now be measured. This display can be powered by connecting terminal 144 of the display to a 4.5-V tap in the battery pack, as shown in Figure 3.24. The black lead of the milliampmeter connects to terminal 55 of the battery pack, and the red lead can successively be contacted to terminals 145 through 151 to mea-

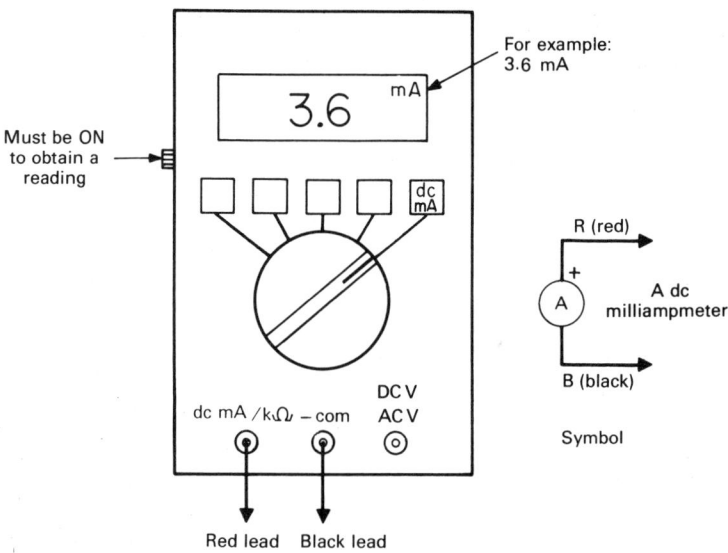

Figure 3-23 Setting up the digital multimeter to measure dc current.

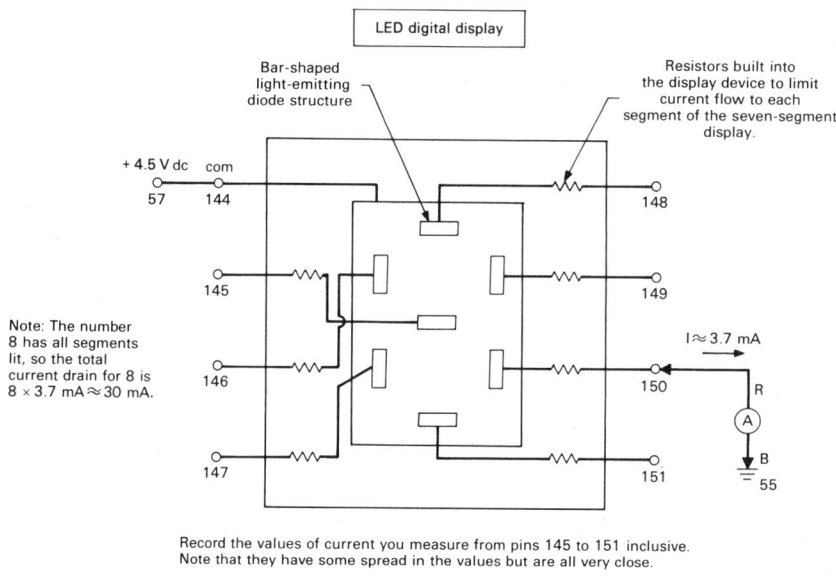

Figure 3-24 Measuring the currents used in a light-emitting diode display.

sure the values of dc current that light up each of the individual seven segments. If the red meter lead is simultaneously connected (using additional hook-up wires) to all of these terminals (145 through 151), all seven segments will be lit. This puts an 8 on the display. By simultaneously contacting to various groupings of these segments, the numbers 0 through 9 can be displayed.

Ohm's law

There is a very important way to relate voltage, current, and resistance. This relationship is called "Ohm's law" in honor of Georg Simon Ohm. If a voltage (V) is developed across a resistance (R), this will specify the current (I) that is flowing $(V = IR)$. Similarly, a current flow from a voltage source would specify the value of resistance that is connected to this voltage source $(R = V/I)$. These examples of Ohm's law only apply for dc circuits (ac circuits are more difficult).

Relationships exist between the three parameters: voltage, current, and resistance. This gives rise to the three expressions of Ohm's law shown in Figure 3.25. The memory aid indicated here is to think of *voltage* as the *vulture* flying high in the sky, *resistance* as the *river*, and *current* (the symbol, I; "intensity," is used to denote current) as the *Indian*. The vulture flying in the sky looks down and sees the *Indian*

60 Chapter Three

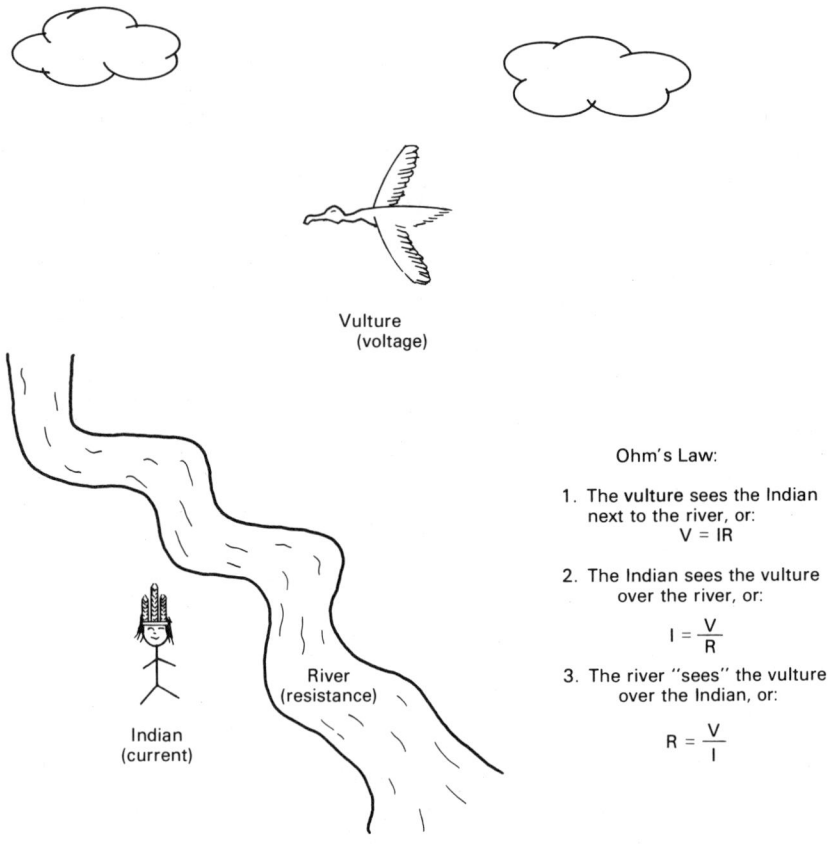

Figure 3-25 A memory aid for Ohm's law.

next to the river (IR), $V = IR$. The Indian sees the *vulture over the river* (V/R), $I = V/R$. In a similar manner, the river "sees" the *vulture over the Indian* (V/I), $R = V/I$. By the use of the appropriate one of these expressions, any of these parameters can be calculated when the other two values are known.

Ohm's law can be used, as shown in Figure 3.26, to provide an indirect way to measure current flow. The multimeter has been previously hooked up as a milliampmeter and used to directly measure current, as shown in Figure 3.26a. Figure 3.26b shows an "indirect measuring technique." The multimeter is configured as a voltmeter, and the voltage that is developed across a current sampling resistor is measured. The current that must be flowing through this resistor can then be calculated using the relationship $I = V/R$.

In this example, the 1.5-V cell is used for the voltage source, so 1.5V is across the 10-kΩ resistor. The calculation shown on this figure indi-

Circuit Components Operating with Direct Current   61

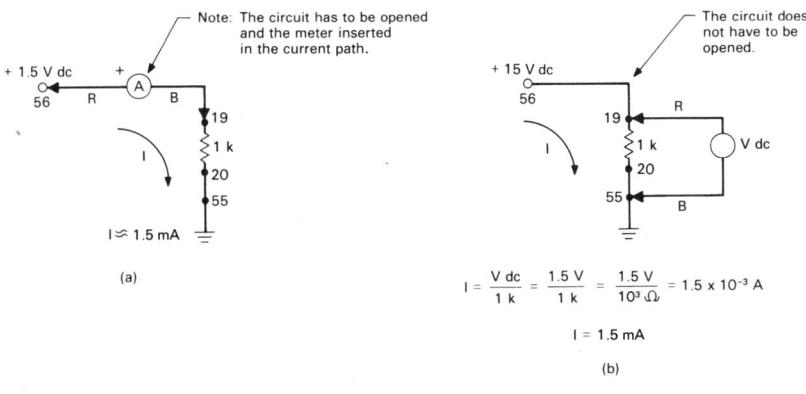

Figure 3-26 Two ways to measure current flow. (a) A direct measure and (b) an indirect measure.

cates that 1.5 mA of current will flow. This is called an indirect measure because a voltage is actually measured, and then the current that flows is calculated. The advantage of this indirect technique is that voltages are easy to measure because the meter probe simply has to contact a circuit node. To directly measure current flow, the circuit has to be opened to insert the meter in series with the circuit. This is more difficult and takes more time. Therefore, this indirect way to measure current is often used.

Figure 3.27 shows that a 100-Ω resistor, when connected across a 1.5-V cell, will create 15 mA of current flow. This is a direct current measurement.

An interesting advantage of the indirect current-measurement technique can be demonstrated if the sampling resistor is changed from 100 Ω to 100 kΩ. The current can be calculated as 15 µA, as shown on the figure. The milliammeter doesn't have enough sensitivity to directly read this small value of current. Smaller values of current can be measured with the indirect technique.

Resistors limit current flow

An example of the use of a resistor to limit current flow to an electronic component is shown in Figure 3.28. Here the 10-kΩ resistor is limiting the current that is flowing through one of the light-emitting diodes (LEDs) that is in the lab kit. The front panel LED labeled No. 1 (available on terminals 153 and 152) is used. The current can be determined by using an indirect current measurement. The value of voltage (V_2) that exists across the 10-k resistor is measured, and then the current is calculated (as shown in the figure) to be 318 µA. The light output from the LED can still be seen even though this small current

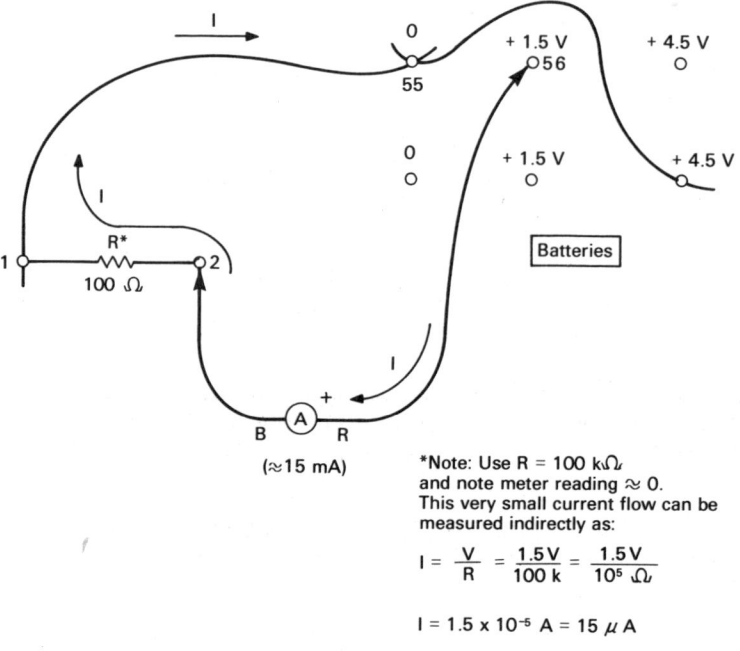

Figure 3-27 Resistors resist current flow.

is flowing (LEDs are usually operated at 10 mA). With optimum viewing conditions, the light output from an LED can be seen at much smaller values of current flow. Increase the resistor value to 100 k and see if light can be detected from the LED. Also, change the resistor to 330 Ω to see a brighter light output.

Voltage sources and current flow

In the previous chapter, "ideal voltage sources," as shown in Figure 3.29a, were assumed. An ideal voltage source will provide any amount of current that is demanded by the circuitry that is connected to it. If a small value of load resistance is connected across an ideal voltage source, a large current will flow, *but the output voltage will remain unchanged.*

Any real voltage source has a "source resistance," a small amount of internal resistance. Therefore the output voltage that is available to a load will fall somewhat because of the voltage drop that results as the load current flows through the source resistance. Larger values of load current create a larger drop in the output voltage.

An example of a voltage source that is *almost* ideal is the 110-V wall outlet in homes. A lot of different electrical appliances can be powered

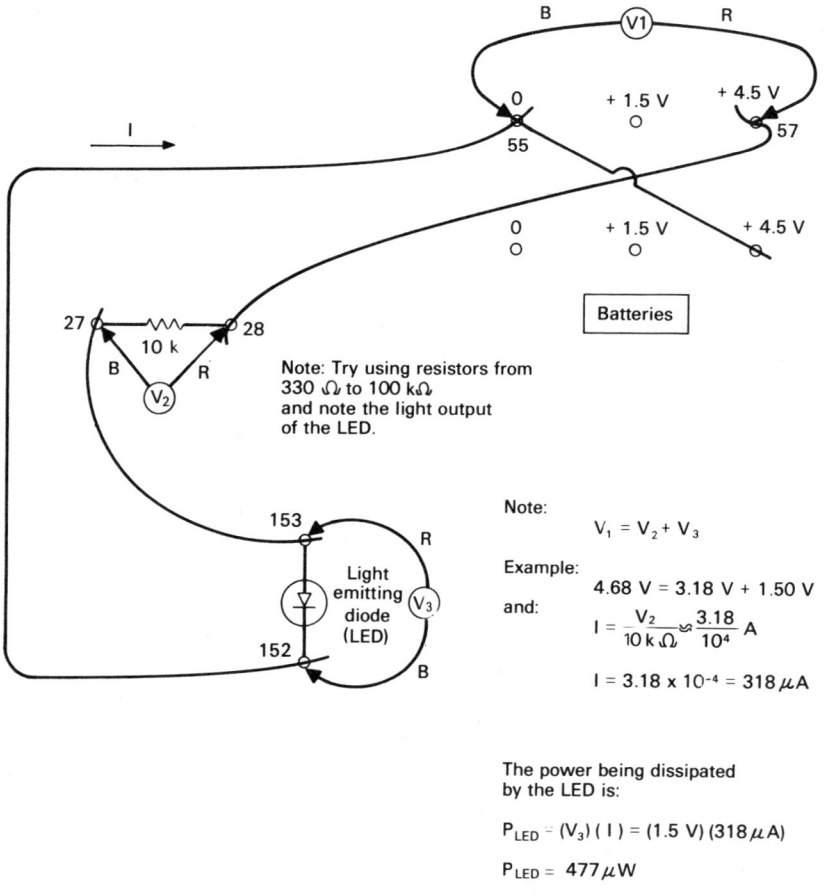

Figure 3-28 Resistors limit current flow to other components.

from a wall outlet and the voltage will still remain at 110 V. However, a radial-arm saw (or any other appliance with a large initial current demand) will cause lights to dim until the saw comes up to speed. Therefore the ac wall outlet is not an ideal voltage source because the source resistance, although small, does cause the voltage to drop when large load currents are demanded.

An example of a more ideal voltage source is a car battery. In fact, a simple way to test a car battery is to turn on the headlights before the car is started. The starter on an automobile draws a large amount of current from the battery. By observing the brilliance of the headlights while the starter motor is engaged, you can determine the condition of the battery. A good battery will provide essentially a constant headlight illumination even though the starter motor is engaged. A bad bat-

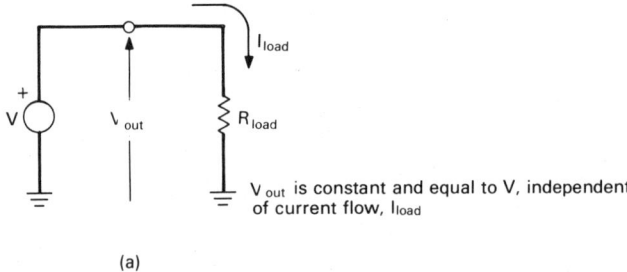

(a)

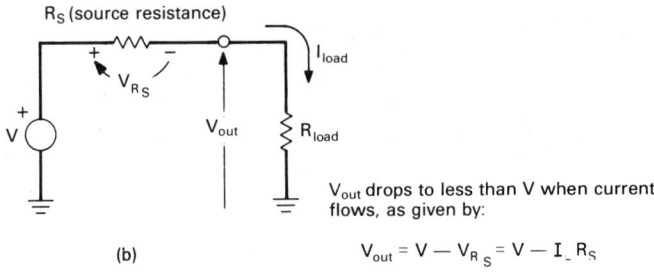

(b)

Figure 3-29 Real voltage sources have a source resistance. (a) An ideal voltage source and (b) a real voltage source.

tery, on the other hand, causes the headlight intensity to decrease (or even change to a yellow shade) while the starter is engaged. Also, the starter motor will not turn the engine over very rapidly. The starter won't crank the engine rapidly because the terminal voltage of the battery falls when high currents are supplied from a bad battery. The reason for this is shown in Figure 3.29b.

Power: Whenever a Current Flows

When a voltage source causes a current flow, power is being delivered to a circuit, as shown in Figure 3.30. In Figure 3.30b, when the switch is closed and current flows, electrical power is being provided to the lamp. This power, in this dc circuit example, is the product of the voltage times the current. The units for electrical power are watts (W), named in honor of the American inventor James Watt. To allow comparisons with other ways of obtaining power, 1 horsepower (hp) is equivalent to 746 W.

All resistors dissipate power when there is a voltage across them, and, because of this, they get hot (although with small power dissipa-

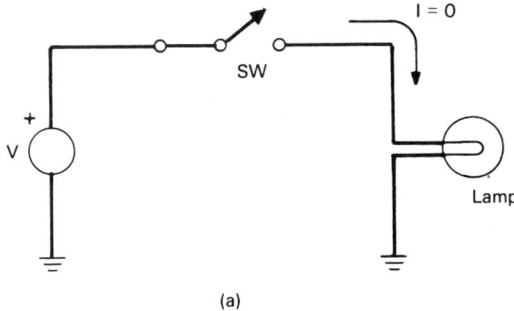

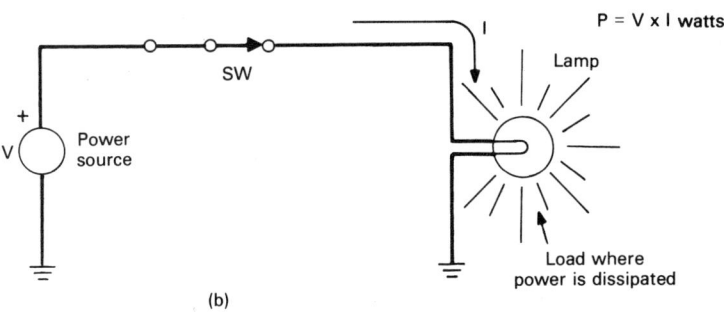

Figure 3-30 Power requires a current flow. (a) No power with $I = 0$ and (b) if I, then P.

tion there may be only a very slight temperature rise). Therefore resistors are provided in many different packages in order to increase the power that can be dissipated. Figure 3.31 shows the smallest-size resistor that is commonly available, and this has a power dissipation rating of one-eighth of a watt. The power dissipation rating for a resistor is an important specification and ranges up to 2 W for the largest-size resistor shown in Figure 3.31 (although resistors with much higher power ratings are also available).

Electrical energy and your electric bill

When you pay for the electrical energy that you use, the energy unit is the "kilowatthour." Electrical energy is the power that is consumed multiplied by the time during which this power is used. One kilowatt of power consumed for 1 hour (h) is 1 kilowatthour (kWh) of electrical energy. Also, 10 kW of power consumed for one-tenth of 1 h is 1 kWh.

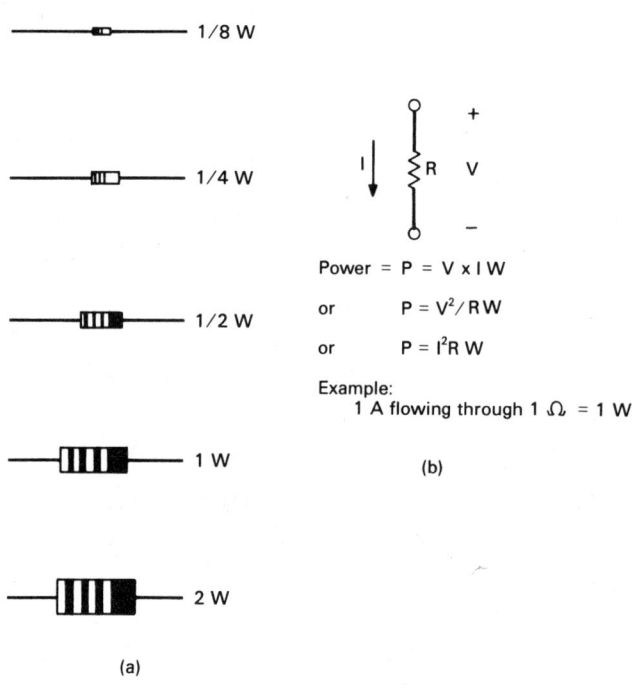

Figure 3-31 Resistors dissipate power: They get hot. (*a*) The larger the physical size, the larger the power that can be dissipated and (*b*) power is dissipated when current flows through a resistor.

The cost of electrical energy ranges from 5 to 10 cents per kilowatt hour (depending on locality), and the cost also increases as more power is consumed. An idea of what it costs to operate home appliances can be determined. For example, the calculation shown in Figure 3.32 illustrates that it costs ½ cent to operate a small 1200-W bathroom heater for 25 minutes (min) if the rate is 10 cents per kilowatthour. It is interesting to consider the relative costs for operating electrical appliances. Pay attention to the high-power-drain appliances. Some of the smaller

Assume the cost of electric energy = 10¢ / kW·h.

Example: What is the energy cost for a small 1200-W bathroom heater if operated for 25 min?

Answer:

$$\text{Cost} = 1200\text{ W} \times 25\text{ min} \times \frac{\$0.10}{\text{kW}\cdot\text{h}}$$

$$= \left(1200\text{ W} \times \frac{1\text{ kW}}{1000\text{ W}}\right)\left(25\text{ min} \times \frac{1\text{ h}}{60\text{ min}}\right)\left(\frac{\$0.01}{\text{kW}\cdot\text{h}}\right) = \$0.005 = ½¢$$

Figure 3-32 Determining the cost of operating an electrical appliance.

appliances don't really matter much one way or the other. Radios, for example, typically draw very small amounts of power; therefore they won't affect your electrical bill in a very dramatic fashion.

The electrical power drain of home appliances

Figure 3.33 shows the range of the power drain, in watts or kilowatts (1000 W), of some of the common home appliances. There is a wide range in the power required. Neon night-lights (that glow with a yellow light) will consume only one-quarter of a watt, whereas incandescent night-lights consume 4 or 7½ W. A total of 400 neon night-lights that are on simultaneously will draw the same power as one 100-W incandescent light bulb. Some appliances consume kilowatts of power. Operating these appliances for extended time intervals rapidly raises the electric bill.

By way of contrast with the large power-consuming appliances in homes, the digital multimeter used in this book consumes 5 milliwatts (mW). This means that only 1.7 mA is taken from the internal 3-V battery while the meter is on.

Capacitors: The Capacity to Store Electrons

The symbol for a fixed capacitor is two parallel lines separated by an air space, as shown in Figure 3.34. This is basically a diagram of how a capacitor is made; two plates of metal are separated by some kind of a nonconductor that is called a "dielectric" material. A wide range of capacitors is shown in Figure 3.35, where it can be seen that many different physical types of capacitors are available.

Appliance	Energy use (kWh/month unless otherwise stated)
Electric heating	
Small home	350-700
Large home	700-2000
Hot water heater	480
Water bed heater	80-120
Central air cond. (3 T)	570-1705
Refrigerator (19 cu ft)	108
Household lighting	100
Radio-phonograph	0.03 kWh/h
Color TV	0.23 kWh/h
Washer, hot wash, warm rinse)	0.25 kWh/load
Clock	2
Electric blanket (king)	1 kWh/night
Night light (4 W)	3
Vacuum cleaner	0.75 kWh/h

Figure 3-33 Power dissipation of some home appliances.

68   Chapter Three

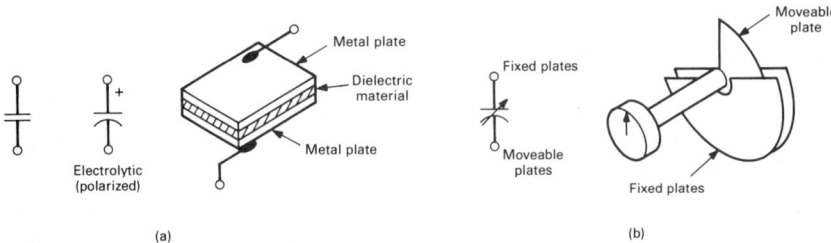

The unit of capacitance is the farad (F, a very large amount of capacitance).
More common units are: 1 microfarad = 0.000, 001 F   = 1 μF = 10^{-6} F
                       1 nanofarad = 0.000,000,001 F = 1 nF = 10^{-9} F
                       1 picofarad = 0.000,000,000,001 F = 1 pF = 10^{-12} F

Figure 3-34   Capacitor symbols. (*a*) Fixed capacitors and (*b*) a variable capacitor.

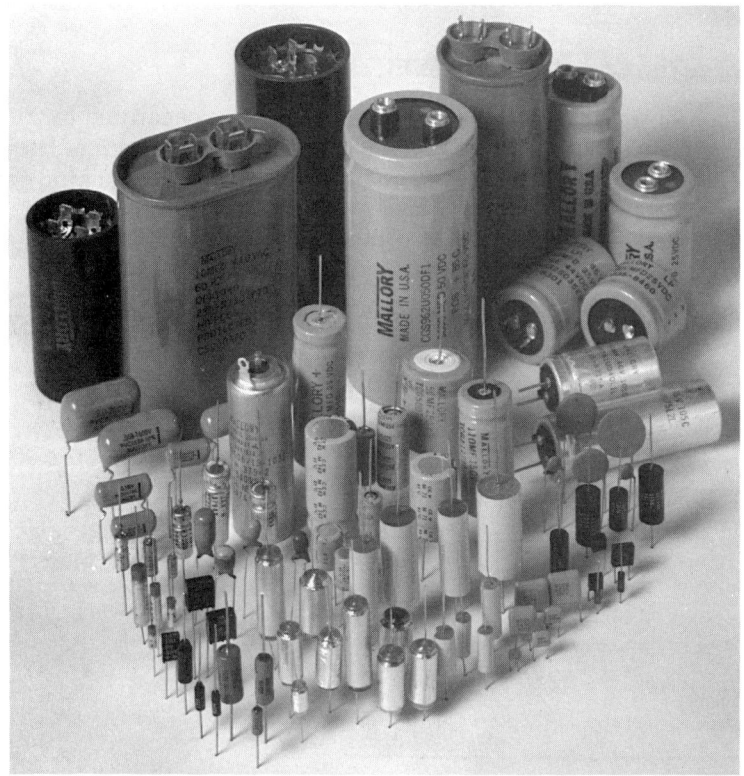

Figure 3-35   Capacitors look like this. *(Courtesy of Mallory Capacitor Company.)*

Capacitors have the basic circuit property that they can store charge and, as a result of this, they tend to maintain a constant voltage across their terminals. A capacitor can accept current from a circuit and relatively slowly "charge up" to a new voltage value. A capacitor can also supply current to a circuit. This "discharging current" also tends to hold the voltage across the capacitor relatively constant. One of the circuit uses for a capacitor, therefore, is to make use of this tendency to resist voltage changes. Large-valued capacitors can act similarly to a battery. An example of this is demonstrated when the plug that was powering a radio is pulled out of the ac wall outlet: the radio will continue to play for a short time. The radio is being powered by internal capacitors that slowly lose their charge. Also, unavoidable "parasitic circuit capacitance" undesirably limits the processing speed of the circuits within a computer because these "stray" capacitors tend to slow down the voltage changes that occur within the circuits.

Discrete component capacitors are supplied in a wide range of values. The basic unit of capacitance is the farad, named in honor of Michael Faraday. One farad (F) is an extremely large value of capacitance. Metric prefixes are used for the smaller capacitor values that are used in electronic circuits. More typical are capacitor values that make use of the following metric prefixes; microfarad (μF), one-millionth part of a farad (10^{-6} F); nanofarad (nF, 10^{-9} F); and picofarad (pF, 10^{-12} F). The abbreviation for picofarad, pF, is often pronounced "puff," as a "10-puff capacitor."

It takes a relatively large chip area to provide what is generally considered a small-valued capacitor within an integrated circuit. A large capacitance value is something like 50 to 100 pF, but in the real world of electronics, 100 pF is considered to be a very small value of capacitance. In contrast to this, resistors can more easily be supplied within integrated circuits. The move to integrated circuits has therefore greatly reduced the number of discrete resistors that are required in electronic systems, but external capacitors are often still needed.

In electronics, small-valued capacitors have values less than 1000 pF (also sometimes designated as 0.001 μF or more properly 1 nF). Medium-valued capacitors have values of capacitance up to 1 μF, and large-valued capacitors have capacitance values in excess of 1 μF.

Relatively large-valued "electrolytic capacitors" are available. These capacitors make use of internal electrolytic action to form a very thin "dielectric film" (an insulating oxide layer) on a metal surface. This thin film of oxide on one of the metal plates of the capacitor allows a very large magnitude of capacitance to fit into a small package. The other plate of an electrolytic capacitor is an electrolyte that is either wet or at least damp to provide an electrical conductor that is next to the thin oxide layer. DC voltage must be applied to an electrolytic capacitor to match the polarity marks that are indicated on the capacitor. A plus (+) sign is associated with one of the terminals of an electrolytic capacitor. The voltage applied to this terminal has to be always kept more positive than the voltage at the other terminal; otherwise the oxide film will be destroyed, and the capacitor will be ruined. It will lose capacitance and eventually conduct dc current.

A "variable capacitor," shown in Figure 3.34b, uses essentially the same symbol as a fixed capacitor but adds an arrow going through the symbol at an angle. The curved line of this capacitor symbol is used to indicate the movable plates. Variable capacitors provide the station tuning control for AM and FM radios. When the knob is turned to tune to a different station, the value of a variable capacitor is typically changed. The knob marked "Tuning," located on the extreme left edge of the front panel, is the control for a variable capacitor (terminals 135 and 136) that has a maximum value of about 265 pF.

There are ten fixed capacitors and one variable capacitor in the lab kit, as shown in Figure 3.36. These capacitors are located near the center of the kit. To the right, within the group of capacitors, are four electrolytic capacitors. Notice that these use a polarity indication. A plus sign appears next to the appropriate terminal for all four of these electrolytic capacitors. The six smaller-valued capacitors are all called "disc ceramics." The ceramic dielectric is a special material that provides large values of capacitance in a relatively small size.

Capacitors in series and parallel

Capacitors can be connected together. Figure 3.37 shows two capacitors connected in series and also in parallel. Capacitors that are connected in series provide a smaller total capacitance (the same as resistors connected in parallel). The total capacitance (C_T) of a series connection of two capacitors is the product of the capacitance values over the sum of these values. In contrast to this, if the two capacitors

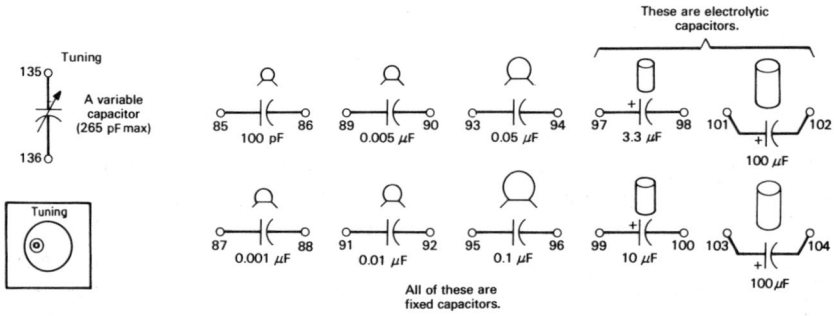

Figure 3-36 The capacitors in the lab kit.

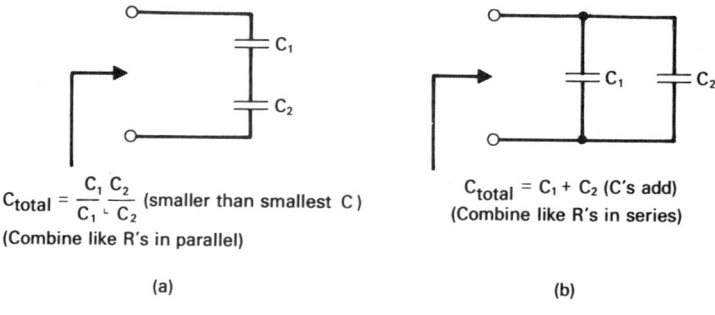

Figure 3-37 Capacitors in series and parallel. (a) Series connection and (b) parallel (shunt) connection.

are connected in parallel, the total value of the resulting capacitance is the sum of the capacitor values (like resistors connected in series).

Comparing an ideal capacitor with a real capacitor

An ideal capacitor does not dissipate any power, as indicated in Figure 3.38. Capacitors will accept a charge and can then deliver this charge back to the circuit at a later time. Real capacitors have some small losses associated with the dielectric material (or with the resistance of the wire connecting leads), so they will dissipate very slight amounts of power. Capacitors can heat up as the frequency of the applied voltage is increased because the dielectric losses of a capacitor often increase with frequency. A power dissipation rating is not used for a capacitor. The two critical specifications of a capacitor are the breakdown voltage and the capacitance value.

There are many additional specifications for capacitors, such as the leakage current (dc current that flows through the dielectric material). An ideal dielectric will not pass dc current. Real capacitor dielectrics sometimes do allow small amounts of dc current flow. If the capacitor

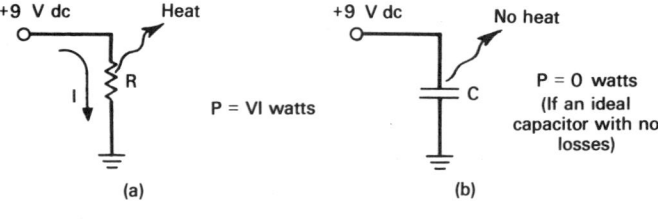

Figure 3-38 Capacitors are energy efficient. (a) Resistors get hot and (b) capacitors stay cool.

72   Chapter Three

is placed across the voltage source that is used to power a circuit, this small dc leakage current flow is not a problem. In some circuit applications, the dc leakage current of a capacitor is a major problem. Additional specifications indicate the time and temperature stability of the capacitance value.

Dielectric constant

In its simplest form, a capacitor has two metal plates that are separated by a dielectric. A dielectric is any material that does not conduct current, an insulating material such as air, mica, glass, plastic film, and special ceramic compounds such as barium titanate. The particular dielectric material that is used affects the value of the capacitance that is obtained.

The value of a parallel plate capacitor with an air dielectric, Figure 3.39a, can be increased if a solid dielectric material is used, Figure 3.39b. This increase is caused by a characteristic of the dielectric material called the "dielectric constant." For example, if the value of capacitance doubles, the dielectric constant of this material is 2. Paper has a dielectric constant of 2 to 3. A lot of plastics have dielectric constants in the 3 to 4 range. Some of the special ceramic dielectrics that are used in disc ceramic capacitors have values of dielectric constant of 1000 or even 10,000! These are known as "super K" (super dielectric constant) materials. A high dielectric constant material is desirable because a large value of capacitance can be obtained in a small-sized package.

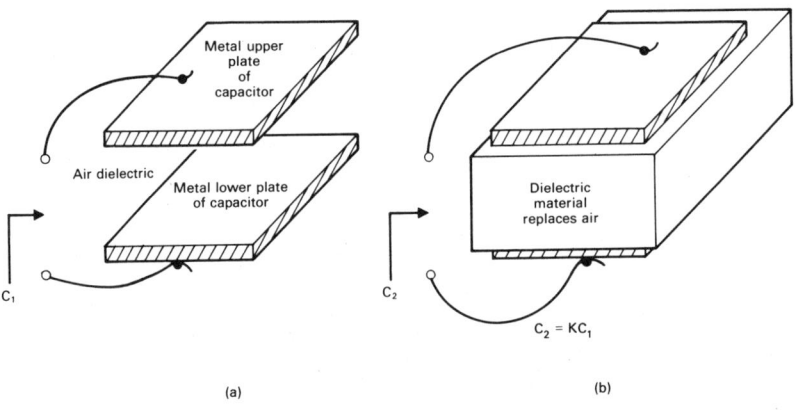

Figure 3-39   The meaning of dielectric constant. (a) Capacitance value with air as the dielectric and (b) capacitance value with dielectric material replacing the air.

The voltage rating of a capacitor

The voltage rating of a capacitor is the most important specification. The next consideration is the value of capacitance. A circuit designer must ensure that the voltages that are applied across a capacitor are always less than the "breakdown voltage rating" of the capacitor.

Electrical breakdown results from the very intense electrical force that tries to reunite positive charges with negative charges. An "electric field" is said to exist within the region between separated groupings of charge. An electric field therefore results between the plates of a capacitor when a voltage exists between these plates, as shown in Figure 3.40. The magnitude of this electric field is given by the magnitude of the voltage divided by the distance that separates the plates. The units for electric field strength are volts per meter. If the electric field gets too high, the dielectric material will undergo an electrical breakdown. Many times this breakdown creates a spark and also a cracking noise. Sometimes a capacitor will even explode because of the internal gas pressure that is generated by the instantaneous decomposition of the dielectric material.

An air dielectric capacitor can momentarily break down, and if the voltage across the capacitor then returns to a much lower value, the spark will extinguish and the capacitor will survive. Oil, used as a dielectric material (an "oil-filled capacitor"), can also undergo momentary breakdowns without permanent destruction.

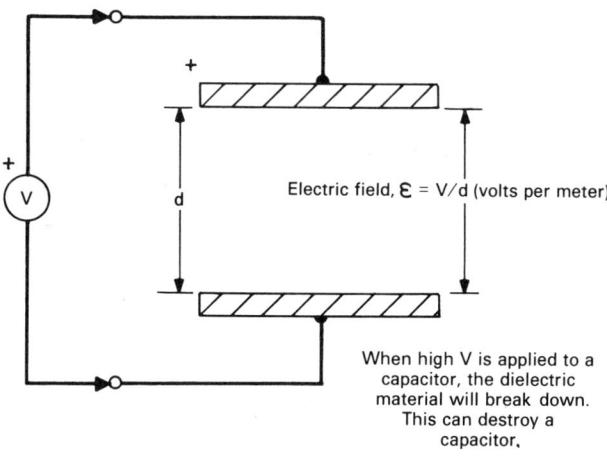

Figure 3-40 The voltage rating of a capacitor.

Lightning and the big capacitor in the sky

A common spectacular example of a capacitor in breakdown is a lightning discharge. This results from charge that the wind picks up from the surface of the earth and moves up onto cloud layers high in the sky, as shown in Figure 3.41.

The charge that is sitting in a storm cloud sets up an electric field between this cloud and the earth, as shown in Figure 3.42. It is this electric field that is trying to return that charge back to the earth where it came from. The presence of this electric field can be felt on a stormy, lightning-type day. Hair will stand up on your arms and perhaps even on your head because you are walking through the air dielectric layer of a large capacitor, a big capacitor in the sky.

When the electric field finally gets intense enough, this capacitor breaks down, and the flow or the return of this charge back to the earth, Figure 3.43, constitutes the large current surge that is the visible lightning spark. Thunder results from the noise the air makes when it abruptly flows back into the "hole" or tunnel that was created in the spark path.

A capacitor made from common materials

A capacitor can be made out of common materials that exist in a home. This is shown in Figure 3.44, in which two sheets of aluminum foil about 2 feet (ft) long and 1 ft wide are used. One of these sheets is put down on a table and is then covered with a dielectric layer (either a

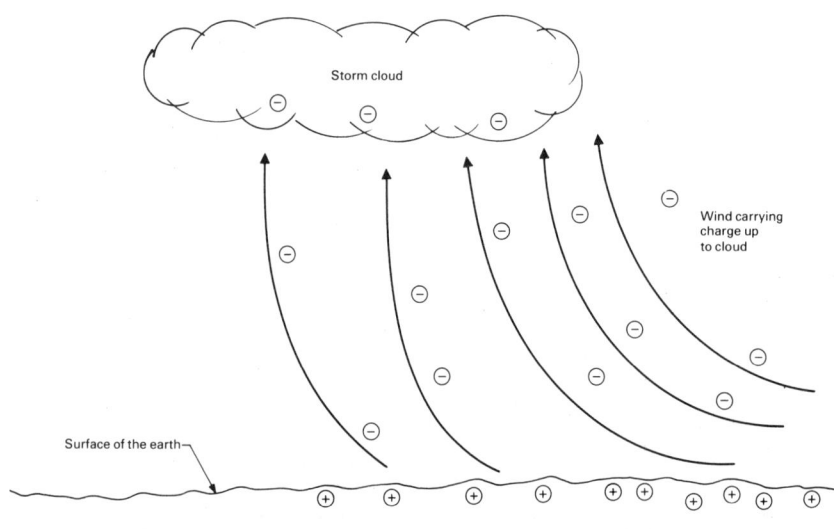

Figure 3-41 Charging the big capacitor in the sky.

Circuit Components Operating with Direct Current 75

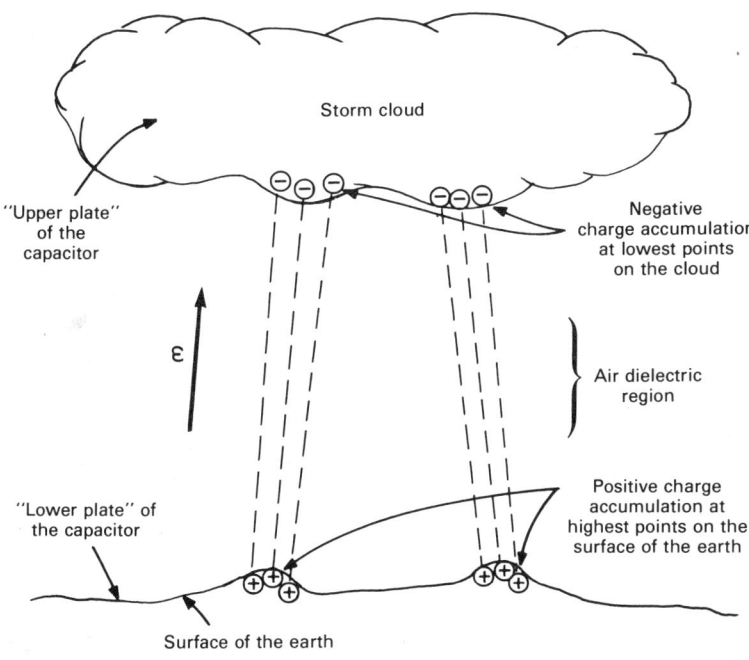

Figure 3-42 The electric field that results and attempts to return the charge to the earth.

thin clear plastic food-storage wrap or waxed paper). The second sheet of aluminum foil is placed on top of this dielectric layer. This second aluminum foil is positioned so that it does not contact the first sheet of aluminum and also so that the long edges of each aluminum sheet extend out without lying over the other sheet (one across the top and the other across the bottom). On top of this second aluminum sheet, a second layer of either the plastic wrap or waxed paper is placed. This "sandwich" is folded up (as shown in Figure 3.45a), or it can be rolled up. The idea is to keep the two aluminum sheets from touching each other; this would short out (and thereby destroy) the capacitor.

One sheet of the aluminum has been shifted up a little bit with respect to the other sheet so that, when folded up, a short part of one aluminum sheet sticks out one end and the other sheet completely covers the rest of this sheet and a contact is made to both ends. These two ends become the contacts to the capacitor.

The value of this capacitor is approximately 0.04 μF. This provides an appreciation for what it takes to make a capacitor of this value. A 1-μF capacitor would require a sheet of aluminum foil that is 25 times larger. Try to imagine this same technique being used to build a 1-F capacitor. This would have to be a million times larger than the 1-μF capacitor or 25 million times larger than the 0.04-μF capacitor!

76   Chapter Three

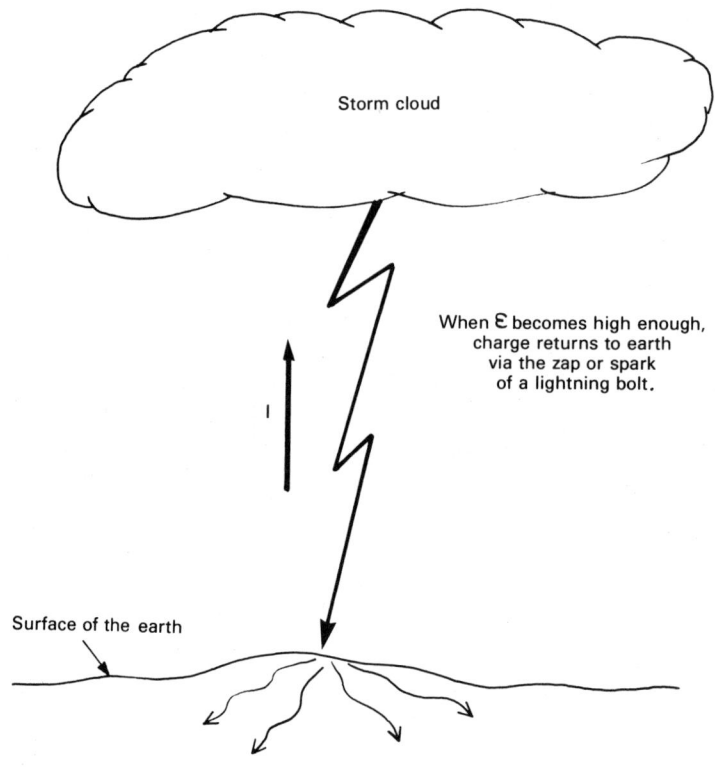

Figure 3-43 The lightning bolt ruptures the dielectric as the charge quickly returns to earth.

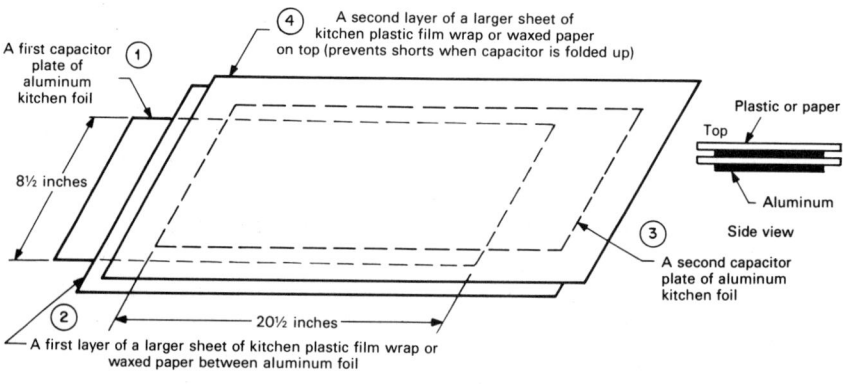

Figure 3-44 Making a capacitor.

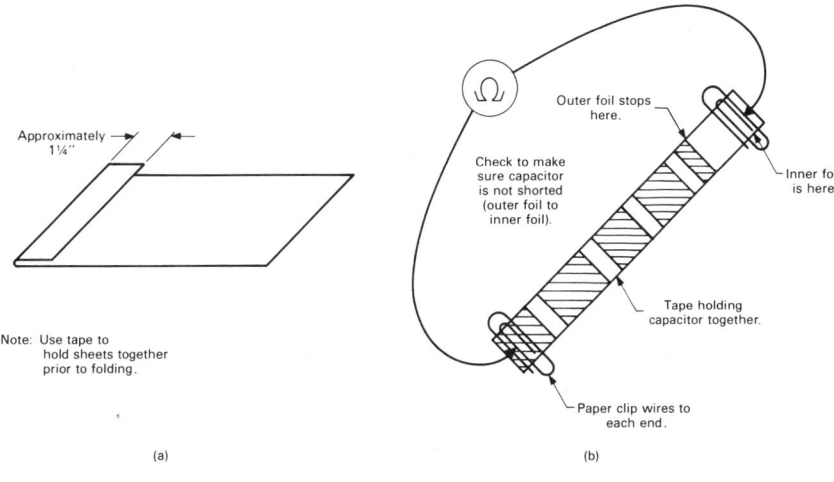

Figure 3-45 Folding up your capacitor. (*a*) Starting the foldup and (*b*) the finished capacitor.

The breakdown voltage of this homemade capacitor will be fairly large because the breakdown of plastic is a few hundred volts per mil (0.001 in). So, even with 0.5-mil plastic wrap, the breakdown voltage will be in excess of 100 V. With 3-mil-thick waxed paper (that has a breakdown rating of approximately 200 to 300 V per mil), the breakdown voltage will be 600 to 900 V. These are large breakdown voltages because of the relatively thick dielectric layers. The benefit of a thinner dielectric layer is that breakdown voltage can be directly exchanged for a larger capacitance value.

Charge and a hydraulic analogy

A capacitor is very similar in its functioning to a water tank that accumulates and stores water. Water can be added to the tank at random times, as shown in Figure 3.46*a*. The tank is a reservoir. A spigot at the bottom of the tank can draw off a continuous stream, a "dc flow" of water, even though water is added to the tank in random quantities and at random times.

A capacitor, in an analogous electronic circuit, is shown in Figure 3.46*b*. "Charge packets" can be added at random time intervals and these charges will accumulate on the capacitor. The capacitor is storing this charge. A steady flow of charge (a dc current) can be extracted from the capacitor. This current can be passed through a resistive load, as shown in the figure. A large current flow (like 1 A) represents 1 C of charge extracted from the capacitor each second (1 A = 1 C of charge flow per second). Such a large current would rapidly discharge the capacitor.

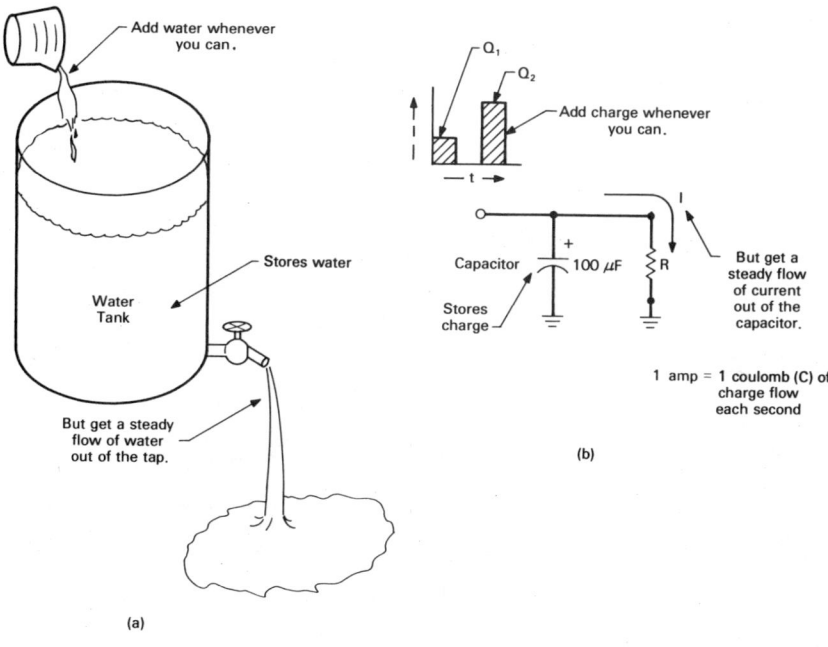

Figure 3-46 Capacitors are like a water tank. (*a*) The water tank and (*b*) the capacitor.

A hydraulic circuit analogy is shown in Figure 3.47. Figure 3.47*a* is a hydraulic circuit that uses an elevated tank of water. The height of this tank provides the *pressure* that forces the water through the pipes and the plumbing fixtures of the hydraulic circuit. An ON/OFF valve is shown at the bottom of the tank. A small-diameter pipe (coming down from the tank) limits the flow of water. This small pipe is analagous to a large value of resistance in an electronic circuit.

A person is shown sitting in a bathtub at the bottom of Figure 3.47*a*. This is the purpose of the water flows and is analogous to a load in an electric circuit. Notice that water is drained at the bottom of the bathtub. A pump is used to lift this water back up to the tank by way of a separate pipe. This provides a closed circuit for the water flow. A relatively small-diameter return pipe is again analogous to a large resistance.

An electric circuit analogy of this hydraulic system is shown in Figure 3.47*b*. The load in this case is a light bulb. Current flow will light the lamp. A battery replaces the water pump and "pumps electrons up," and the voltage created by these displaced electrons causes them to flow through the circuit so that they can return to the battery. As in the hydraulic circuit (which had a continuous flow of water), this electric circuit has a continuous flow of electrons (current).

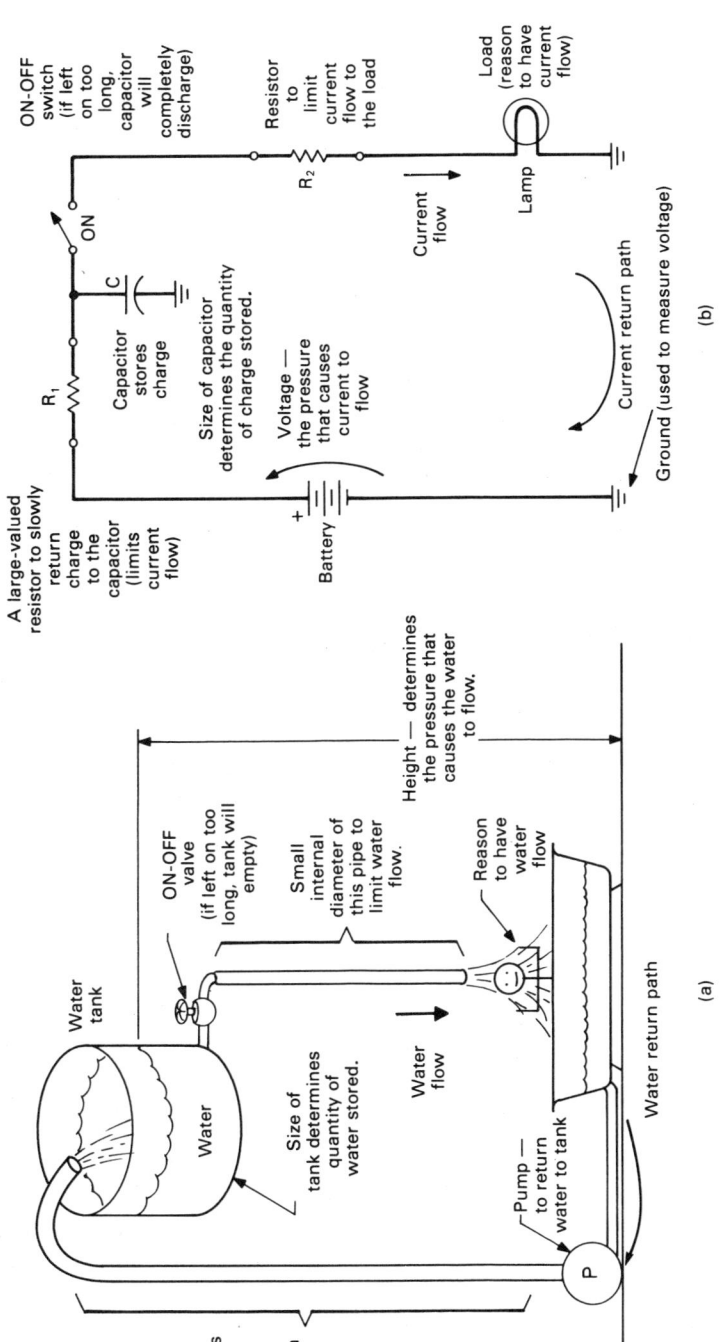

Figure 3-47 The analogy between a hydraulic circuit and an electrical circuit. (*a*) A hydraulic circuit and (*b*) an electric circuit.

80   Chapter Three

A resistor (R_1) tied between the battery and the capacitor is analogous to the small-diameter return pipe between the pump and the top of the water tank in the hydraulic analogy. This resistor is limiting the rate at which charge is returned to the capacitor. The resistor, R_2 tied between the battery and the lamp is analogous to the small-diameter exit pipe that limited water flow to the bathtub.

Capacitors accumulate and store "charge." Charge is sometimes a hard thing to think about. Voltage, current, and resistance are easier concepts, but what is charge? A current flow for a time interval constitutes a movement of a quantity of charge.

A couple of current waveforms are shown in Figure 3.48. Many different types of current waveforms exist. In the example shown in Figure 3.48a, the current is considered to start flowing at time 0 and is a constant current of 1.2 A up to time t_1. At t_1, the current linearly increases and has a value of 1.6 A at time t_2 and then linearly decreases to 0.6 A (600 mA) at time t_3, where it levels off and holds constant.

Charge is the area under a current curve, as shown in Figure 3.48a. Charge depends on how much current flows and also the time duration during which the current flows. Charge is the product of current and time. The units of charge are coulombs. One coulomb of charge exists when 1 A of current flows for 1 second (s). Figure 3.48b shows the example of a constant current flow of 1 A of current from time 0 to 1 s. This is the movement of 1 C of charge.

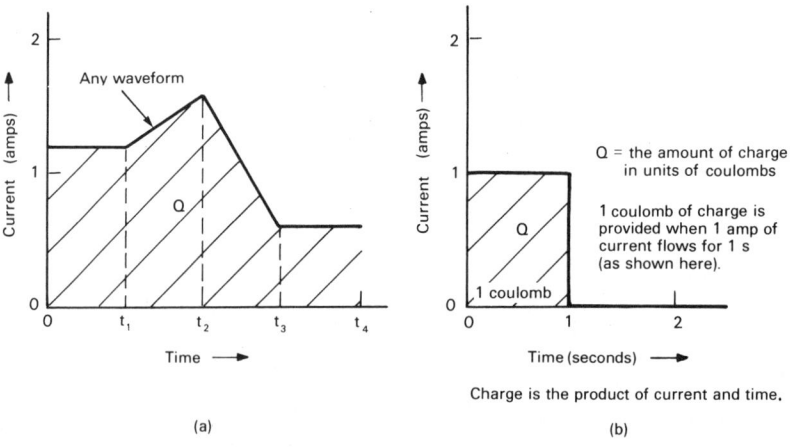

Figure 3-48 The relationships between current and charge. (*a*) A varying current and the resulting charge (*b*) One coulomb of charge.

Capacitors as charge reservoirs

Capacitors can be used as charge reservoirs as shown in Figure 3.49. The Select switch (SW_1) of the lab kit is used to first charge (while in position A) both of the 100-μF capacitors to approximately 9 V. These capacitors are wired in parallel to provide a total capacitance of 200 μF.

When SW_1 is switched over to the B position, these capacitors will discharge through a 10-kΩ resistor and a light-emitting diode (diode No. 6 that is available via terminals 162 and 163). This LED is a way to provide a visual indication of the flow of current. The brighter the illumination, the higher the current flow.

Keep your eye on the LED as switch SW_1 is moved to the B position. The LED comes on most brilliantly at the start and then slowly tapers off in light intensity, but it does stay lit. Light is provided by this diode for a relatively long time interval. This light is provided by the charge that was stored on the capacitors. These capacitors are acting like a battery (they provide a source of voltage and current) but only for a relatively short interval of time. Capacitors cannot act like a battery over long time intervals unless only a very small amount of current is extracted. Capacitors store charge. They first accumulate this charge from a voltage source and then, at a later time, they can deliver this charge to an electronic circuit.

In the application of integrated circuits, a capacitor is usually needed from the power-supply voltage pin of the IC to ground, as shown in Figure 3.50. This capacitor typically has been called a "reservoir capac-

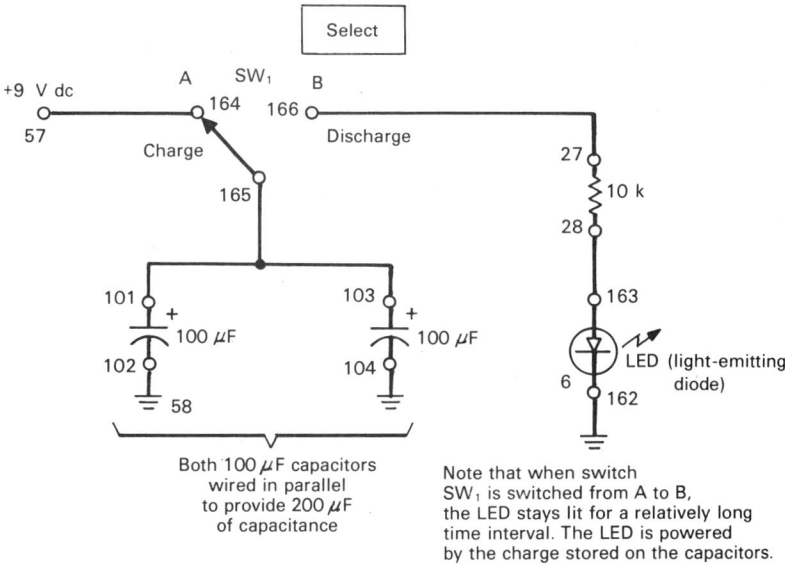

Figure 3-49 A capacitor used as a charge reservoir.

82   Chapter Three

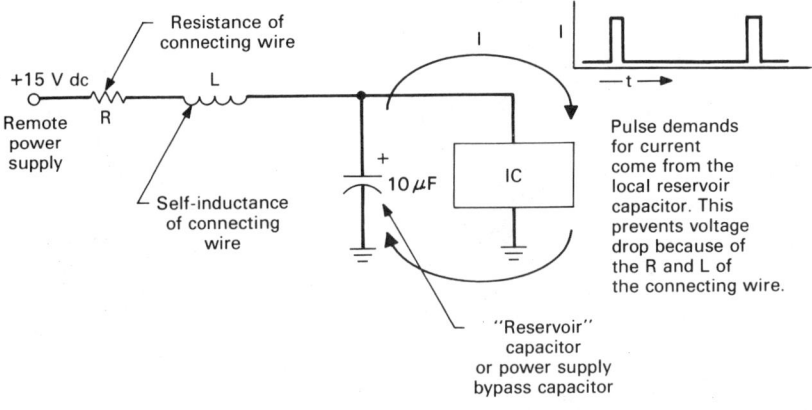

Figure 3-50 The capacitor reservoir for an integrated circuit.

itor" because its function is to hold charge in reserve. If the IC has an instantaneous requirement for a large quantity of charge (a short burst of current flow), this charge will be supplied by the local reservoir capacitor. This prevents the relatively large voltage loss that could otherwise result if a large transient current were drawn through the long wires that connect to a remotely located power supply.

Charging a capacitor

Figure 3.51 shows a test setup that is used to charge a capacitor. All of the cells in the battery section have been placed in series to obtain the highest voltage possible, 9 V. Also, the largest resistor available in the lab kit is used, 470 kΩ.

The capacitor uses the Key switch (with a 100-Ω series resistor) to discharge this capacitor (to bring the voltage across this capacitor back to approximately zero). When the Key is opened, the capacitor again will charge up. The dc voltmeter can be connected across the terminals of the capacitor to allow this charging to be observed.

When the Key is first opened, the voltage across the capacitor will increase relatively rapidly and then will slowly taper off and increase only very slowly as time goes on. This resistor-capacitor (RC) network allows the capacitor to be slowly charged from the 9-V dc voltage source.

The voltage across the capacitor in this RC network follows a very precise exponential curve as shown in Figure 3.52a. The time units on this graph are given as multiples of the RC product (it may seem strange that when ohms are multiplied by farads, the units become seconds, but this is the case). This RC product is often called the "time constant" of an RC network. In one time constant the voltage across the capacitor will increase from 0 to about 63 percent of the final volt-

Circuit Components Operating with Direct Current   83

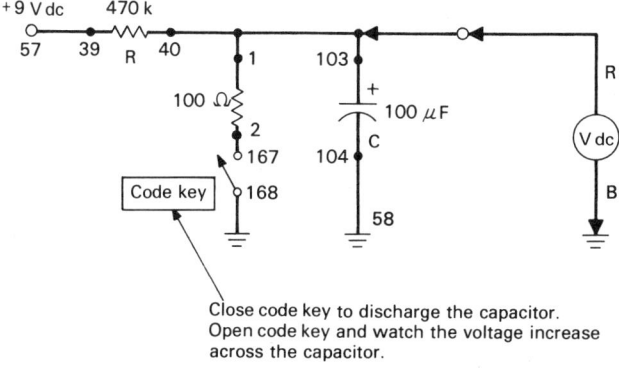

Close code key to discharge the capacitor.
Open code key and watch the voltage increase
across the capacitor.

Figure 3-51 The test setup to charge a capacitor.

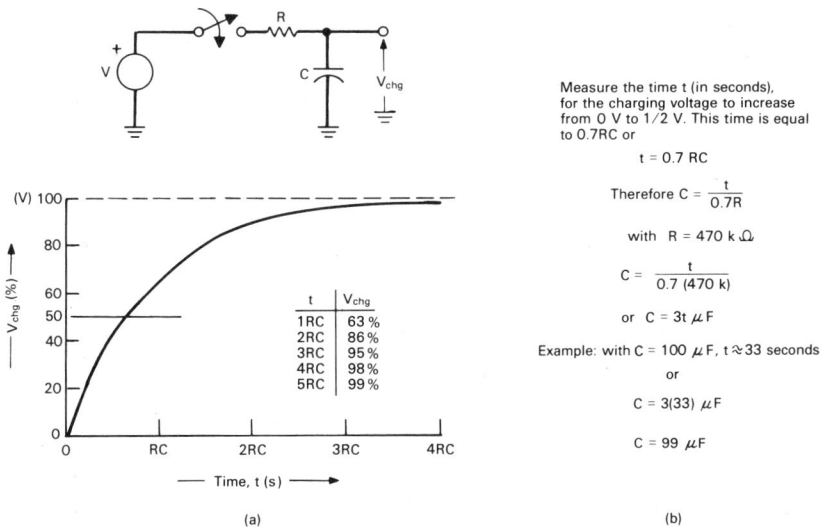

Figure 3-52 Measuring the charging time to determine capacitance value. (a) The charging waveform and (b) determining the value of capacitance.

age. After two time constants, the voltage will be up to 86 percent. After three time constants, to 95 percent, and after five time constants, to 99 percent of the final voltage.

The capacitor will have acquired 50 percent of the final voltage after a time interval of approximately $0.7\,RC$. This can be used as a way to measure the value of a capacitor. If an R of 470 kΩ is used, the equation in Figure 4.53b shows that the capacitance value (in microfarads) is simply equal to 3 times the time (in seconds) that it takes for the capacitor to charge from 0 V to half of the final voltage. As an example, if one of the 100-μF capacitors is used, the time to charge from 0 V to half of the final voltage (4.5 V using a 9-V supply) would be 33 s. With a time of 33 s, the capacitance value can be calculated to be 99 μF.

Stray capacitance delays voltage changes

Capacitors tend to resist voltage changes. This creates a major problem in the design of high-speed digital circuits. Even when capacitors are not specifically used, there is undesired "stray," or "parasitic," capacitance associated with the circuit interconnect wiring (the transistors and resistors that are used to build circuits). The effects of this stray capacitive loading on a logic circuit are shown in Figure 3.53. In Figure 3.53a, with no stray capacitance (an idealization), the logic voltage changes are very abrupt. With stray capacitance present, Figure 3.53b, the voltages cannot change as rapidly. This more slowly changing logic voltage waveform undesirably reduces the speed of the propagation of logic signals (voltage changes) through a digital system and therefore slows down the processing speed.

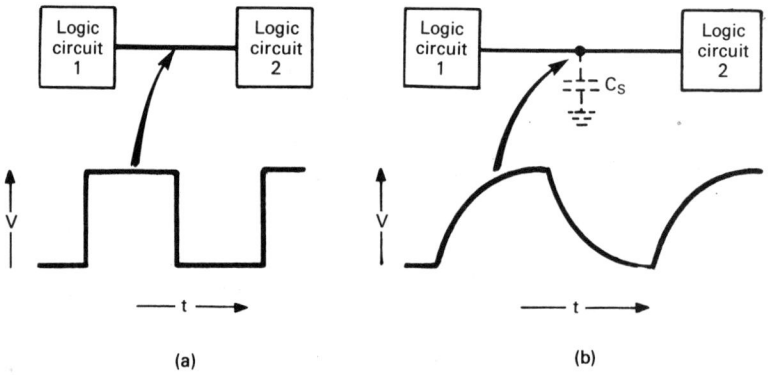

Figure 3-53 Effects of stray capacitance. (a) Ideal—no stray capacitance and (b) actual—with a very large amount of stray capacitance.

Capacitors sharing charge

A water analogy of capacitors sharing charge, Figure 3.54, shows how water is shared between two equal-sized glasses. Figure 3.54a shows one glass initially filled with water and the second glass initially empty. When the water is shared between the two glasses, both glasses end up half full.

In Figure 3.54b, a large glass and a small glass are used. At the start, the large glass is full and the small glass is empty. The water is shared by bringing the level in both glasses up to the same height. The water level of the large glass will not change much because the small glass does not hold much water.

In Figure 3.54c, the small glass is initially full of water and the large glass is initially empty. When the water is shared, the small glass will lose a considerable amount of the original water level because the large glass takes a lot of water to increase its water level.

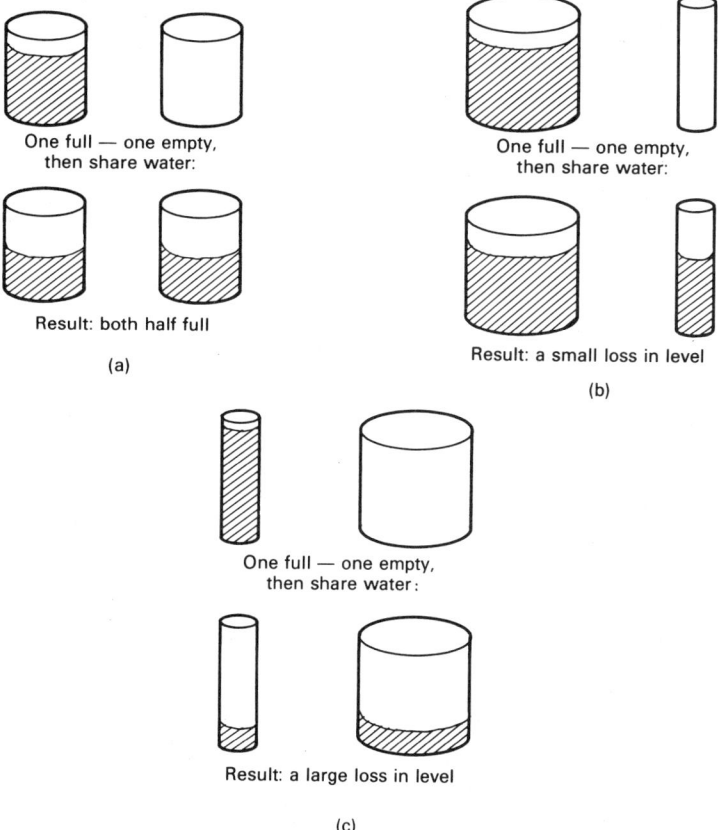

Figure 3-54 Sharing water between various-sized glasses. (a) Equal-sized glasses sharing, (b) a large glass sharing with a small glass, and (c) a small glass sharing with a large glass.

86 Chapter Three

This water-glass analogy holds up identically with capacitors when they share charge. The analogy of the water is charge: glasses store water and capacitors store charge.

In Figure 3.55, two equal-valued capacitors are used. Both are 100 µF. With the Select switch (SW_1) in the A position, one of the 100-µF capacitors is fully charged to the 1.5-V level. While this capacitor is charging, close switch SW_2 (the Key switch) to discharge the second capacitor to make sure that it is initially completely "empty."

Notice that whenever a capacitor is discharged, a 100-Ω resistor is placed in the discharge path. The purpose of this small-valued resistor is to provide a limit on the maximum discharge current that is allowed to flow. Without this resistor, the contacts of the switch could be damaged because of the large initial surge current. It is always advisable to place some resistance in series with switches that are used to discharge capacitors, provided that no detrimental effects in the overall performance of the circuit result.

Close the Key discharge switch (SW_2) and watch the voltage across capacitor C_2 go to zero. Open the Key switch, then slide the Select switch (SW_1) over to the B position. Notice that equilibrium will be immediately reached. Both capacitors will have a voltage of about half of the starting voltage (something close to 0.75 V). This experiment consists of two equal-valued capacitors sharing charge and is analogous to two equal-sized glasses sharing water.

A second example, shown in Figure 3.56, is a large-valued capacitor sharing charge with a small-valued capacitor. Notice that the large-valued capacitor is 100 µF and the small-valued capacitor is only one-tenth as large (10 µF). In this case, when the charge is shared, the

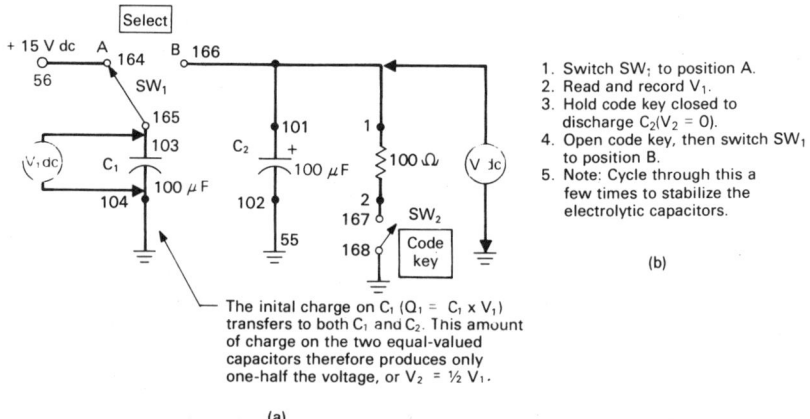

Figure 3-55 Sharing charge between equal-valued capacitors. (*a*) Test setup and (*b*) procedure.

Circuit Components Operating with Direct Current 87

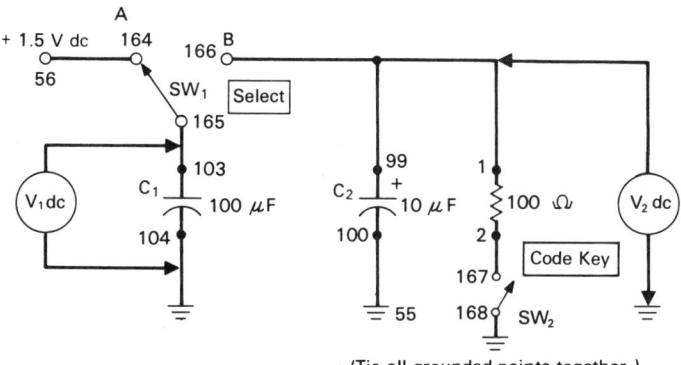

Follow same switching sequence as on previous figure. Note that not much additional capacitance is added now (C_2 is only 10 μF and C_1 is 100 μF), so V_2 is only slightly less than V_1.

Figure 3-56 Sharing charge from a large-valued capacitor to a small-valued capacitor.

voltage across the large capacitor will not fall very much because only a small charge is supplied to the small-valued capacitor.

Capacitors provide voltage memory

A water tank can be filled up, and if left alone, it will "remember" the amount of water that it contains. In an analogous way, capacitors can "remember" voltages. Capacitors are commonly used to store voltage levels. In dynamic random access memory (RAM) ICs, the digital memory is obtained by using many small-valued capacitors to store voltages.

As an example of voltage memory, Figure 3.57 shows that the 100-

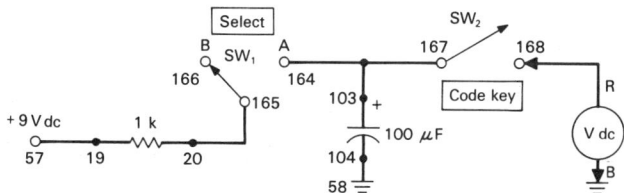

Procedure:
1. Charge the capacitor to the maximum voltage (hold code key switch closed and read on meter) by closing SW_1 (to position A).
2. Open the code key switch, then open SW_1 (to position B).
3. Momentarily close the code key switch long enough to read the voltage across the capacitor—then open the code key switch again.
4. Wait many seconds.
5. Again, repeat step no. 3 and note how much voltage remains across the capacitor.
6. Again, wait; and again read the voltage. Notice how long the voltage is maintained by this 100-μF capacitor.

Figure 3-57 Capacitors provide voltage memory.

μF capacitor can be charged when the Select switch (SW_1) is in the A position. While switch SW_1 is still in the A position, the Key switch (SW_2) can be closed and the voltmeter will indicate that the full 9 V is across this capacitor. Then the Key switch is opened, and the Select switch (SW_1) is moved to position B. The capacitor is now sitting with nothing connected to it, so it will remember or retain this initial voltage.

The voltmeter can be connected to the capacitor via the Key switch to momentarily read the voltage. The reason for using this momentary connection of the voltmeter to the capacitor is because the voltmeter does draw a small amount of current and therefore slightly discharges the capacitor. The voltmeter has an input resistance (between the red and black measuring leads) of about 10 MΩ. The Key switch keeps this 10-MΩ load away from the capacitor: it connects the voltmeter for a short time interval, only long enough to obtain a reading.

The capacitor is charged and the initial voltage is measured. Then, after each of a sequence of long time intervals, the voltage is quickly measured. Notice that not much loss in voltage takes place between these measuring intervals.

Capacitor specifications often indicate this ability to retain voltage for long time intervals by a parameter that is called the "self-time constant." A self-time constant (RC) of a capacitor represents the product of the capacitance value (C) and an equivalent external resistor (R) that would draw a current equal to the internal dc leakage current of the capacitor. Self-time constants of the best storage capacitors (Teflon capacitors) can be 50 years! This means that after 50 years, a capacitor with a Teflon dielectric, left alone with nothing tied to it, will lose 63 percent of its initial voltage. The self-time constant is usually highly temperature dependent. If the temperature is elevated, the self-time constant will be reduced because leakage resistance typically decreases as temperature increases.

Capacitors can provide time delays

Capacitors are often used in electronic circuits to provide time delays. A circuit that demonstrates one way of doing this is shown in Figure 3.58. When the Select switch (SW_1) is moved to position A, the capacitor initiates a time delay before the LEDs light. Two LEDs are connected in series so that the LEDs will take twice the voltage of a single diode before these diodes turn on. In this example, to get a large-valued capacitance, the two 100-μF capacitors of the lab kit are connected in parallel.

Start with the Select switch (SW_1) in the B position to fully discharge the capacitors. After the capacitors are fully discharged, move the Select switch (SW_1) to the A position (which will apply 9 V to this RC network). The 22-kΩ resistor is creating a slow (exponential) buildup

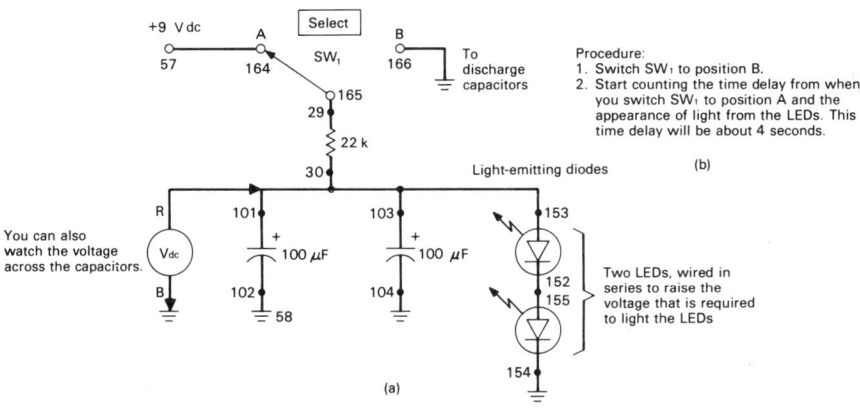

Figure 3-58 Capacitors causing a time delay. (a) Test setup and (b) procedure.

in the voltage across the capacitors. The turn-on voltage of the LEDs keeps them off until about 3 V has been accumulated across the capacitors. This creates the time delay. Change SW_1 from position B to position A and start counting time. Notice that about 4 s goes by before the LEDs turn on. This circuit has a 4-s time delay from the closure of the switch to the appearance of light out of the LEDs.

Capacitors block dc current

Good capacitors do not pass dc; dc current does not flow through a capacitor. Once a capacitor charges up, there will no longer be any current flow from a dc voltage source.

Electrolytic capacitors, on the other hand, often pass a dc leakage current. The oxide layer in an electrolytic capacitor is constantly being formed while the capacitor has a voltage across it. The forming of this oxide creates a small current flow. But even after this oxide layer is completely formed, a small-valued current will still flow. This small current flow can be determined *indirectly* by measuring the voltage that this current develops across a 100-kΩ current-sampling resistor.

Piezoelectric Quartz Crystals: The Frequency References

When mechanical forces are applied to crystals that exhibit what is called the "piezoelectric effect," voltages are generated on opposite faces of the distorted crystal, as shown in Figure 3.59. There are many applications in electronics for these piezoelectric crystals, such as phonograph cartridges, earpieces (as in the lab kit), microphones, the new flintless and batteryless cigarette lighters, and the quartz crystals that

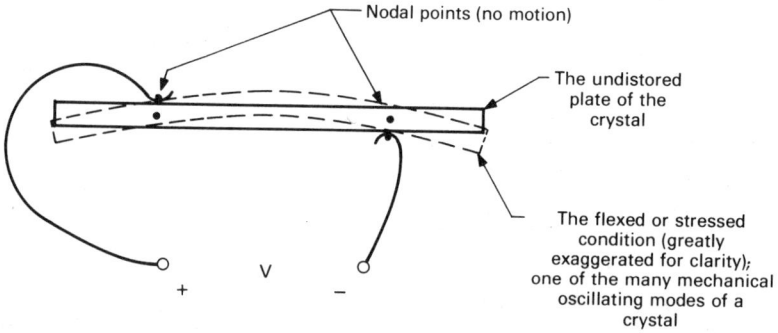

Figure 3-59 Voltages are generated by a stressed crystal.

are used to provide stable frequency references. The symbol, the physical mounting, and the use of a crystal are shown in Figure 3.60.

Quartz is the crystalline form of the oxide of silicon (SiO_2). It has very good dimensional stability during temperature changes. The mechanical resonant frequency of a quartz crystal depends on its physical dimensions and is therefore stable over both time and temperature changes.

Many radio receivers (and also radio transmitters) make use of quartz crystals, especially when operating on fixed frequencies (channels) as in citizens' band radio. Also, the basic clock circuit in digital computers and digital communications circuits uses a quartz crystal because of the low initial tolerance and the excellent temperature stability that is obtained.

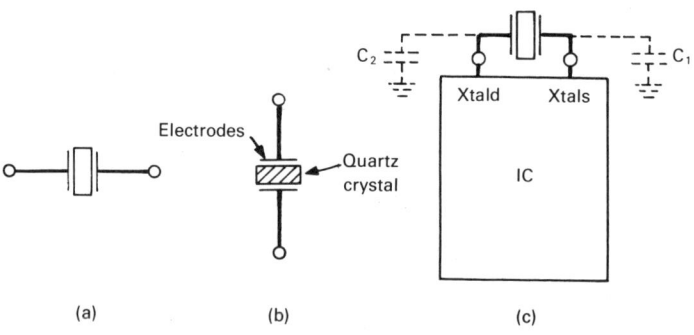

Figure 3-60 The piezoelectric quartz crystal. (*a*) Symbol, (*b*) actual arrangement, and (*c*) connection to an IC.

Diodes: The Two-Terminal One-Way Devices

A diode is like a one-way street. Diodes allow current to flow in one direction but prevent current from flowing in the opposite direction. This action and the electronic symbol for a diode are shown in Figure 3.61. Notice that both an arrowhead and a bar make up the diode symbol. The arrowhead is the "anode," and the bar is the "cathode" of the diode. In less formal discussions, people might refer to the "arrow" and the "bar" because the words "anode" and "cathode" don't come to mind anymore. These words were common in the days of vacuum diodes. The direction of the arrowhead in a diode is the direction of the easy flow of current. Current will not flow in a direction opposite to this arrow.

This directionality of a diode is shown in Figure 3.62, in which an LED is again used as a visual indication of current flow. A 10-kΩ current-limiting resistor is placed in series with the LED. When the diode is connected as shown in Figure 3.62a, the current flow is blocked. If the connections are reversed (as in Figure 3.62b), current flows.

Some "logical" uses for diodes

Diode-logic circuits have been used in digital computers. Two diode-logic circuits are shown in Figure 3.63. Figure 3.63a shows an OR gate with two inputs, *A* and *B*. Each of these digital input voltages can be either 0 or 4.5 V (4.5 V is the closest voltage that is available in the lab kit to the standard 5-V power-supply voltage). If the *B* input happens to be at 0 V and the *A* input is at 4.5 V, the diode tied to the *A* input will pass the 4.5 V over to the output. So, the output will be very close to 4 V (approximately 0.6 V is lost in going through a conducting silicon diode). The diode on the *B* input is reverse biased. The anode (arrow) is at ground, and the cathode (bar) is up at +4 V (so this diode is not conducting). This allows the *B* input to be at 0 V without disturbing the output voltage level. For this OR gate, if either input *A* OR input B (*OR both* of them) is the high voltage of 4.5 V, the output

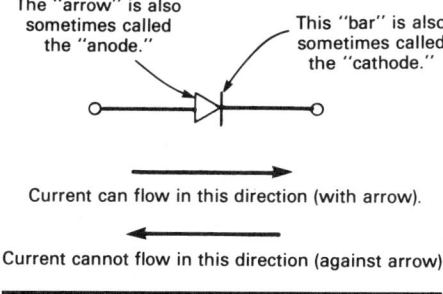

Figure 3-61 The symbol for a diode.

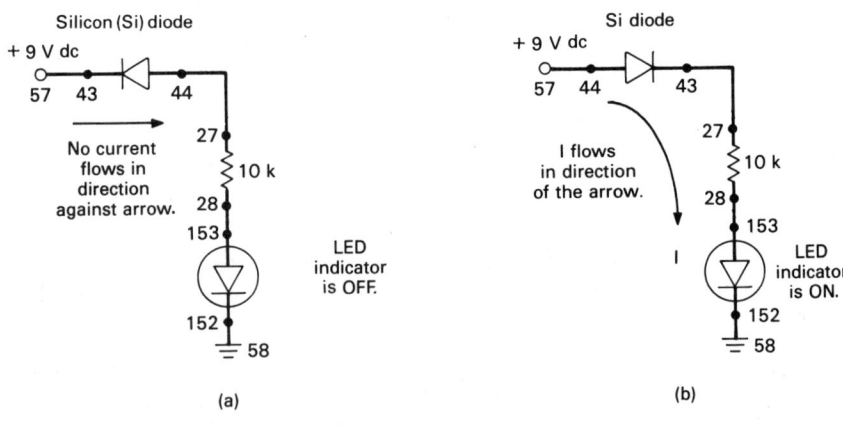

Figure 3-62 Verifying that diodes conduct current in only one direction. (a) Diode blocks current flow and (b) diode allows current flow.

will be in the high-voltage state. This is called the logical "OR function" (there is more about logic in Chapter 4).

An AND logic gate is shown in Figure 3.63b. The 10-kΩ resistor now ties to the 4.5-V power supply and the diodes are reversed. If either input A or input B is at 0 V, the output will be pulled down to very nearly 0 V (it will actually be one diode drop above 0, or about 0.6 V). Both A AND B must be in the high-voltage state to get the output in the high-voltage state. When both A AND B are at 4.5 V, the output

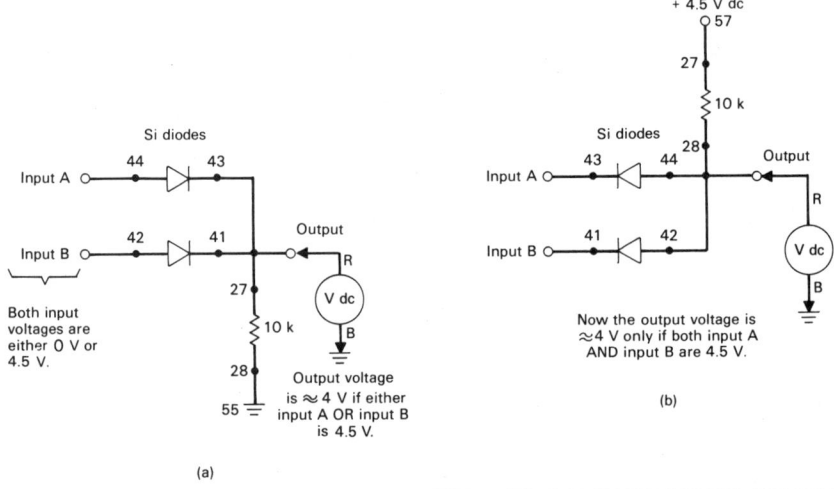

Figure 3-63 Diodes used in logic circuits. (a) The OR gate and (b) the AND gate.

will also be at 4.5 V because both diodes are blocking. This allows the output voltage to rise to the power-supply voltage level.

A closer look at semiconductors

To understand the internal action of a diode, the earlier discussions of silicon will be reviewed. Silicon forms a crystal like carbon forms a diamond. A pure silicon crystal is not a good conductor. To be of use in electronics, other elements must be substituted for a few of the silicon atoms within an otherwise perfect crystal structure.

Figure 3.64 shows two useful elements, boron and phosphorus. The outermost shell of a boron atom has only three electrons (one less than the four that exist with silicon). Conversely, the outermost shell of a phosphorous atom has five electrons (one more than the four that the silicon atom has).

As shown in Figure 3.65, if a boron atom can somehow be substituted for a silicon atom, the three electrons that are provided by the boron atom will be shared by three of the adjacent silicon atoms. A problem occurs with the silicon atom shown to the right because this silicon atom has an electron to share but the boron atom does not. This represents a distortion in the crystal lattice because *a place exists for an electron*. If an electron can be found wandering around within the crystal structure, this place for an electron (called a "hole") can capture this extra electron and thereby satisfy the Si atom to the right. This hole (this absence of an electron) is acting like a positive charge. Doping of silicon with boron is therefore said to produce "P-type" silicon (the "P" is for positive).

Figure 3.66 shows a phosphorus atom replacing one of the silicon atoms. There are five electrons in the outermost shell of a phosphorus atom. A phosphorus atom is therefore able to provide one electron in a covalent bond with each of the four neighboring silicon atoms and have one *spare* electron left over. This electron is shown very close to the phosphorus atom. In actuality, this spare electron can be located any-

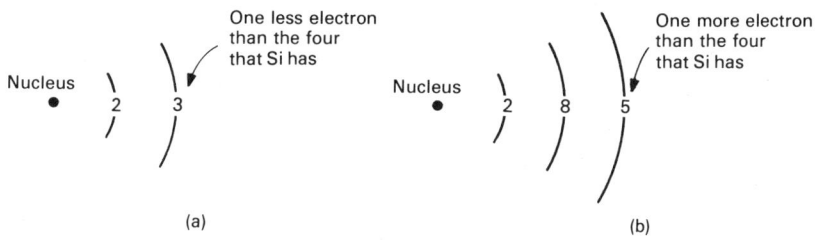

Figure 3-64 Dopants for silicon. (*a*) Boron (B), a P-type dopant and (*b*) phosphorus (P), an N-type dopant.

where within a vicinity of a few thousand silicon atoms away because this electron is not very tightly held to the phosphorus atom. This extra electron is therefore easily dislodged, and it is then available to conduct current. Because of this extra electron and its negative (N) charge, phosphorus provides what is called "N-type doping."

By using controlled doping, both N-type and P-type regions can be formed within a silicon crystal. This is how PN diodes, NPN transistors, PNP transistors, N-type resistors, and also P-type resistors are made. All of these designations refer to the types of doping that were used in the silicon.

When silicon is doped, it is changed from a "semiconductor" to a "conductor" of electricity. A heavily doped silicon crystal is indicated as N^+ or P^+. Heavy doping provides low values of resistance. An N^- or a P^- designation represents light doping concentrations. Lightly doped silicon is not a very good conductor of electricity.

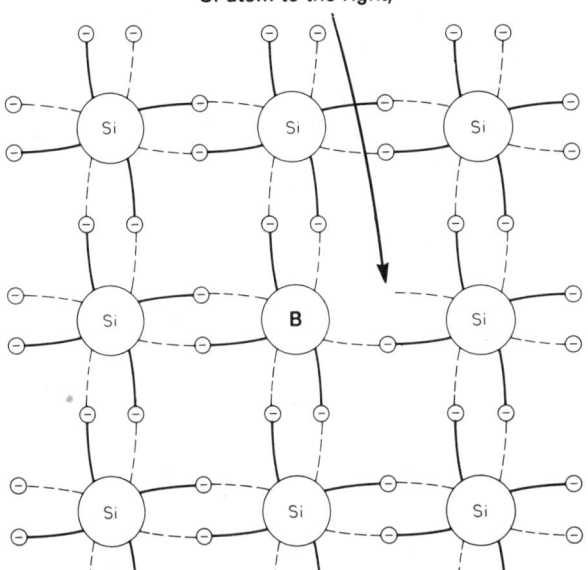

A place for an electron
(to fill the bond to the unsatisfied
Si atom to the right)

If an electron occupies this place,
an unbalanced charge of -1 results
that is fixed in the crystal lattice.

Figure 3-65 P-type doping of silicon.

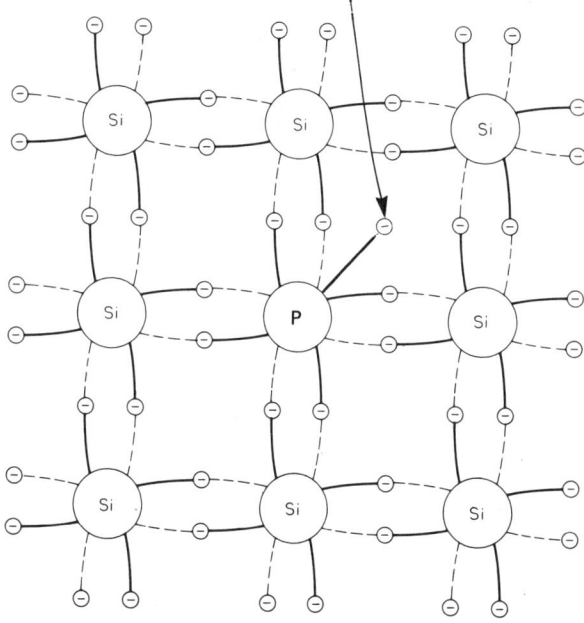

An extra or spare electron that is bound only lightly to the phosphorus atom

If this electron is lost, an unbalanced charge of +1 (from the P nucleus) results that is fixed in the crystal lattice.

Figure 3-66 N-type doping of silicon.

The PN diode

If two separate blocks of silicon, one doped P type and the other doped N type (as shown in Figure 3.67a), are fused together (Figure 3.67b), a PN diode is formed. The spare electrons that are available in the N-type side will immediately flow across the PN junction between these two blocks of silicon and fill the holes in the P-type side. An equilibrium condition is rapidly reached after some of the available electrons from the N-type side have initially moved over to the P-type side.

When the N-type side loses those electrons, the phosphorous doping atoms (that are fixed in the crystal lattice, the "fixed charges") are unbalanced. The nucleus of these phosphorus atoms has a charge of +5. The fifth electrons of these phosphorus atoms are now gone and are no longer exactly balancing the total positive charge that exists in the nucleus of each phosphorus atom. These positive fixed charges are embedded in the silicon crystal lattice on the N-type side.

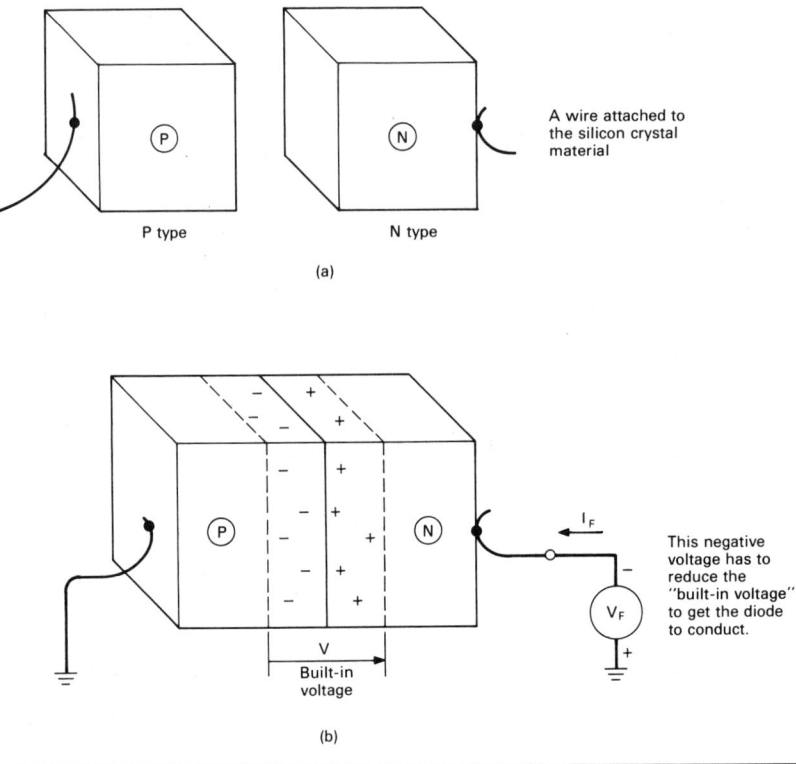

Figure 3-67 Making a PN diode. (*a*) Two separate crystals of doped silicon and (*b*) on contact, a PN diode is formed.

Those electrons that moved over and filled the holes on the P-type side provide an equal number of fixed negative charges near the boron atoms on the P-type side. This initial charge separation (that was caused by the electrons that moved across the PN diode) is now fixed in the crystal. These fixed charges, which are located on both sides of the diode, create a "built-in voltage" (and also a built-in electric field) that *prevents any further flow of electrons across the junction.* Therefore, to get a PN diode to conduct current, an external voltage has to be applied in the direction that will *reduce* this built-in voltage and thereby allow electrons (and holes) to constantly flow through the diode. This is called the "forward voltage," or "forward bias," that must be applied to a diode to get it to conduct current.

If the polarity of the external biasing voltage is reversed, called a "reverse voltage," this adds to the built-in voltage and continues to prevent the flow of current through the diode. This is why diodes conduct current in only one direction.

The forward characteristics of diodes

The forward voltage that has to be applied to a diode to get it to conduct current can be measured as shown in Figure 3.68. Notice that two values of voltage (1.5 and 4.5 V) are used. A series resistor (R) limits the current flow to the diode and will be changed over the range from 470 kΩ to 470 Ω as larger forward current flows through the diode. The multimeter is set up to read dc volts and provides the data shown in Figure 3.68b.

The potentiometer labeled "Control" is adjusted to sequentially obtain the values of forward voltage (V_1) shown. First, adjust for $V_1 = 200$ mV, and then record the second voltage (V_2). Then adjust to obtain a forward voltage of 300 mV, and so on. V_1 steps of 100 mV are used over the range from 200 to 800 mV. The current flow (I) in the diode is calculated by differencing the two voltages ($V_2 - V_1$) and then dividing this difference voltage (the voltage across the resistor R) by the value of the resistor R. This is an *indirect* way to measure the current I.

Looking at these data in a tabular form does not provide much of a "feel" for what is going on. It is better if these data are plotted so that relationships can be seen more clearly. Therefore the previously tabulated data on the silicon diode are plotted in Figure 3.69. Notice that a silicon diode requires a forward voltage of approximately 580 mV before any significant current flows, but when the diode does start to conduct, it has a fast turn-on characteristic.

The effects of ambient temperature on the forward voltage characteristics of a diode can be demonstrated with the circuit shown in Figure 3.70. A silicon diode is used and is biased with a 10-kΩ resistor from a 9-V power supply. The value of the forward voltage of this diode

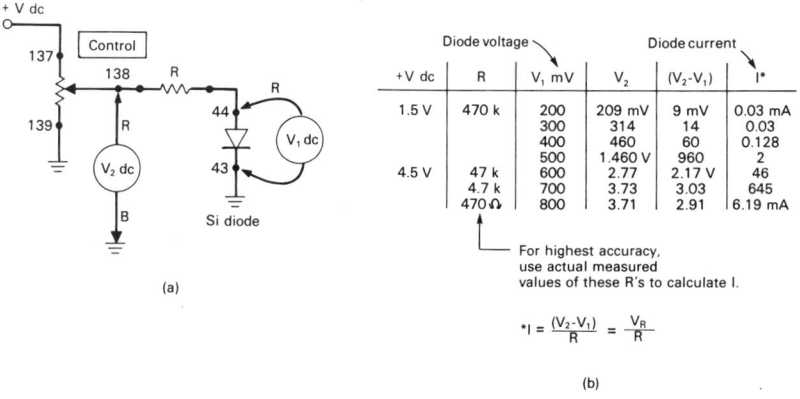

Figure 3-68 Obtaining data on the forward characteristics of a silicon diode. (a) Test setup and (b) tabulating the data.

98 Chapter Three

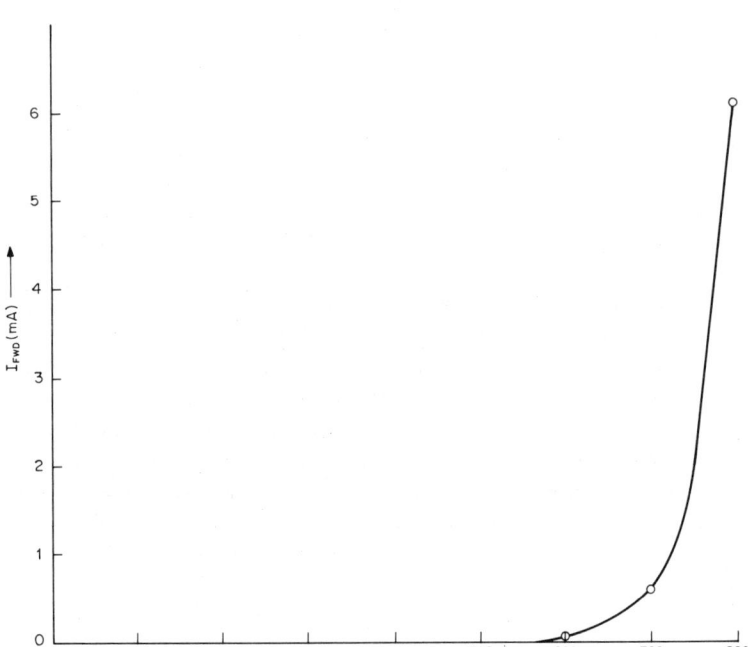

Figure 3-69 The forward characteristics of a silicon diode.

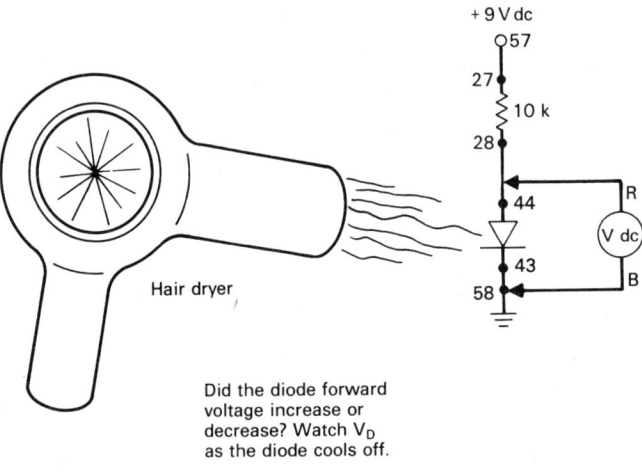

Figure 3-70 Measuring the effects of temperature on the forward voltage of a silicon diode.

at room temperature is first recorded. Then the hair dryer is turned on and held about 2 or 3 in from the silicon diode. Notice that the forward voltage falls as the temperature of the diode increases. A good rule of thumb is that the diode forward voltage falls at the rate of about 2 mV for every degree Celsius (centigrade) increase in the temperature of the diode.

The reverse characteristics of diodes

When a diode is reverse biased, large values of current no longer flow. An experiment to measure this reverse current is shown in Figure 3.71. If a silicon diode is used, the reverse current would be too small to measure with this meter.

If the germanium diode in the lab kit is used, the reverse current will be found to be approximately 25 μA. Now if the hair dryer is used (keep it 2 or 3 in away) and the germanium diode is heated while it is under reverse bias, the reverse current will increase. The forward voltage decreases and the reverse leakage current increases when the temperature of a diode is increased.

Transistors: The Three-Terminal On-Off Amplifying Devices

Now that diodes have been considered, some experiments have been performed, and the operation of diodes has been determined, we will turn our attention to something a little more complicated, a "bipolar transistor." There are basically two types of transistors available in electronics. One general type is the bipolar transistor, which will now be considered. A different type is the "field-effect transistor." Field-effect transistors aren't available in the lab kit and therefore won't be used in experiments. The basic operation of the metal-oxide semiconductor

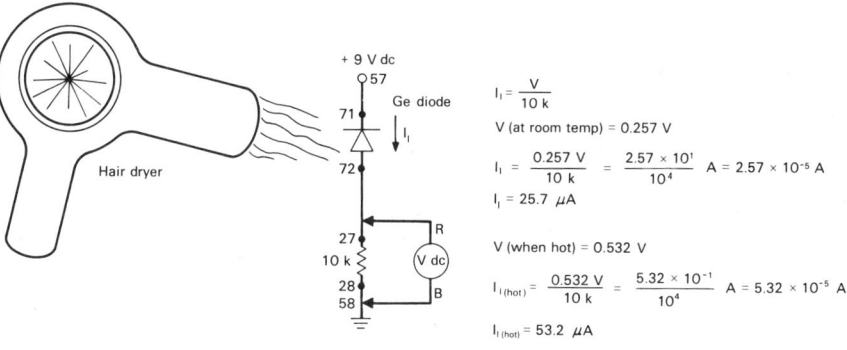

Figure 3-71 Measuring the leakage current of a germanium diode.

100 Chapter Three

(MOS) type of field-effect transistor will be described in Chapter 4 because these transistors are very popular in digital circuits.

Bipolar transistors are supplied in many different packages. Figure 3.72 shows the large metal TO-3 package (TO is an abbreviation for Technical Outline, the mechanical drawing on the package), smaller metal "cans" like the TO-5 and the TO-46, and some of the plastic packages that are used for transistors. The metal packages are generally supplied for high-operating-temperature applications. Plastic packages are used for low-cost systems.

Similar to a resistor, transistors can get hot, and some applications require a large package because the package is used to keep the transistor cool. In many applications there are such small voltages and currents involved that the power that is being dissipated in the transistor is not a concern. Near the output stages of an electronic system, like the output stage of a hi-fi power amplifier (that is providing the audio output power for a loudspeaker), large transistors are used that have to be bolted to special metal "heat sinks." In low-power circuitry, heat sinking of the transistors is usually not needed. Therefore, both small-sized (the physical size) transistors, and large-sized transistors are generally used in an electronic system. A large transistor (like a TO-3) indicates that there is a lot of power associated with that section of the system.

In the center region of the lab kit there are four transistors (as shown in Figure 3.73) that are available for experiments. The two on the left side have the symbol for a PNP transistor. Notice that the arrowhead (which indicates the "emitter") is pointing into the bar (the symbol for the "base"). The two transistors on the right have the arrowhead reversed: the arrow is pointing away from the bar for these NPN transistors.

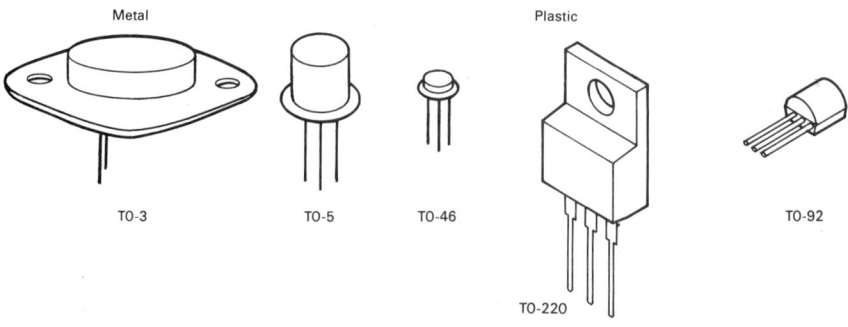

Figure 3-72 Transistors look like this.

Circuit Components Operating with Direct Current   101

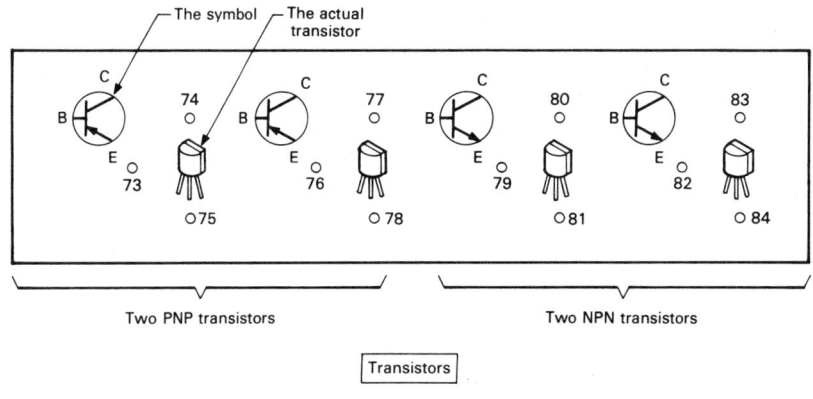

Figure 3-73 The four transistors in the lab kit.

The small plastic TO-92 package is used. These transistors are therefore not capable of much power dissipation. In the experiments this will not be a problem because only relatively small voltages and currents will be used.

In electronic schematic diagrams, the symbol for a transistor should be drawn so that the emitter arrow points down the page. The emitter current then always flows from the top to the bottom of the page. This convention makes schematics easier to follow. The symbol for an NPN transistor should therefore be drawn with the emitter at the bottom, and a PNP transistor should be drawn with the emitter at the top, as shown in Figure 3.74.

The three leads of a transistor are the base, emitter, and collector. On the NPN transistor of Figure 3.74a, the base current and the collector current are seen to enter the transistor; the emitter current leaves. This means that the sum of the base current and collector cur-

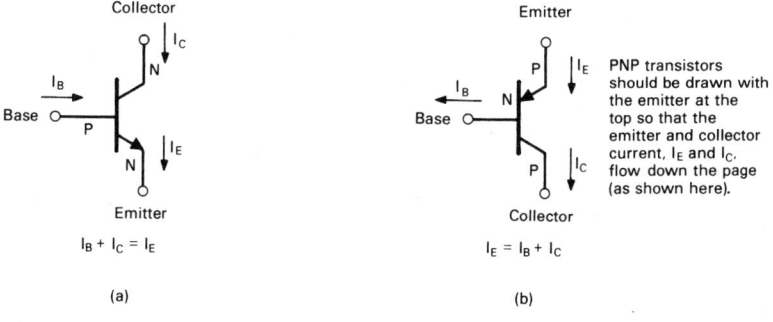

Figure 3-74 Symbols for bipolar transistors. (a) An NPN transistor and (b) a PNP transistor.

rent must equal the emitter current; that is, the current *going in* must equal the current *coming out* (this basic relationship will be used later on).

A PNP transistor is shown in Figure 3.74*b*. Notice the direction of the currents for this transistor. Also notice that the emitter has been located at the top of the symbol. The emitter current, therefore, flows down, from the top of the paper to the bottom.

The two diodes in a transistor

There are two diodes associated with a bipolar transistor, as shown on the PNP transistor of Figure 3.75. One of these diodes is the emitter-base diode. Notice that the emitter-base symbol is very close to a diode symbol. The arrowhead indicates the forward direction for current conduction in this diode.

The other diode is the "collector-base diode." It is indicated with a dotted arrowhead in Figure 3.75*a*. This arrowhead is usually not shown so that there will be no confusion as to which lead is the emitter. Both the emitter and the collector of any bipolar transistor are always made of the same dopant type. In this PNP example, that dopant is P type.

The forward voltages of these diodes can be measured as indicated in Figure 3.75*b*. The 100-k resistor is used to limit the diode current flow. To the left is the circuitry to measure the voltage of the emitter-base diode, and to the right is the circuitry to measure the collector-base diode. These diodes are very similar to the silicon diodes that are available in the lab kit.

These two diodes can be drawn in a different way, as shown in the PNP transistor of Figure 3.76. This drawing uses the same cathode sym-

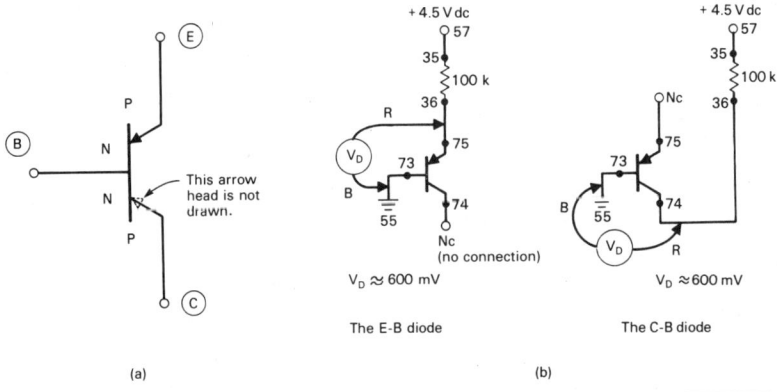

Figure 3-75 The two diodes in a transistor. (*a*) The PNP transistor and (*b*) measuring the forward voltage drop of each diode.

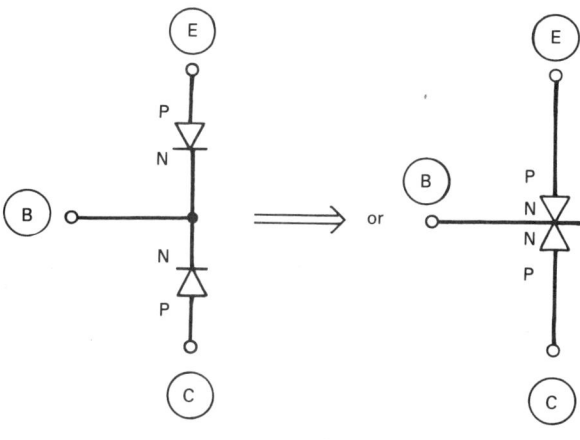

Figure 3-76 Drawing a PNP transistor as two back-to-back diodes.

bol and locates the anodes on both sides. Some originally unexpected action between these two diodes ("transistor action") is the key to bipolar transistor operation.

Demonstrating transistor action

Transistor action can be demonstrated by hooking up the test circuit shown in Figure 3.77. In Figure 3.77a, notice that the base lead is grounded. The emitter lead of the transistor is supplied with a forward current. This current is established by the 2.2-kΩ resistor that is connected to the 4.5-V power supply. The emitter current is about 1.8 mA.

With the multimeter set up as an ampmeter (tied between the negative 4.5-V power-supply voltage and the collector), the collector current can be measured. Notice that *the collector current is essentially equal to the emitter current*. Almost all of the emitter current appears in the collector. This is "transistor action." Transistor action takes place when the collector "steals" essentially all of the emitter current away from the base. As a result, the base current is very small (it is the difference between these currents, $I_B = I_E - I_C$).

In Figure 3.77b, the two diodes that are within a transistor are replaced with the two discrete silicon diodes that are in the lab kit. A similar demonstration circuit is used to see if transistor action takes place when using these two *separated* diodes. The same current is entered into one of the diodes and the common cathode point is similarly grounded. The ampmeter is connected in series with the lower diode to see if current flows (this would indicate the existence of transistor action).

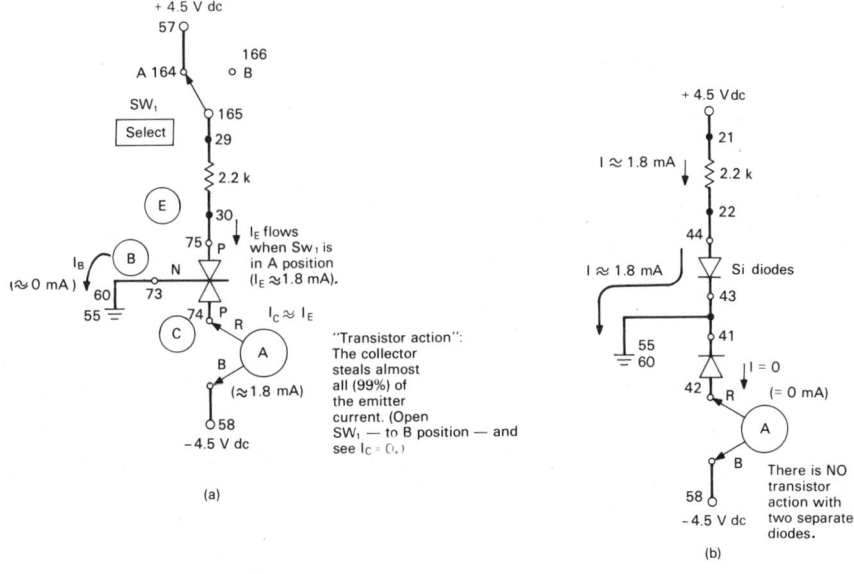

Figure 3-77 Demonstrating transistor action. (a) Transistor action and (b) using two separate Si diodes there is no transistor action.

Notice, in this case, that the ampmeter reads zero, indicating that none of the forward current of the upper diode is "stolen" by the lower diode. Therefore, transistor action does not exist between two separated diodes. The junctions of these diodes are too far apart. In fact, these junctions exist in separate packages. So, *transistor action occurs only when two diodes are built very closely together.*

Current gain (β) of a transistor

A small base current can control a much larger collector current. This can be demonstrated with the experimental setup indicated in Figure 3.78. The 1.5 V that is available from a single cell in the battery section is used, and a 100-kΩ resistor limits the current flow into the base lead. The base-emitter junction is a silicon diode, so the base lead will be about 600 mV above ground. The base current that flows can be determined by using the multimeter as a dc voltmeter to measure the voltage drop across the 100-kΩ resistor. This indicates about 10 μA of base current. If the multimeter is then connected as a dc ampmeter and put in the collector lead (as shown in Figure 3.78b), about 2 mA of current can be measured. This demonstrates the current gain of the transistor. The 10 μA of base current is multiplied by the current gain of 200 to become 2 mA of collector current.

A transistor as an electronic switch

In digital circuit applications, the transistors are simply turned on or off. The transistors are used as electronically controlled switches. An example of a transistor used as a switch is shown in the simplified representation of Figure 3.79. In Figure 3.79a, the collector-emitter circuit of the transistor has been replaced with a switch. This switch is controlled by the magnitude of the base voltage. With a base voltage of zero, there is no base current. The transistor is off and the switch is open. Because the switch is open, the output voltage will be the full power-supply voltage (5 V dc). That is one of the two possible states of the output voltage. This represents a logical 1, the high-voltage state.

If a large control voltage, say 5 V, were applied (an input resistor is used to limit the base current), the transistor would be turned on. This conducting transistor would be in saturation (operating just as if a switch between the collector and emitter leads were closed). A short circuit now exists between the collector and the emitter. This ties the collector to ground, so the output voltage is 0 V. An output voltage of zero is called a logical 0.

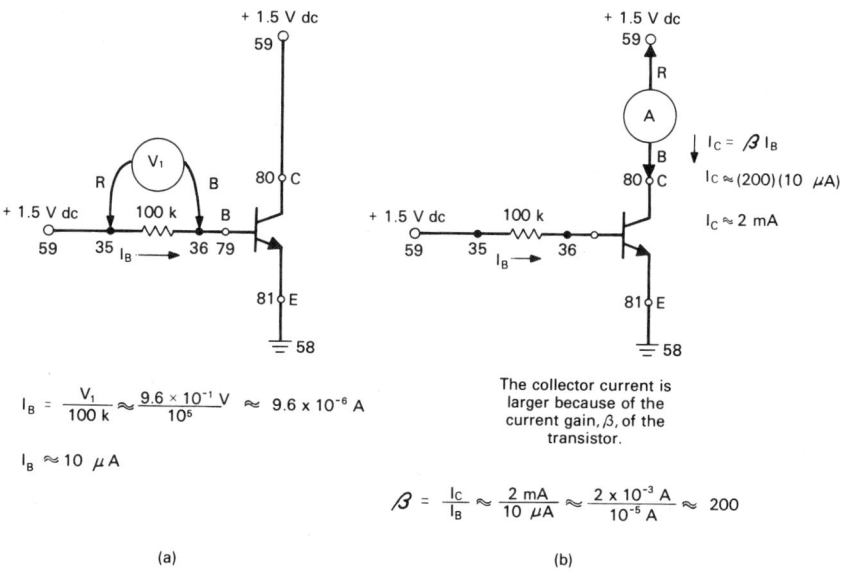

Figure 3-78 Measuring the current gain of a transistor. (a) Measuring the base currents and (b) measuring the larger collector current.

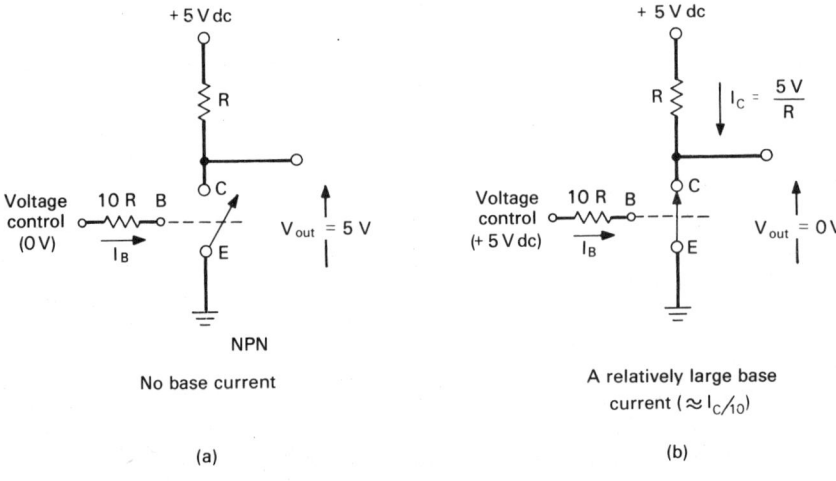

Figure 3-79 A transistor as a switch. (*a*) Transistor (switch) off and (*b*) transistor (switch) on.

A primitive *RS* flip-flop

An example of a logic circuit that has electronic "memory" is the direct-coupled Reset-Set (*RS*) flip-flop shown in Figure 3.80. This circuit is easy to construct and is relatively easy to understand. This flip-flop uses the two NPN transistors that are available in the lab kit. Notice

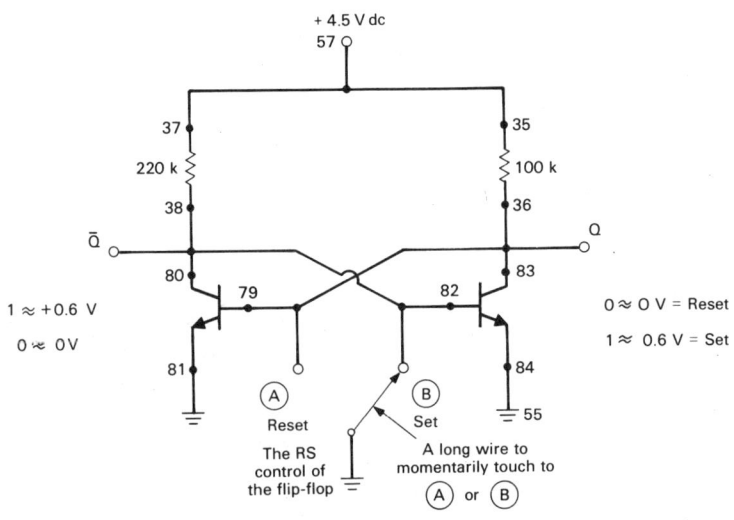

Figure 3-80 A primitive *RS* flip-flop using direct-coupled transistor logic (DCTL).

the crossing of the wires in the center of the circuit diagram. The collector of one transistor ties over to the base of the other, and vice versa. This "cross coupling" is characteristic of a flip-flop circuit.

If the collector output on the left is arbitrarily called $\bar{Q}$, (pronounced "Q bar") and the collector output on the right is called Q, whatever signal exists at Q, the complement or the opposite logic state always exists at $\bar{Q}$. The bar over the symbol Q implies the complement of whatever logic state Q is in. For example, if the transistor on the right side is conducting, the voltage at Q will be approximately 0 V (representing the *reset state* of this flip-flop). Zero volts at the collector of the right-side transistor means that the base voltage for the transistor on the left will also be zero. With 0 V on the base, the left-side transistor will be off, so this collector voltage will try to rise to 4.5 V.

Notice that the collector of the left transistor ties back to the base of the right transistor. That base (also called point B) is the "Set input." Therefore, as the collector voltage attempts to move up to 4.5 V, the base-emitter diode of the other transistor catches it and limits it to about 600 mV. When the Q output is zero, the $\bar{Q}$ output is in the logical 1 state at 600 mV.

If the Set input is momentarily grounded (with a wire that is touched to ground), the base of the right-side transistor goes to zero (which shuts off that transistor). Therefore, the collector voltage of this transistor rises. The base of the left-side transistor (the point marked A) clamps this rising voltage at one diode drop (600 mV). This turns on the left-side transistor. The wire that was used to set the flip-flop is therefore no longer needed, and this logic state will remain as long as the power-supply voltage is applied. Therefore, a flip-flop has memory. It remembers whatever logic state it was forced into. This flip-flop can be set or reset by shorting alternate bases to ground. In the Set state, the Q output is a logical 1 (600 mV) and the $\bar{Q}$ output will be a logical 0 (0 V). This RS flip-flop is called a "bistable circuit" because it has two stable states.

The astable multivibrator

An "astable" multivibrator circuit has no stable states. It constantly changes from one state to the other: it "oscillates." An astable multivibrator is sometimes used as a clock circuit for a simple digital system.

An astable multivibrator can be built using the components that are in the lab kit, as shown in Figure 3.81. The two 100-μF capacitors provide a low-frequency oscillation that can easily be observed using the dc voltmeter. The time that this circuit remains in each state can be determined by counting seconds.

The cross coupling is now provided by capacitors. This is the reason that stable states are not achieved. These capacitors (C_1 and C_2) are

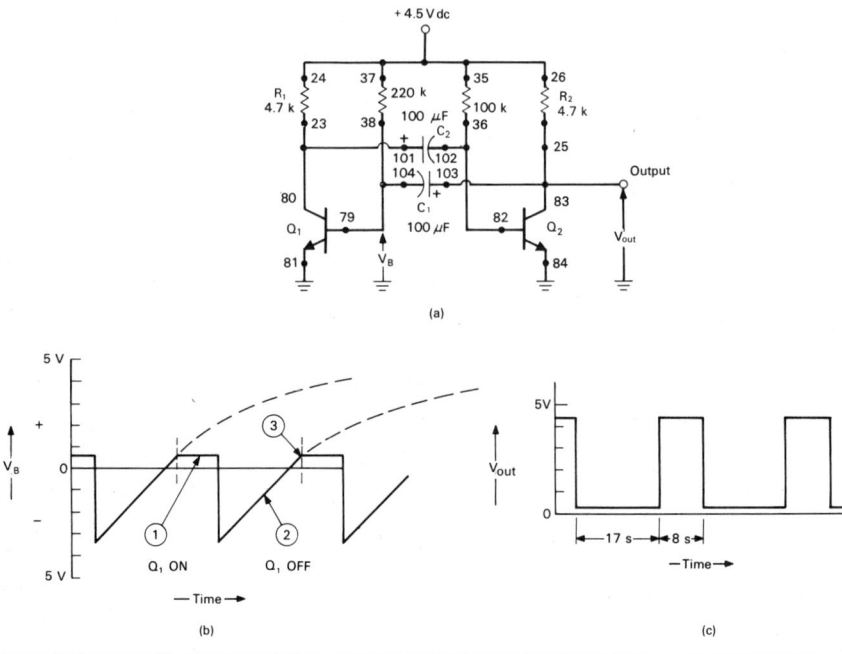

Figure 3-81 An astable multivibrator. (a) The circuit diagram, (b) the V_b waveform, and (c) the output waveform.

the key to the circuit action. Initially, assume that the transistor on the left (Q_1) is on. The current through the 220-kΩ resistor keeps it on. This is region 1 on the V_B waveform shown in Figure 3.81b.

While Q_1 is on, Q_2 will be off (because of a negative voltage that appears at the base of Q_2; this will be discussed shortly). With Q_2 off, C_1 is charged up to nearly the 4.5-V supply voltage by R_2. The left side of C_1 is tied to the base of Q_1, which provides a voltage of approximately 0.6 V, so C_1 will charge up to 4.5 V minus 0.6 V, or 3.9 V. The negative voltage at the base of Q_2 is slowly increasing because of the current flow through the 100-kΩ resistor. Eventually this voltage will become positive and large enough (0.6 V) to turn Q_2 on. This then causes a change of state.

When the circuit changes states, Q_2 goes on and Q_1 goes off. Notice that when Q_2 goes on, the right side of C_1 (being tied to the collector of Q_2) goes to essentially 0 V. The voltage stored on C_1 therefore causes the base of Q_1 (V_B on Figure 3.81b) to abruptly swing to a negative value (approximately -3.3 V, the region labeled "2" on the V_B waveform). It is this negative voltage at the base of Q_1 (or Q_2 for the opposite state) that keeps this transistor off.

During this quasi-stable state, the 220-kΩ resistor is providing a current flow into C_1 that is charging this capacitor toward 4.5 V. The negative plate of the electrolytic capacitor (C_1) is now on its way to +4.5 V. This voltage change on C_1 follows the exponential curve shown as region 2 of Figure 3.81b. When V_B increases to +0.6 V, Q_1 is no longer held off and therefore is turned on by the current coming from the 220-kΩ resistor. This is the point labeled "3" on the V_B waveform of Figure 3.81b and terminates that quasi-stable state.

In this astable multivibrator, one of the base voltages is always negative. This provides the quasi-stable states. Use the dc voltmeter to observe the V_B voltage and also the output voltage (V_{out}) shown in Figure 3.81c. This output voltage is not symmetric because unequal base resistors are used (100 and 220 kΩ). This provides the approximately two-to-one difference in the on-off timing. Equal-valued base resistors and equal-valued capacitors would provide a symmetrical square wave output voltage waveform.

The monostable multivibrator

A "monostable" multivibrator has *one* stable state. This circuit, shown in Figure 3.82, uses a resistor (22 kΩ) to cross couple on one side and a capacitor (100 μF) to cross couple on the other side. Therefore, this is a combination of a bistable with an astable circuit. The new thing is the trigger input that is used to initiate the quasi-stable state.

At rest, Q_1 is on and Q_2 is off. Momentarily closing the Key switch causes the voltage at the base of Q_1 to swing negative (as in the previous astable circuit). This negative voltage at the base of Q_1 turns Q_1 off, and the rising V_1 voltage couples through the 22-kΩ cross-coupling resistor to turn Q_2 on. Because Q_2 rapidly goes on, only a short-time-duration trigger is needed. This quasi-stable state persists while the 470-kΩ resistor charges the 100-μF capacitor and eventually causes

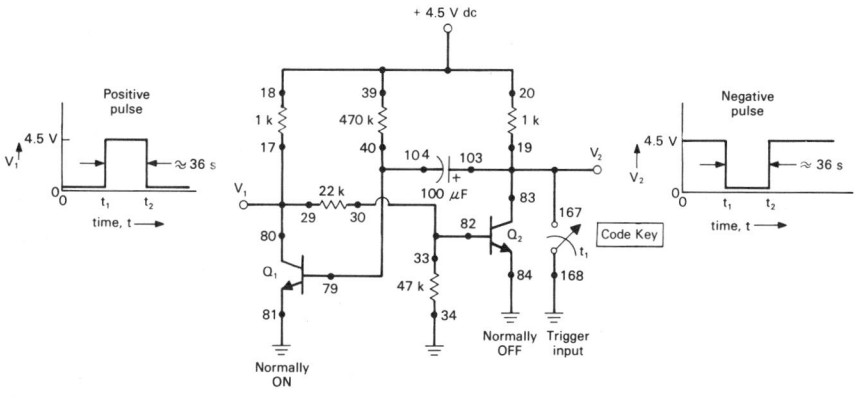

Figure 3-82 A monostable multivibrator.

the base voltage of Q_1 to increase to $+0.6$ V. At this time the circuit returns to its reset state. This produces an output pulse for each trigger input. This circuit is also known as a "one-shot multivibrator."

A toilet is a hydraulic analogy of this monostable multivibrator. The flushing lever is the trigger input. The flushing action continues until the local reservoir of water in the tank is drained, which ends the quasi-stable state. The system then "recharges" by again filling the tank and then returns to its stable rest state, awaiting the next input trigger.

The Silicon-Controlled Rectifier

A number of specialized semiconductor devices (in addition to diodes and transistors) have appeared over the years. One of the more successful of these is the silicon-controlled rectifier (SCR) that is used in power-control applications. A similar device, the "triac," is also available for ac power-control applications. The SCR will be described because undesired parasitic SCRs exist within digital ICs.

The symbol for an SCR is shown in Figure 3.83a. A sequence of three regions of alternating doping types is needed to make NPN or PNP bipolar transistors. If an additional layer is added, to provide an NPNP or PNPN structure, an SCR can be created. Therefore, an SCR can be considered as a special "hook connection" of a bipolar NPN and PNP transistor, as shown in Figure 3.83b.

This is a "regenerating" circuit. Initially, consider that current is somehow being supplied out of the collector of the PNP. This becomes base current for the NPN. The collector current of this NPN is larger

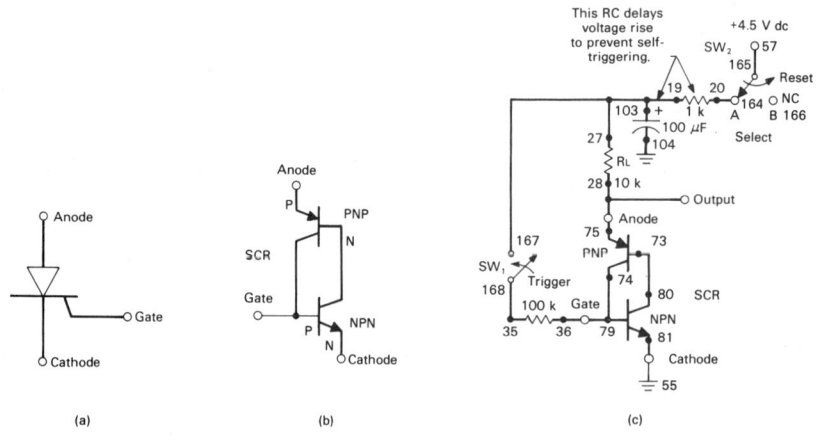

Figure 3-83 Making a silicon-controlled rectifier out of two transistors. (a) The symbol for an SCR and (b) the hook connection of two transistors to make an SCR

because of the current gain of this transistor. This increased collector current flow is base current for the PNP. Again, this PNP base current is increased by the current gain of the PNP to provide a larger collector current. This reinforces the initially assumed current flow. If either transistor is momentarily turned on, this circuit will regeneratively "latch up" so that both transistors are conducting very large currents (limited *only* by the external circuitry).

An SCR can be built out of the NPN and PNP transistors that are available in the lab kit, as shown in Figure 3.83b. The 10-kΩ resistor (R_L) tied to the anode of this simulated SCR establishes the current limit when this SCR latches.

To trigger this SCR, the Key switch (SW_1) inputs an initial base current to the NPN transistor. The Key switch needs only a very quick tap because a short-duration current pulse is enough to get the rapid regeneration mechanism started. The 100-kΩ resistor in series with the Key switch limits this triggering base current flow.

An SCR, once latched, will stay in the latched-up mode. To reset this SCR, the Select switch (SW_2) has to momentarily remove the power by being switched to position B. The 1-kΩ and 100-μF RC network on the A side of this switch slowly reapplies voltage to the SCR. Remove the ground lead of this capacitor and notice that the abrupt application of anode voltage to the SCR will also trigger it on.

The output of the SCR (the anode) will be at +4.5 V until the SCR is triggered on. While on, the output voltage will be slightly larger than one forward diode drop (or about 650 mV).

Complex IC processes, such as all of the bipolar and the complementary MOS (CMOS) processes, provide adjacent regions in silicon that follow this NPNP or PNPN sequencing. Therefore, undesired parasitic SCRs become a problem in the applications of these ICs.

Special processing steps have been taken in some of the newer CMOS processes that eliminate this parasitic SCR problem. The simplicity of the wafer processing that was used for the older PMOS and the newer NMOS digital processes does not provide parasitic SCRs. Therefore, for MOS digital circuits, this SCR problem first appeared with the introduction of CMOS logic circuits.

Now that a good background has been provided in electronics, we'll take a look at some of the basic concepts that are used in digital computers.

Chapter

4

Learning to Think Digital

When you first hear the word "digital," you might think that people are talking about something to do with their fingers. In electronics, the word digital refers to "digits" in the computational sense. For example, in the decimal system the digits are the numbers 0 through 9. Computers and digital circuits don't work with anything as complicated as the decimal system; they instead operate with a simpler "binary" number system in which only two digits are involved, 0 and 1. These *bi*nary dig*its* are called "bits."

Fitting Things into a Two-State World

To represent the binary digits, only two conditions are needed that can be easily separated from each other.

On-off, open-closed, and high-low

A few ways to represent binary digits are shown in Figure 4.1. For example, a switch can be either open or closed, a light can be on or off, or a statement can be true or false. Typically the on and true states are called a "logic 1" state which corresponds to the highest digit in the binary system. The closed state of a relay is also considered a logic 1. A light that is off, a switch that is open, or a statement that is false represents the "logic 0" state.

In the binary electronic circuits that are used in digital systems, only two voltage levels are needed to represent the binary digits. This was done to simplify things, because these voltage levels correspond to a transistor either being driven strongly on or being held completely cut

114   Chapter Four

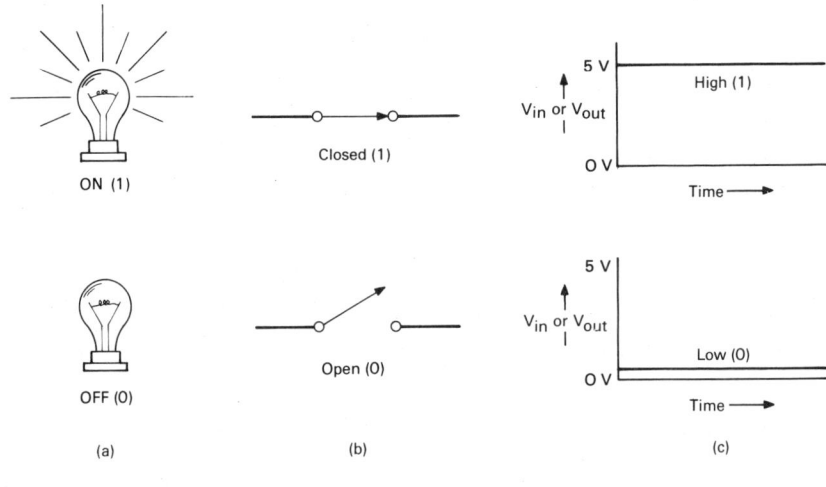

Figure 4.1 Binary events in electronics. (*a*) Lamps, (*b*) switches, and (*c*) voltage levels.

off. The high voltage state of 5 V is called the "logical 1 level." If a voltage in a digital system is close to zero, that represents the "logical 0 level" and corresponds to an output transistor that is driven strongly on.

Counting in the binary number system

Before considering counting in the binary number system, we will first review counting in the decimal number system. The decimal system originally got started because people have a total of 10 fingers and thumbs on both of their hands. Historically, people have counted things using their fingers, much like small children do today. Having the fingers all clenched into a fist represents the count of 0, as shown in Figure 4.2. As the counting starts, an index finger is extended to represent a count of 1. Then the index finger and a thumb are both extended to represent 2, and so on. The count can go from 0 through 10 and will be indicated by the total number of fingers and thumbs that are extended.

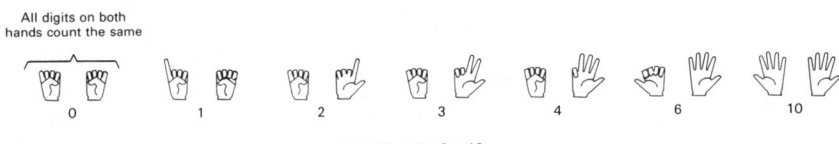

Figure 4.2 Counting with your hands.

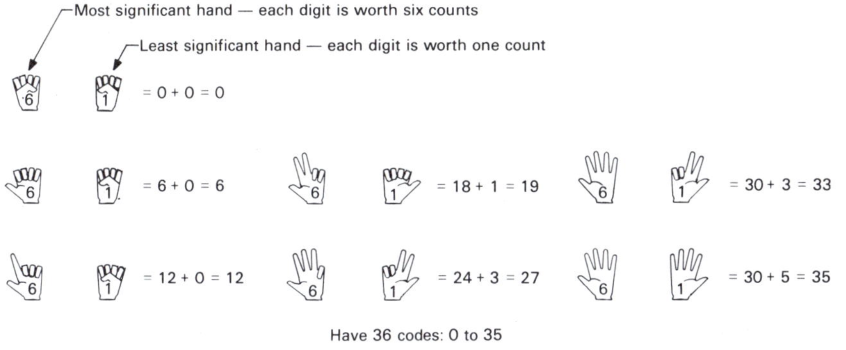

Most significant hand — each digit is worth six counts
Least significant hand — each digit is worth one count

= 0 + 0 = 0

= 6 + 0 = 6   = 18 + 1 = 19   = 30 + 3 = 33

= 12 + 0 = 12   = 24 + 3 = 27   = 30 + 5 = 35

Have 36 codes: 0 to 35

Figure 4.3 A more efficient way to count with your hands.

It is interesting that there is a much more efficient way to count with your hands, as shown in Figure 4.3. This is a little more difficult, so it is not a natural way to count. (I don't know of anyone who has ever used this, but it provides an interesting example.) Rather than saying that every digit (every finger or thumb) on both of your hands is only worth a count of 1, higher numbers can be reached if the digits on the left hand have a higher significance. So, a thumb or a finger on the left hand would represent a count of 6, and the digits on the right hand would still have a significance of only 1. Clenching both fists would still represent a count of 0.

Counting would then start with the least-significant right hand. The thumb would be extended to represent a count of 1. All of the fingers and the thumb of the right hand finally being extended would represent a count of 5. To indicate the next count (6) the right hand would *reset to 0,* and the thumb would be extended from the left hand. By making use of "positional weighting" (saying that digits on one hand are more significant than those on the other hand), counts from 0 through 35 (36 different numbers; 0 is counted as a number) can be represented. For equal weighting of both hands, only 11 numbers can be represented. Positional weighting therefore greatly increases the capability to represent numbers with our hands.

Counting, using only your thumbs

A binary number system would have been more common if people did not have any fingers at all. With only thumbs (one thumb on each hand), as shown in Figure 4.4, the number 0 would be represented by both thumbs being retracted. Assume that the right thumb represents the least-significant digit and the left thumb the most-significant digit. The count of 1 would then be indicated by simply extending the least-

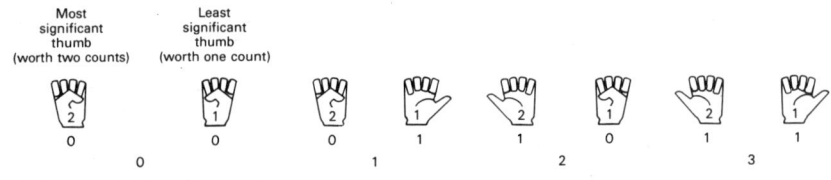

Figure 4.4 Use the binary number system if you are all thumbs.

significant thumb. To indicate 2, nothing more can be done with the right thumb (that already is indicating its highest count of 1), so that thumb is reset to 0, and the left thumb is extended to indicate a count of 2. A count of 3 would then be indicated with both thumbs extended. Even if you only had thumbs, you could represent four numbers (0 through 3) in this binary number system.

Positional weighting of the digits

The concept of positional weighting of digits is used in our standard decimal system. For example, a 1 by itself is only a 1. But a 10 (a 1 moved over one place to the left) represents ten. Moving it another place to the left represents 100.

As an example of positional weighting in the decimal number system, consider the odometer shown in Figure 4.5. To simplify, only the three least-significant digits are shown. As these digits go through a counting sequence, the right-most digit goes from 0 through 9. Every time this digit resets to 0, a 1 is "carried" to the next digit position to the left. So, the 9 to 0 transition carries a 1 to the next most-significant digit position. The next time a 1 is added to this digit position occurs after the count of 19. The next count will again make a 9 to 0 transition in the least-significant digit, and this will cause another carry of 1 to make the next most-significant digit increment to 2.

This type of counting continues until the second digit position accumulates a count of 9. Then, after the count of 99, a carry will "ripple" across these two digit positions. This carries a 1 to the next adjacent digit column to the left (the hundreds column). This is called a "major carry" because the carry rippled through to the most-significant digit position.

With this in mind, look at a binary number system using three digits, as shown in Figure 4.6. Positional weighting is used in a manner similar to the way it is used in the decimal system. The digit positions are no longer in steps of 10 or powers of 10, like $10^0 = 1$, $10^1 = 10$, and $10^2 = 100$. Rather than having 10 as the base of this number system, 2 is used. Now the digit positions are based on 2 being raised to various powers such as $2^0 = 1$, $2^1 = 2$, and $2^2 = 4$. The three-digit columns in a binary number system have the least-significant column as the

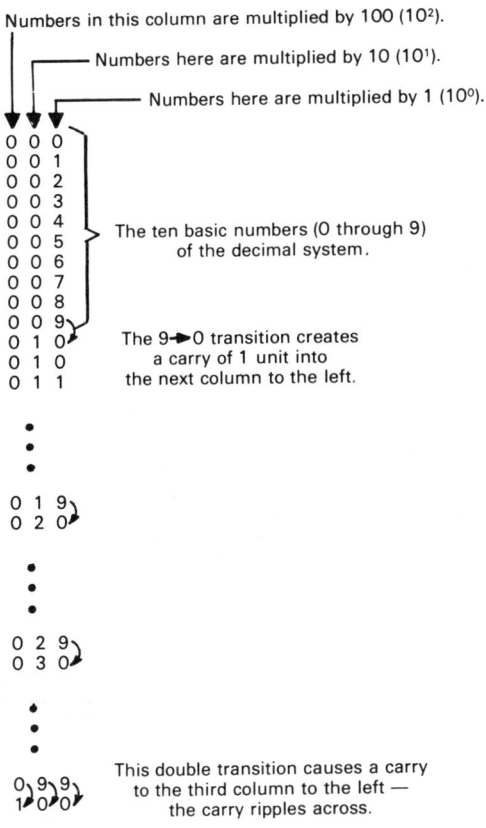

Figure 4.5 A look at an odometer.

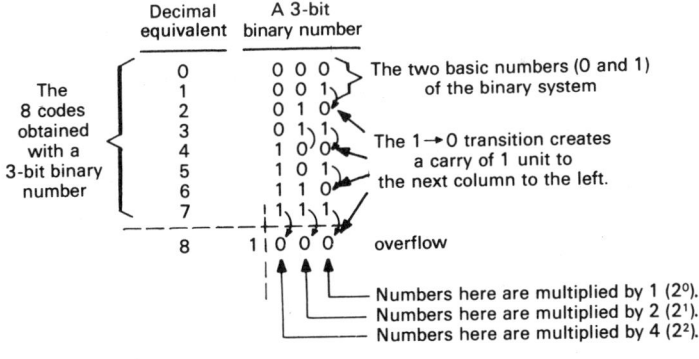

Figure 4.6 The 8 codes of a 3-bit binary number.

units column, $2^0 = 1$ (a positional weight of 1), and the next column to the left has a positional weight of $2^1 = 2$. Counts in the next adjacent column to the left have a weight of $2^2 = 4$.

Carries occur more frequently in digital systems. For example, the least-significant binary digit is creating a carry on every other count. In each column, as the 1 to 0 transition is made, a carry propagates to the next more-significant column to the left. When the highest number (111) for this 3-bit example is reached, the carry propagates clear across and generates an "overflow." This last carry is lost (an overflow) because the next binary number (1000) is larger than can be represented with only 3 bits.

In Figure 4.7, the positional weighting that is involved with an 8-bit binary number is shown. The binary number used in this example is 11010011. The least-significant bit is to the right and has a weight of 2^0 or 1. The positional weight doubles each time the bit position moves one place to the left. The most-significant bit in an 8-bit binary number is seen to have the positional weight of 128.

It becomes a little difficult to express this binary number in a decimal equivalent. The most-significant bit is 1; therefore at least a count of 128 is represented. The next most-significant bit is also 1; so its positional weight of 64 must be added. Every time there is a 1 in a digit position, the decimal weight of that bit is added. The sum of all of these individual positional weights provides the equivalent decimal number. Therefore, 11010011 (binary) is equal to 211 (decimal).

The number of bits that are available indicates how many different numbers can be expressed. Digital numbers are often used to represent various other things. The digital numbers are then called "codes." For example, digital numbers can represent the letters of the alphabet. This means that a particular "decoding" scheme will interpret each unique grouping of 1s and 0s in a predefined way.

The number of unique codes or numbers that are possible can be determined in advance by knowing how many bits are available. In

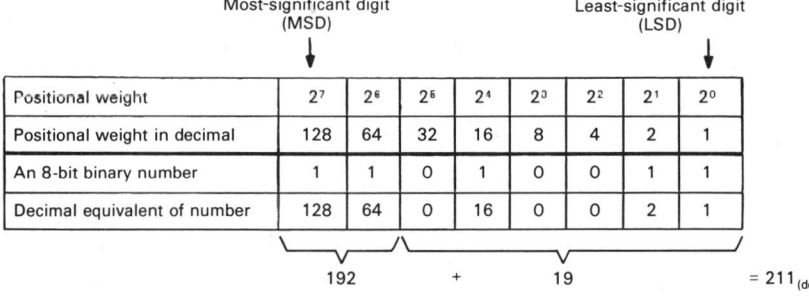

Figure 4.7 Positional weighting in an 8-bit binary number.

```
0 0
0 1    The four possibilities
1 0    with a 2-bit number
1 1
```
(a)

```
0 0 0
0 0 1
0 1 0
0 1 1   The eight possibilities
1 0 0   with a 3-bit number
1 0 1
1 1 0
1 1 1
```

In general: have $2^{No.\,of\,bits}$ different numbers.

(b)

Figure 4.8 The number of bits specifies the number of different numbers. (a) With 2 bits there are 2^2, which equals four different numbers and (b) with 3 bits there are 2^3, which equals eight different numbers.

the example of Figure 4.8, if 2 bits are available (Figure 4.8a), only four numbers can be represented. If one more bit is added (Figure 4.8b), the allowable number of codes doubles from 4 to 8. Each added bit always doubles the number of available codes. To determine the number of codes that are possible, take the total number of bits that are available as an exponent on 2. So with 4 bits, $2^4 = 16$, and therefore the total number of unique codes is 16. With 10 bits, $2^{10} = 1024$ so there are 1024 (also called 1K but not 1k, which is the metric prefix for 1000), and 11 bits will double this to 2048 or 2K unique codes.

Adding binary numbers

In the decimal number system there are certain rules that must be applied when adding numbers. These rules for addition are generally memorized in the early grades. Similarly, to add two binary numbers (A added to B) as shown in Figure 4.9a, rules for binary addition must be used. Notice that whether or not a carry is being generated by the next-lower bit position has to be considered. The rules for binary addition, Figure 4.9b, go through the four combinations of A and B with the carry in the 0 state and then go through these same combinations of A and B a second time, with the carry in the 1 state. Notice how the sum is generated and also how a carry is generated. When A, B, and C are all in the 1 state, this generates not only a sum of 1 but also a carry of 1. These are the rules for binary addition.

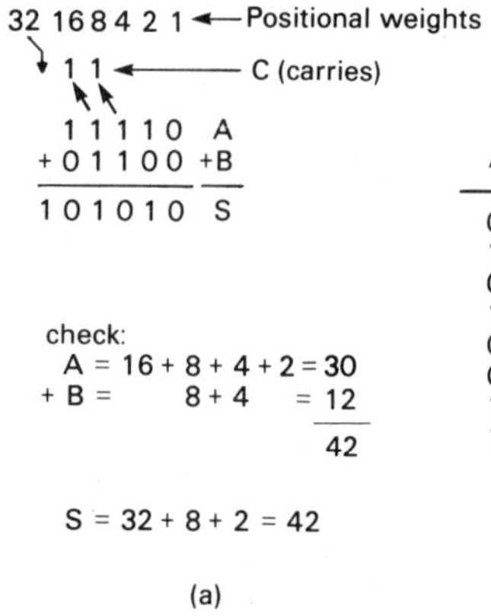

```
32 16 8 4 2 1  ←— Positional weights
  ↓ 1 1 ←——— C (carries)
    ↖↖
    1 1 1 1 0   A
  + 0 1 1 0 0  +B
  ───────────
    1 0 1 0 1 0   S

check:
  A = 16 + 8 + 4 + 2 = 30
 +B =       8 + 4    = 12
                    ────
                     42

S = 32 + 8 + 2 = 42

(a)
```

A	B	C_P (previous carry)	$S_{(sum)}$	C_N (new carry)
0	0	0	0	0
1	0	0	1	0
0	1	0	1	0
1	1	0	0	1
0	0	1	1	0
0	1	1	0	1
1	0	1	0	1
1	1	1	1	1

(b)

Figure 4.9 Adding binary numbers. (*a*) Adding two binary numbers, *A* + *B*, and (*b*) rules for binary addition.

Subtraction can be done in a way that is similar to this, but multiplication and division are more complex. There are a number of ways to achieve binary multiplication and division that make use of "algorithms." An algorithm is an ordered collection of simple steps, like how to bake a cake from scratch, that must be gone through to arrive at a result. If these steps are sequentially followed, an answer will be obtained. Programming a digital computer involves algorithms. Computers go through the steps that are specified by the program to provide a desired result.

Complementing binary numbers

In digital systems, you'll often hear of "complementing" a binary number. There are two types of complements that can be done. Both of these are shown in Figure 4.10. Figure 4.10*a* shows the 1's complement, in which all the bits are inverted.

The 2's complement, Figure 4.10*b*, is the 1's complement with the additional step that 1 is added. The act of taking the 2's complement of a binary number changes the sign. The 2's complement code is used to represent negative numbers and is also very useful in handling subtraction (as we'll see later in the chapter).

Doing It with Logic

Digital circuits and systems make use of logic circuits (often abbreviated as "logic"). You'll hear references like, "This is the logic that was

```
1 0 1 1 0 1 — A binary number
0 1 0 0 1 0 — The 1's complement
     1 ⟶ 0
     0 ⟶ 1  } Rules
```

(a)

```
1 0 1 1 0 1 — A binary number
0 1 0 0 1 0 — The 1's complement
+         1 — Add 1 to 1's complement
_____
0 1 0 0 1 1 — The 2's complement
```

(b)

Figure 4.10 Complementing binary numbers. (*a*) 1's complement and (*b*) 2's complement.

used," to imply the representation of the circuit interconnections and the types of logic circuits that were used to accomplish a particular digital function.

The inputs to logic circuits are usually named by using the letters of the alphabet, as *A, B, C,* etc. These are called "discrete variables" because they can only take on one of two possible values, 0 or 1. They are sometimes also referred to as "Boolean variables" in honor of George Boole, an early contributor to computer basics.

These logic inputs exist as voltages: 0 V for a logical 0 (or false), and +5 V for a logical 1 (or true). These voltages can represent various inputs to a digital system such as, "It is now raining," "The car is out of gas," "The proper number of digits has been dialed," "This machine is out of change," etc. Digital voltages representing these true/false statements can then be combined in a number of logical ways, as we will now consider.

Logic voltage waveforms

There are two conventions associated with logic voltage levels, as shown in Figure 4.11. "Positive logic" implies that the most positive voltage (of the two voltages that the circuits provide) will be considered the logical 1 level. In contrast with this, "negative logic" implies that the most negative voltage is the logical 1 level. Negative logic was used in the early days of PMOS ICs which required negative power supplies. Most modern logic circuits operate from a single positive 5-V, power-supply voltage; therefore, negative logic is now rarely used.

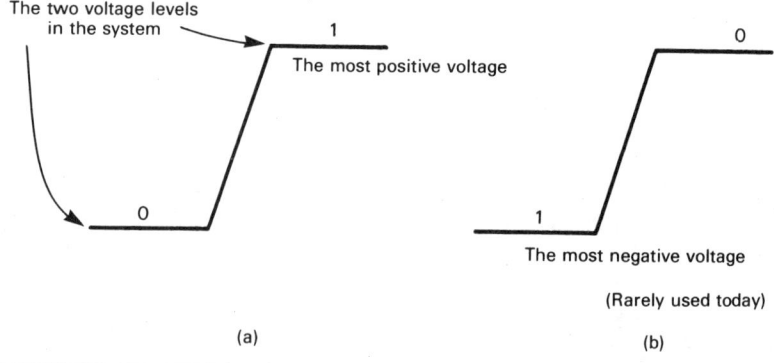

Figure 4.11 Logic levels versus voltage levels. (a) Positive logic and (b) negative logic.

The timing parameters that are associated with the changes of a digital voltage waveform are defined in Figure 4.12. Notice that both the rise and fall times are referenced from the 10 and 90 percent points on the voltage waveform. This convention is used so that the measurements will be made from more well-defined parts of the waveform. The rise time is the time it takes a voltage waveform to move in a positive direction from the 10 percent to the 90 percent points of the total voltage excursion. The fall time is the time taken for the voltage waveform to fall from the 90 percent to the 10 percent points.

Many logic families specify that the input digital voltages should have both rise and fall times less than some small number, such as 500 ns (this is the specification for 74HC CMOS logic circuits). Specifications like this are used to make the logic inputs more definite and to limit

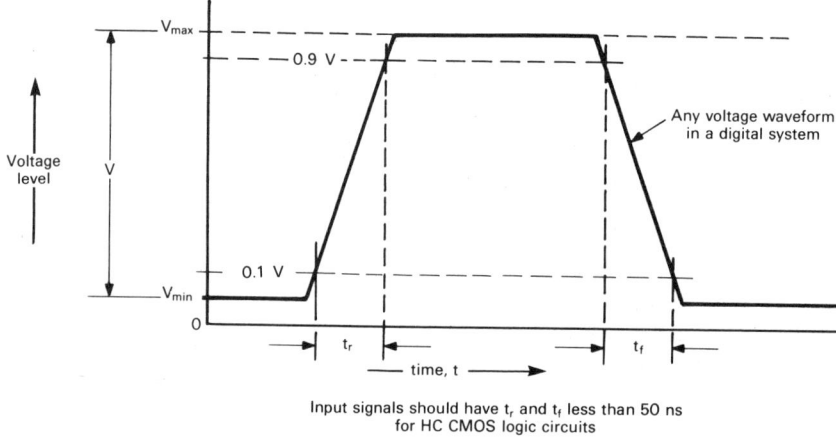

Figure 4.12 The rise and fall times of a digital voltage waveform.

the power drain that exists while the input voltages are changing. There is undesired "indecision" in digital systems if the voltage waveforms have extended rise and fall times, because the circuitry cannot interpret these in-between voltage levels and can therefore malfunction. In digital systems, if the rise and fall times of the voltage waveforms become degraded, Schmitt-trigger logic circuits can be used to "square up" the voltage waveforms, to restore abrupt changes between the two logic-voltage levels.

The logic inverter

One of the simplest of the logic circuits is the inverter. Inverters are used to complement a digital signal. They change a 0-input signal into a 1-output signal, and vice versa, as shown in the "truth table" of Figure 4.13a. Truth tables are generally supplied for logic circuits. This is a concise way to indicate the output states that will result from all of the possible combinations of logic states at the inputs. The inverter truth table indicates that the output function (f) is the complement of the input (A). An inverter is also called a "NOT gate."

This logic inversion function is indicated as a switch shunting a LED in Figure 4.13b. When the switch is open, the light is on. When the switch is closed, the LED is shorted out, so the light goes off. This function is opposite to that of a normal switch, where closing the switch lights the light.

The symbol for a logic inverter is shown in Figure 4.13c. It is a triangle with a small ball (either at the output or at the input) that signifies inversion.

There is a major interest in the time that it takes a digital signal to propagate through a logic circuit. This is called "propagation delay" and is usually measured in the very small time units of nanoseconds (light travels 1 ft in 1 ns). The propagation delay through an inverter is indicated in Figure 4.14, where the input signal is shown using the

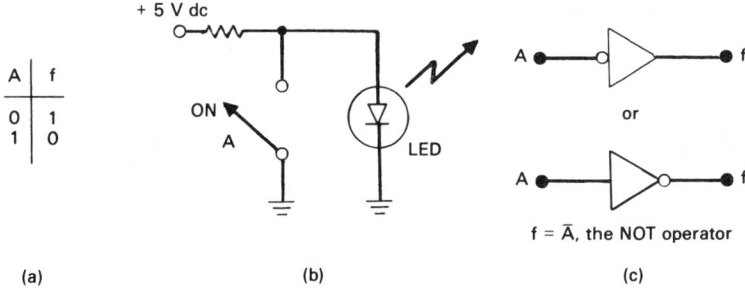

Figure 4.13 The logic inverter. (a) Inverter truth table, (b) inverter function, and (c) inverter symbols.

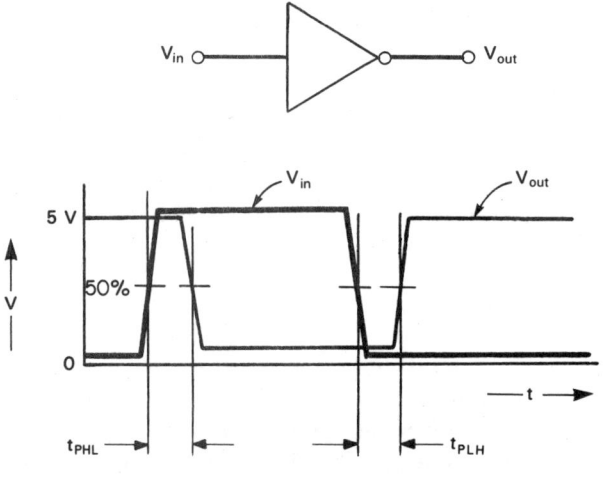

Figure 4.14 The propagation delay through an inverter.

wide line, and the resulting inverted output signal is drawn with the narrow line. Notice that whenever the input signal is low, the output signal is high, and vice versa. There is a finite time, the propagation ("prop") time delay, that exists before the output follows a change made at the input.

Prop delay is measured from the 50 percent voltage values of the waveforms. The propagation delay for the high-to-low transition of the output is abbreviated as t_{PHL} (HL implies the high-to-low transition). When the input signal falls (and makes a high-to-low transition) the inverted output voltage will then rise. This is the propagation delay low to high, t_{PLH}.

This AND that

One way of logically combining digital input signals is provided by the logical "AND" gate shown in Figure 4.15. The two input signals (A and B) are indicated in the functional diagram of Figure 4.15a. Notice

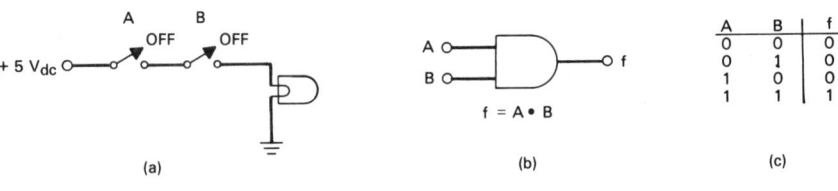

Figure 4.15 The AND gate. (a) AND function, (b) AND symbol, (c) AND truth table.

that both of these switches have to be closed before the light comes on. This means that A AND B have to be true in order to have the output in the logical 1 state. An AND gate can perform the decision implied in statements like, "If I have both time AND money, I will take a vacation." The inputs are digital signals that have been designed to electrically represent the existence of time and money, and the output is a digital signal that represents whether or not you will take a vacation. If both inputs are logical 1s, indicating that you have both time and money, the output will also be a logical 1 to indicate that you will take a vacation.

The symbol for the AND gate is also shown on this figure. Notice that the AND function is indicated by a dot between the A and B, as $A \cdot B$ or simply AB. The truth table shown in Figure 4.15c is a concise way to show the functional relationships. The output is true only when both inputs are simultaneously true.

In addition to the AND gate, a "NAND" gate also exists. A NAND gate is simply the inversion of the AND function, as shown in Figure 4.16. Now when both switches are on, the light is off. The symbol, shown in Figure 4.16b, has a little ball at the output signifying inversion. The complement or inversion is also indicated by $\overline{AND}$. The bar across the top signifies the complement. The NAND truth table, shown in Figure 4.16c, has the output function inverted when compared with the truth table for the AND gate. Now, when both A and B are true, this is the only time that the output is in the low state.

This OR that

The logical "OR" function is indicated in the diagram of Figure 4.17a. Notice that now the two switches are placed in parallel (rather than in series as they were for the AND gate). In this case, closing either switch will light the light. That implies that if A OR B is true, the light will be on. An OR gate can perform the decision implied in statements like, "If I have time OR money, I will take a vacation."

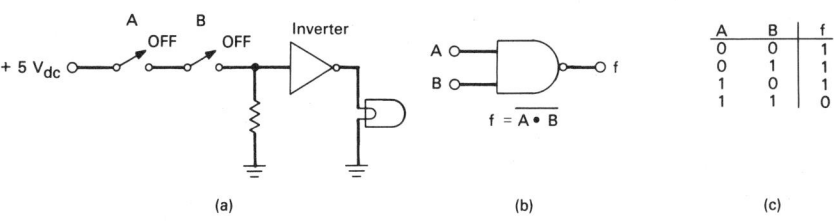

Figure 4.16 The NAND gate. (a) NAND function, (b) NAND symbol, (c) NAND truth table.

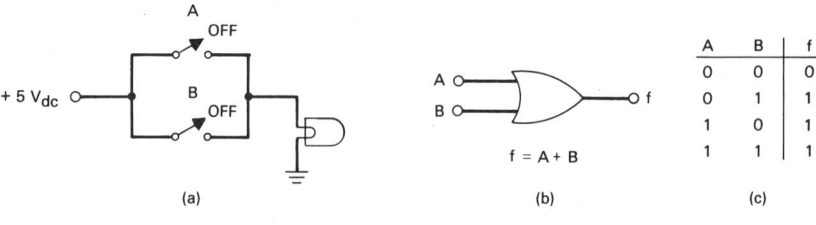

Figure 4.17 The OR gate. (*a*) OR function, (*b*) OR symbol, (*c*) OR truth table.

The OR symbol is shown in Figure 4.17*b*, and the OR operation is indicated with a plus sign. So, the functional relationship will be $f = A + B$, but this is not read as the *sum* of A and B; it is read as A OR B. Unfortunately, it is the same symbol as is used for addition in conventional mathematics.

The OR truth table of Figure 4.17*c* shows that the output function (f) is true when either A OR B or *both* are true. (There is a different logic gate, the exclusive OR gate, which will provide a 0 output if both A AND B are simultaneously true. We will discuss this gate in the next section.)

Similar to the NAND gate, there also exists a NOR gate, as shown in the functional diagram of Figure 4.18*a*. If either A OR B is true (if either switch is closed), the light will be off. Both switches have to be open for the light to be on.

The symbol for the NOR gate is shown in Figure 4.18*b*. This is the OR symbol modified with the small inversion ball at the output. The NOR truth table of Figure 4.18*c* shows the inverted functional relationship when compared to the OR truth table. The only time the output of a NOR gate is true is when A AND B are both false.

The exclusive OR and NOR circuits

The diagram of an exclusive OR gate is shown in Figure 4.19*a*. This is a rather complicated interconnection of the two switches. Each switch

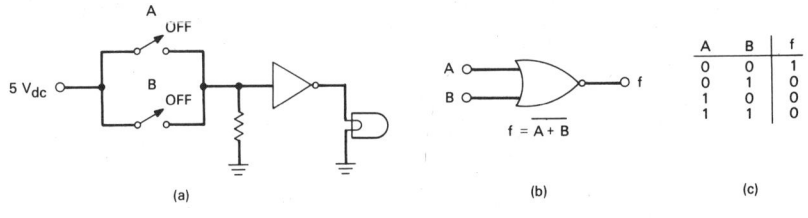

Figure 4.18 The NOR gate. (*a*) NOR function, (*b*) NOR symbol, (*c*) NOR truth table.

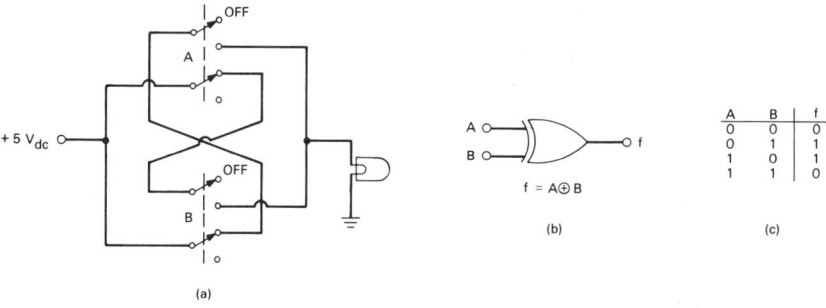

Figure 4.19 The exclusive OR gate. (*a*) Exclusive OR function, (*b*) exclusive OR symbol, (*c*) exclusive OR truth table.

is a double-pole, double-throw (dpdt) switch. This is a more complex gate. Trace the diagram through and notice that each switch is powered only when the opposite switch is in the OFF state. This ensures that if both switches are in the ON state, neither switch is powered, and the light is then not lit. This complication was necessary to provide a modification to the OR gate that disallows the output from being true if both inputs are *simultaneously true*.

The symbol for the exclusive OR gate is shown in Figure 4.19*b*. A second curved line is used at the input that is spaced away from the main symbol. The symbol for the exclusive OR function is a plus sign with a circle around it.

The truth table, shown in Figure 4.19*c*, indicates that the output is true if only one of the inputs (at a time) is a 1. When both inputs are simultaneously true, the output is a 0.

In addition to the exclusive OR function, there is also the exclusive NOR function shown in Figure 4.20*a*. This is the complemented out-

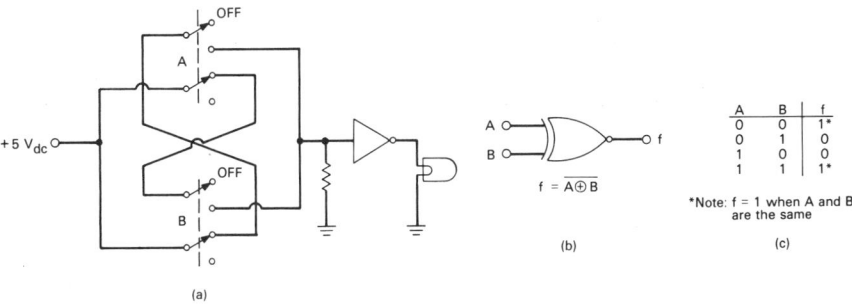

Figure 4.20 The exclusive NOR gate. (*a*) Exclusive NOR function, (*b*) exclusive NOR symbol, (*c*) exclusive NOR truth table.

put of the previous exclusive OR gate. The symbol shown in Figure 4.20b includes the small inversion ball at the output, and the truth table for the exclusive OR gate is given in Figure 4.20c.

One of the uses for the exclusive NOR gate is to indicate that both inputs are the same, because the output is true if both inputs are simultaneously 0s or 1s. So, exclusive NOR gates can be used to indicate equality, the fact that the A and B inputs are logically the same.

The standard logic gates have been described. You might ask, "What are all of the logical output possibilities with a two-input gate?" This is indicated in Figure 4.21, in which there are 16 possible functional relations that can be associated with the two inputs.

The six standard logic gates are indicated on this diagram. Notice that the X in front of the OR and the X in front of the NOR are the exclusive OR (XOR) and the exclusive NOR (XNOR) gates, respectively. Only six of these functions are named. The first of the functions, where the output remains zero for all input states, is simply a null function. A zero output exists independent of the states of the inputs. That is not useful. The sixteenth possibility is similarly locked up in the 1 state. This, again, is not useful. The functional relations indicated as "not standard logic" appear in two groups of four and are also not used.

Fanout

In designing digital systems, consideration has to be given to the maximum number of inputs that can be driven by the output of a gate. This is called the "fanout" of the logic gate and is shown in Figure 4.22 in which a NAND gate is driving 10 different inputs. This is a fanout of 10.

In the bipolar logic families, T^2L, Schottky T^2L, and advanced Schottky T^2L, fanout is typically limited to 10 because of dc current

Inputs		The 16 possible functional output possibilities															
		1	2	3	4	5	6	7	8	9	10	11	12	13	14	15	16
A	B	0*	NOR	← Not standard logic →				XOR	NAND	AND	XNOR	← Not standard logic (complements of 6→3) →				OR	1*
0	0	0	1	0	1	0	1	0	1	0	1	0	1	0	1	0	1
0	1	0	0	1	1	0	0	1	1	0	0	1	1	0	0	1	1
1	0	0	0	0	0	1	1	1	1	0	0	0	0	1	1	1	1
1	1	0	0	0	0	0	0	0	0	1	1	1	1	1	1	1	1

*Note: Not useful

Figure 4.21 All of the functional responses to two inputs.

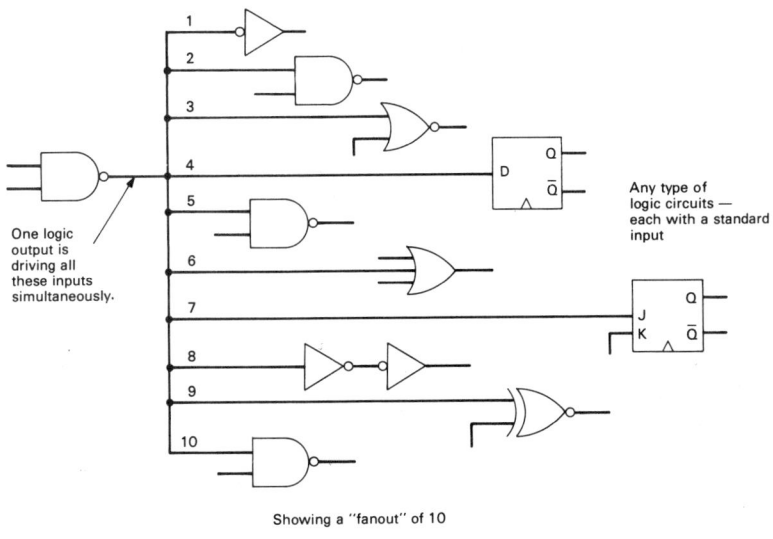

Figure 4.22 Fanout in logic.

flow at the inputs of the logic gates. Fanout considerations differ depending on the technology that is used to make up the logic circuitry. For example, with CMOS logic there is essentially no dc input current flow; so fanout is limited only by the stray capacitance that accumulates at the output node of a gate and eventually limits the rise and fall times.

This difference between bipolar and CMOS, as far as fanout is concerned, is shown in more detail in Figure 4.23. In the bipolar logic gates of Figure 4.23a, each logic input will supply 0.4 mA to the output of the driving gate. This dc input current has to be absorbed by the output of this one driving gate without producing an excessively high voltage while in the logical 0 state. A fanout limit exists because each gate output is specified to sink 4 mA and still maintain a proper logical 0 voltage level. This is why bipolar logic families have a fanout of 10.

As shown in Figure 4.23b, with CMOS logic there is almost no dc input current (it is just reverse-biased junction leakage current and can be neglected). So, the thing that limits fanout in CMOS logic is the degradation of rise and fall times that results from the input capacitances of the driven gates and the stray wiring capacitance.

Some logical examples

A diagram of the logic that is necessary to make a decision for a space flight vehicle is shown in Figure 4.24. This is just a hypothetical example to show how logic can be used in an electronic system. The main

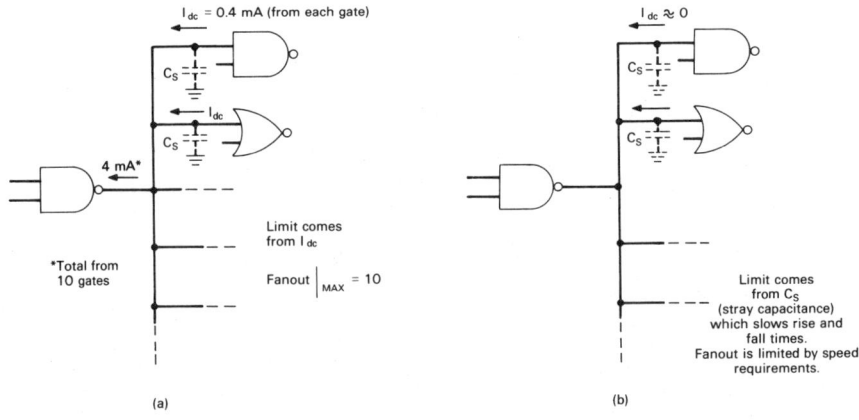

Figure 4.23 Fanout limitations in logic circuits. (a) T²L (bipolar) logic and (b) CMOS logic.

output on the right side of this diagram answers the question, "Should the spacecraft make another orbit?" If this output is in the high state, that indicates, "Yes, make another orbit." If this output is in the low state, it indicates, "No, don't make another orbit, return to Earth."

The various logic inputs are shown on the left side of this drawing. At the top are the life signs of the astronaut: heart rate, blood pressure, and respiration. If these three signals are in the high state, the life signs are acceptable. Any one of these in a 0 state implies trouble with that input condition. The output of the upper three-input AND gate (No. 1) is an indication of all three of the life signs of the astronaut.

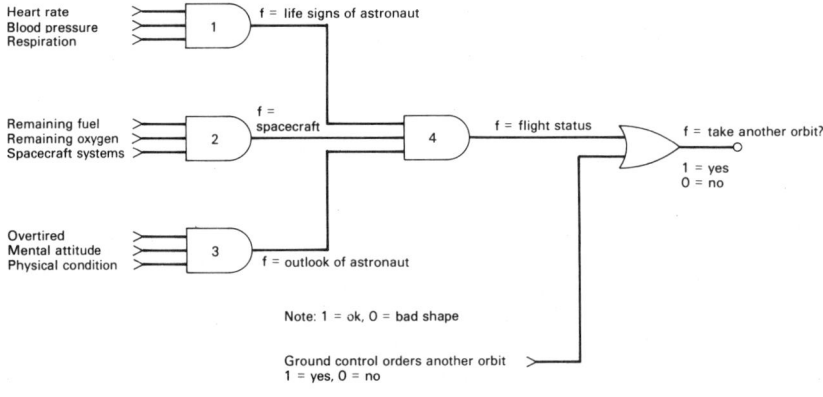

Figure 4.24 Arriving at logical decisions.

Below this, another three-input AND gate (No. 2) is used to indicate the condition of the spacecraft. The inputs here indicate remaining fuel, remaining oxygen, and the condition of the spacecraft systems. The output of this gate represents the general condition of the spacecraft.

Below this, the last AND gate (No. 3) indicates the outlook of the astronaut: rested or tired, mental attitude, and physical condition. If all of these three inputs are in the high state, the outlook of the astronaut will be in the 1 state.

These three separate signals are combined again in a fourth AND gate (No. 4) to provide the overall flight status. This is an indication that, as far as everything associated with the orbiting vehicle is concerned, it is okay (if a 1) for another orbit.

This logic signal then goes into a final two-input OR gate. Notice that the other input to this OR gate is a Control Command from the ground that has an overriding control. With this type of a logic diagram, if the ground control ordered another orbit, that digital input signal would go true and force the spacecraft into an additional orbit, even if the flight status was in the 0 logic state (indicating that the flight status was unacceptable). This overall logic may not be good because the flight status should perhaps have a higher vote. This can be changed by simply making the output OR gate an AND gate. Then the airborne flight status *and* the ground control would have to be in agreement. This is a big difference in the control of the spacecraft.

Simplifying logic diagrams

In order to make logic diagrams easier to follow, two types of logic diagramming are used. One explains the system operation, and the logic symbols that are used on these drawings are quite different from the logic that is available with the standard ICs that are used to implement the system.

This difference is illustrated in Figure 4.25. In the upper left of this figure is a two-input NAND gate. If this NAND gate symbol were to appear on a "functional logic diagram," it would imply that the system is "looking" for both A and B to be true to cause the output to be low.

This NAND gate will also function as shown in the upper right of this figure. Equivalent logic gates can be drawn by simply changing the AND gate to an OR gate, or vice versa, and removing any inversion balls at the inputs or output, or if they didn't exist, adding them.

Applying these rules to the NAND function, an OR function results in which both inputs have inversion balls. This implies that the use of this NAND gate is to detect when either A OR B is low and to then provide a high output. A basic NAND gate provides both of these functions. Drawing the symbol in a particular way can indicate what coin-

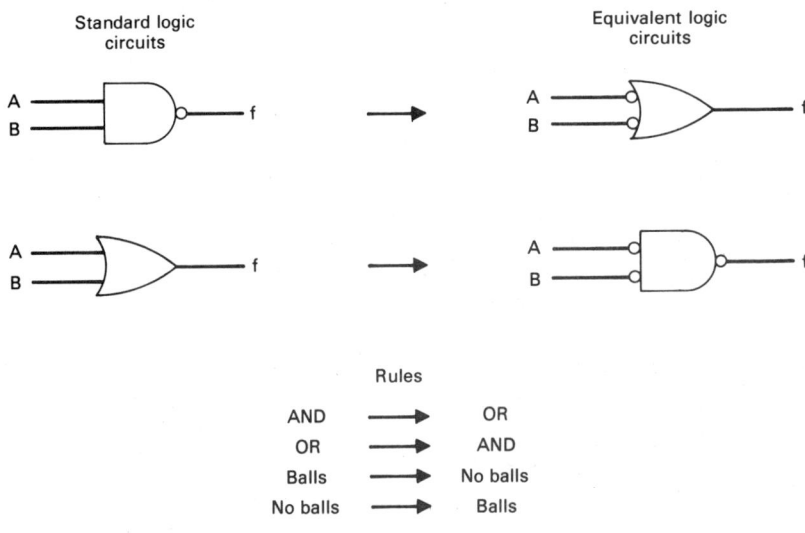

Figure 4.25 Conversions to equivalent logic gates.

cidence of input conditions the gate is being used to detect. This helps to understand a logic diagram.

Just under the NAND gate of Figure 4.25 is a two-input OR gate. If this were shown on a functional logic diagram, it would imply that this gate is looking for A or B to be true to provide a high output. If this is not the desired condition, the OR gate should be drawn as shown to the right: a NAND gate with inversion balls everywhere. This implies that the system is "looking" for A AND B both to be low to provide a low state at the output. The particular input and output conditions that are important are more clearly identified if functional, rather than actual, logic diagrams are used.

A collection of the symbols that are used to indicate these functional relationships is shown in Figure 4.26. The statement underneath each one of these diagrams indicates the functional logic that is provided. To the right of this are the actual logic gates that would be used.

It is very helpful to have two logic diagrams, one to show the functional relationships and the other to show the actual logic gates that are used. To understand the logic, the actual logic gates are not the most helpful; but to find signals on a PC board that contains ICs, the actual logic diagram is most useful.

Simplifying logic expressions

We have discussed simplifying logic diagrams from the standpoint of functional versus actual logic diagramming. When we talk about sim-

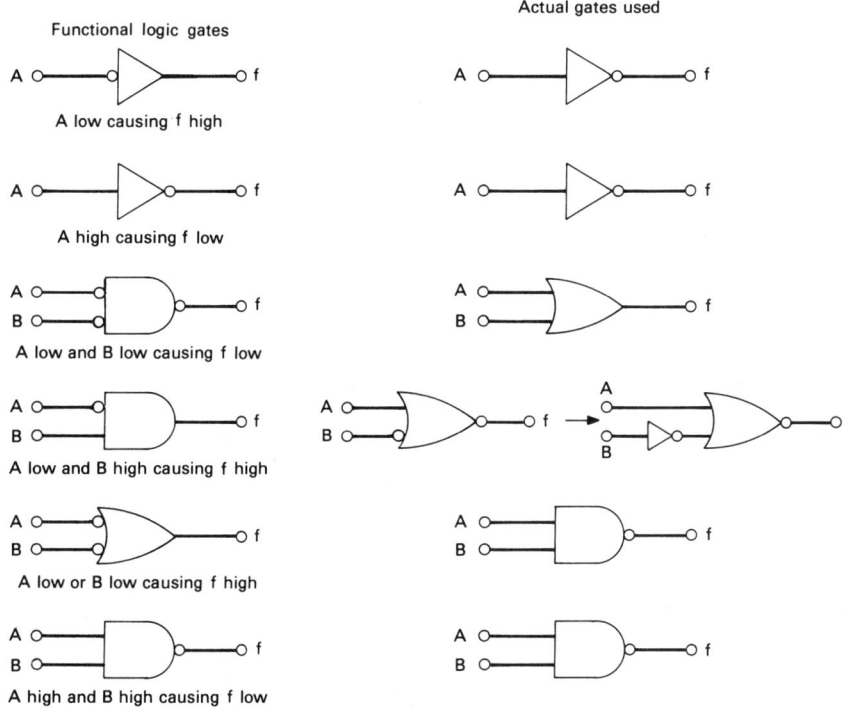

Figure 4.26 Functional logic gates versus actual logic gates.

plifying "logic expressions," we are interested in reducing the total amount of circuitry that is necessary to accomplish the given logic that is needed for a system.

There are a number of ways to simplify logic expressions, some of which are handled on digital computers. An indication of how and why this logic simplification can take place is best demonstrated by using graphical techniques for simplifying logic expressions.

A diagram for simplifying logic expressions is shown in Figure 4.27. The logic inputs $A, B, C,$ and D are written in "minterm" form in Figure 4.27a. Notice that the chart of Figure 4.27b has a particular location for each of the 16 minterm possibilities of these four inputs. Within each small box is shown the logic conditions on the inputs that are necessary to "address" that box. The logic expressions that address each box are called minterms because they involve this minimum area, one-sixteenth of the total area of the diagram. This diagram is a map that shows the addresses of each box.

Figure 4.28 shows the sequence of steps that are used to locate the minterm $AB\bar{C}\bar{D}$. A is true; therefore, this indicates that the address is

$$F = AB\overline{C}D + \overline{A}BCD + AB\overline{C}\overline{D} + \overline{A}B\overline{C}D + \ldots$$

(a)

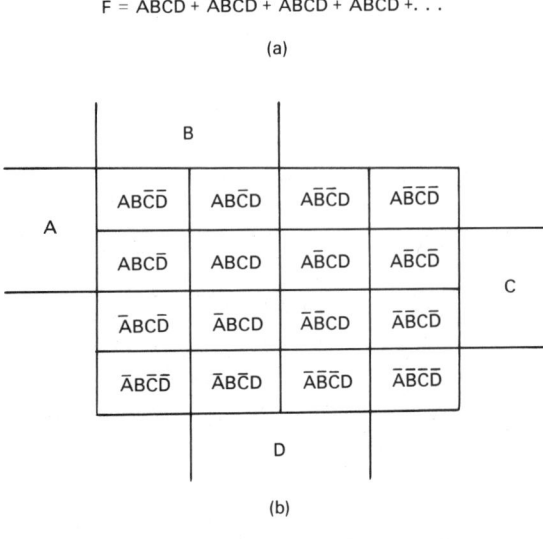

(b)

Figure 4.27 Minterm locations on a 4-literal diagram. (a) Logic expressed in minterm form and (b) locating minterms on a diagram.

somewhere in the upper two rows because all six of these small boxes have A true (the lower two rows are not $A, \overline{A}$).

Similarly, as shown in Figure 4.28b, the two columns on the left are in B; therefore, with B true this further restricts the location to one of the four boxes on the left. The center two rows are included in C, and the top row and the bottom row are not C; therefore, $\overline{C}$ restricts the location to be one of the upper two boxes. The center two columns are included in D, and the left column and the right column are not D. So this minterm ($AB\overline{C}\overline{D}$) is located in the upper left-hand corner.

This may sound a little complicated, but once experience is gained, any minterm on the diagram can be rapidly located. We will now see why we want to locate these minterms and be able to place a 1 in a particular address on the diagram.

If a logic expression existed that included every one of the minterms (all 16 of them) this would place a 1 in every one of these squares as is shown in Figure 4.29a. This overall logic expression is truly independent of the logic states of the four inputs. That is not a useful logic function. It is an extreme case.

In Figure 4.29b, the lower half of the diagram is shown filled up with 1s. It takes eight individual minterm expressions to represent this logic, but a logical equivalent can specify these lower two rows as simply $\overline{A}$. This is a tremendous simplification in the logic circuitry that would

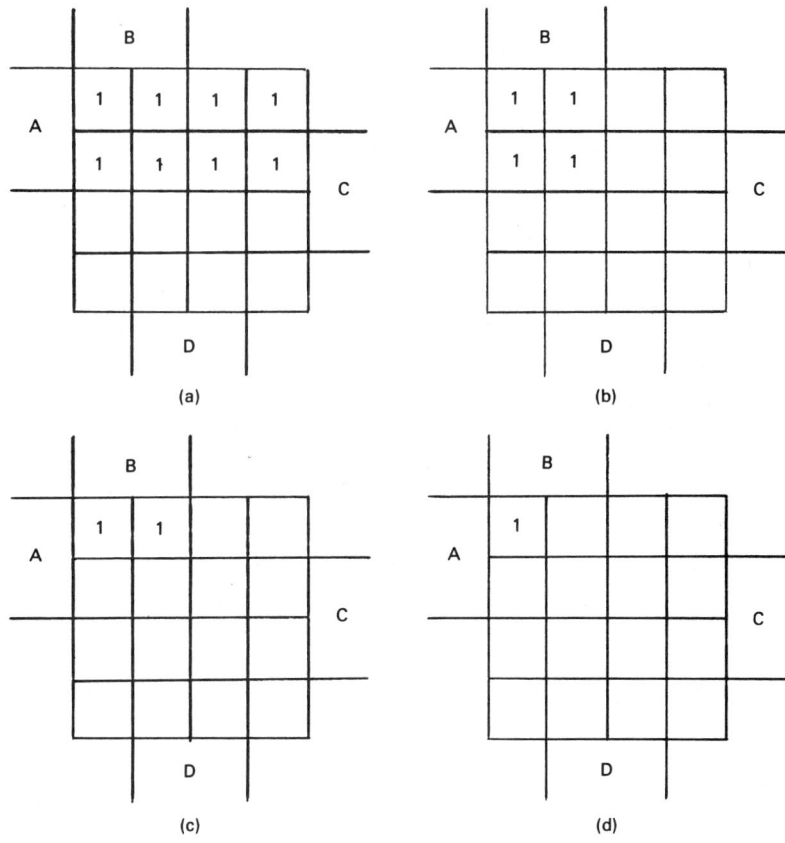

Figure 4.28 The steps in locating the minterm $ABCD$. (a) A is true—A, (b) and B is true—AB, (c) but C is false—$AB\bar{C}$, and (d) and D is false—$A\bar{B}C\bar{D}$.

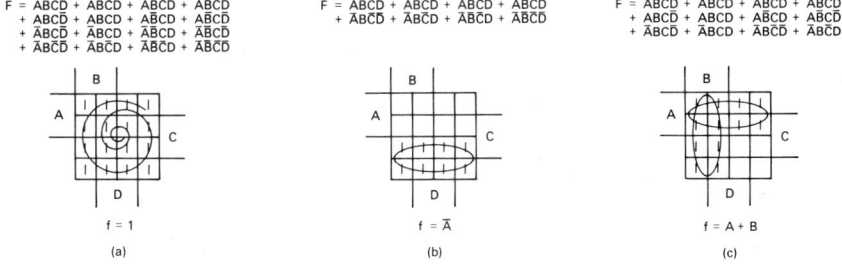

Figure 4.29 Some logic reductions. (a) Every minterm, (b) the lower half, and (c) upper half and left half.

be required to respond to the eight 4-input minterms. An inverter on the A input will provide an equivalent logic function.

Something a little more complicated is shown in Figure 4.29c in which 12 of the minterms are present in the initial logic expression. Notice that the simplified logic expression is obtained by picking up the 1s that have been plotted on the diagram that are adjacent or by picking up even larger groups of 1s that are adjacent.

The four minterms in the upper left-hand corner are picked up twice. It wasn't necessary to pick them up a second time, but a logic simplification results if these are picked up, both as part of the upper two rows and also as part of the left-most two columns. Even though this is redundant, a simpler logic expression results: $f = A$ OR B. For example, if A were true, that would map into the upper two rows; if B were true, that would map into the left-most two columns.

Another example of the use of a diagram to simplify a logic expression is shown in Figure 4.30. Notice that the expression to be simplified (shown at the top of this figure) involves six minterms. These minterms are first plotted on the diagram. The little number on the diagram shows where each one of the numbered minterms has been plotted.

Notice that minterm Nos. 3 and 1 are adjacent at the top center of the chart. This means that they are independent of B. The input B is

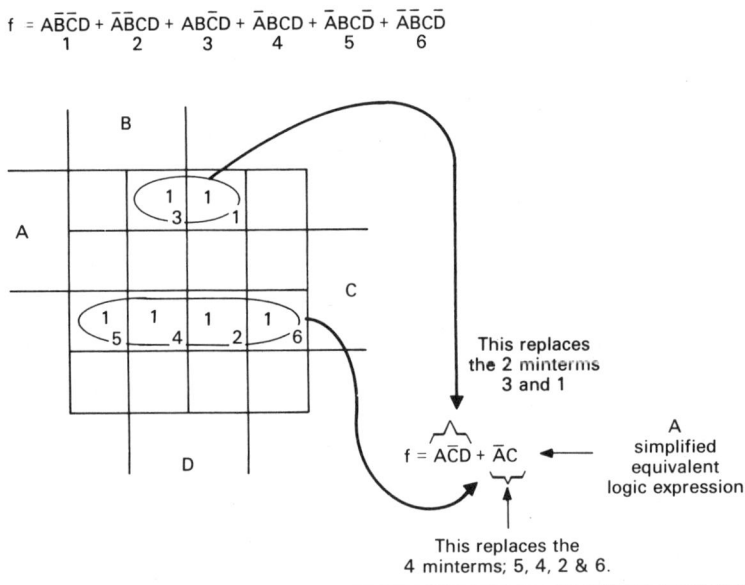

Figure 4.30 Simplifying logic using a diagram.

not needed, so these two minterms can be picked up as $A\bar{C}D$. That is the first term in the simplified expression.

Notice that minterms Nos. 5, 4, 2, and 6 are also all together. When more minterms group together, more of the inputs can be eliminated. For example, this group of four minterms is independent of B because the group is in both the B and the $\bar{B}$ areas. This minterm group is also independent of D because it is in both the D and the $\bar{D}$ areas. So, B and D do not have to appear. A simplified expression for these four minterms is $\bar{A}C$. That rather complicated logic expression shown at the top of the figure can be simplified to the equivalent logic expression, $f = A\bar{C}D + \bar{A}C$.

Codes that Aren't Secret

In digital systems, there are many different codes that are used. Many of these codes are standardized for both numeric (numbers only) and alphanumeric (numbers and letters) applications and use 4- or 8-bit binary numbers.

Encoding so these bits mean something

The process of generating the digital representation of a code is called "encoding." For example, encoding often takes place within the electronics of a keyboard, where depressing a key automatically generates a digital code to represent that character.

Two's complement: To allow negative numbers. In digital computer circuitry, to be most general, a way is needed to handle both positive and negative numbers. This is provided by the 2's complement code in which the most-significant bit is the "sign bit." A sign bit of 0 signifies a positive number and a 1 signifies a negative number. There is an additional benefit with the 2's complement code because the circuitry that is used to add can also be used to subtract.

In Figure 4.31 an 8-bit 2's complement code is listed. Note that there are actually 256 unique codes, ranging from -128 up through 0 to $+127$. The 2's complement code is peculiar. It starts in the middle of this chart with the all-0s code representing 0 (as may be expected). The codes increase from 0 in a standard binary fashion until the code 01111111 is reached. The most-significant bit is still a 0 and this represents positive full scale ($+127$).

One more count would generate a carry that would ripple clear across and change the most-significant bit (the sign bit) to a 1, indicating a negative number. This cannot be allowed to occur in the range of positive numbers, so the code is "folded" at this point. Notice that this next code (the 1 with all trailing 0s) represents negative full scale (the

138 Chapter Four

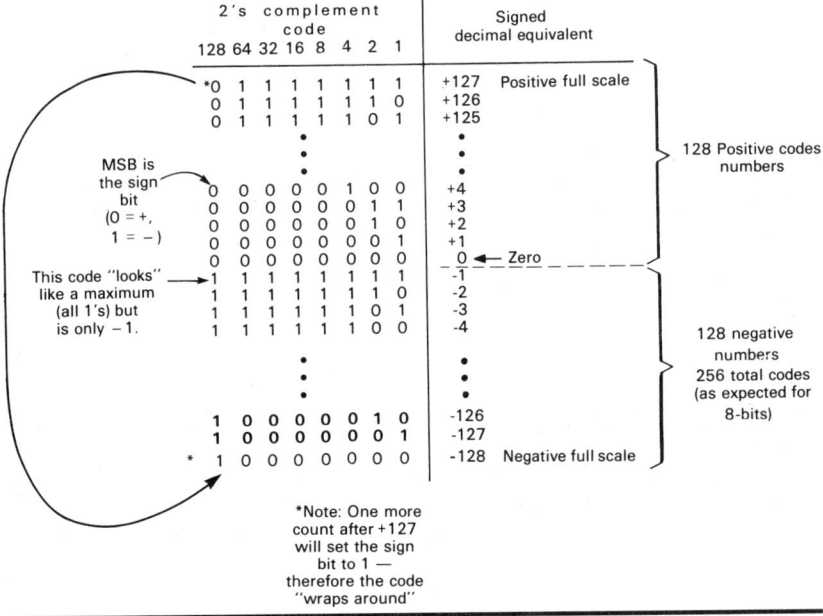

Figure 4.31 Representing negative numbers: The 2's complement code.

largest negative number, -128). From here the 2's complement code again counts up in a binary fashion until it gets to the all-1s code. This looks like full scale because of all of the 1s. The strange thing is that this all-1s code represents 1 bit below 0, which is -1. One more count will make this all-1s code reset to the all-0s code (which is zero).

To subtract two numbers expressed in 2's complement code, take the 2's complement of the subtrahend and then add. Subtraction is therefore performed by 2's complement addition and uses the same circuitry as is used to add two numbers.

Binary-coded decimal. A very popular code to represent decimal digits is shown in Figure 4.32. This is the binary coded decimal (BCD) code. BCD coding is used because people like to work in the decimal number system; therefore, applications for this code are in the interface of computers to human beings, such as displays and other outputs of digital systems.

To represent 10 unique codes, slightly more than 3 bits are required. But 4 bits can count beyond what is needed. Notice (in the bottom of the table of Figure 4.32) that there are six unused codes in BCD coding.

The BCD code counts up from 0 in a binary fashion to 9. The rest of the higher-valued six codes are not used; they are illegal codes for BCD.

"8421" binary-coded decimal (BCD) MSB → b_3 b_2 b_1 b_0	Decimal equivalent
0 0 0 0	0
0 0 0 1	1
0 0 1 0	2
0 0 1 1	3
0 1 0 0	4
0 1 0 1	5
0 1 1 0	6
0 1 1 1	7
1 0 0 0	8
1 0 0 1	9
1 0 1 0	⎫
1 0 1 1	⎪
1 1 0 0	⎬ Six unused codes
1 1 0 1	⎪ (illegal codes)
1 1 1 0	⎪
1 1 1 1	⎭

Figure 4.32 A popular binary-coded decimal code.

Hexadecimal for 8 and 16 bits. Another popular code is the "hexadecimal code," shown in Figure 4.33. Hexadecimal is a way to represent binary bits four at a time and therefore make it easier to work with large binary numbers. The hexadecimal codes for each 4-bit group are taken together to represent large binary numbers.

Hexadecimal is a 4-bit code; so, it provides 2^4 or 16 possible numbers. Using the standard decimal digits, only the first 10 of these (0 through 9) can be represented. To represent the other six, the first six letters of the alphabet are used. So, the hexadecimal number "F" represents all 1s in the group of 4 binary bits.

Decimal equivalent	4-bit binary code MSB LSB	Hexadecimal code	
0	0 0 0 0	0	
1	0 0 0 1	1	
2	0 0 1 0	2	
3	0 0 1 1	3	
4	0 1 0 0	4	
5	0 1 0 1	5	
6	0 1 1 0	6	
7	0 1 1 1	7	
8	1 0 0 0	8	
9	1 0 0 1	9	
10	1 0 1 0	A	⎫
11	1 0 1 1	B	⎬ Have to use letters to represent these six numbers
12	1 1 0 0	C	
13	1 1 0 1	D	
14	1 1 1 0	E	
15	1 1 1 1	F	⎭

Figure 4.33 Basic hexadecimal coding of groups of 4 bits.

Hexadecimal coding for both 8- and 16-bit binary numbers is shown in Figure 4.34. Working with 8-bit binary numbers gets to be a little confusing because there are a lot of individual 1s and 0s that have to be written down. Therefore, there is a large chance for error in handling all of this busywork, even with only 8-bit binary numbers. By grouping the 8-bit binary numbers into two groups of four, two hexadecimal numbers can be used, one for each 4-bit group. The hexadecimal character to the left represents the most-significant 4-bit group, and the hexadecimal character to the right represents the least-significant 4-bit group of the 8-bit binary number. So, the code starts with 00 (where all of the binary bits are 0) and goes to FF (where all of the 8 binary bits are 1). Strange numbers like B6, DA, and 5F are all valid hexadecimal representations for 8-bit binary numbers.

Hexadecimal encoding can be extended to represent a 16-bit binary word as shown in Figure 4.34b. Writing down sixteen 1s or 0s is a large problem, and it is also hard to refer to binary numbers as large as this. These numbers cannot be pronounced, so the string of 1s and 0s must be called out. It is much more convenient to group this 16-bit binary word into four groups of 4 bits each and then represent each of these subgroups with a hexadecimal character. For example, ABCD is a 16-bit binary number, as are 1234, 81FF, and B9F6. All of these strange-looking things are hexadecimal representations for 16-bit binary numbers.

To help avoid confusion, a final "H" is often appended to the hexadecimal number representation (as 4BA5H). Another convention is that

8-bit binary		Hexadecimal
0000	0000	00
0101	1111	5F
1011	0110	B6
1101	1010	DA
1111	1111	FF

(a)

16-bit binary number				Hexadecimal
0000	0000	0000	0000	0000
0001	0010	0011	0100	1234
1000	0001	1111	1111	81FF
1010	1011	1100	1101	ABCD
1101	1001	1111	0110	D9F6
1111	1111	1111	1111	FFFF

(b)

Figure 4.34 Hexadecimal simplifies 8- and 16-bit binary numbers. (a) Using hexidecimal for 8 bits and (b) using hexidecimal for 16 bits.

all hexadecimal codes must start with a number. If a letter comes first, a zero is added at the start (as 0FFFF).

American Standard Code for Information Interchange (ASCII). One of the standard codes uses digital bits to represent all of the characters that are available on a typewriter. This code is used so a computer can process printed words in the English language. Because of the large number of characters that have to be represented (such as both uppercase and lowercase letters, numbers, punctuation, and even some additional control characters, such as carriage return and line feed), 7 bits are needed. These groups of encoded data are often referred to as "strings" because of the relatively long strings or sequences of character bytes that are regarded as a single entry in textual material.

The American Standard Code for Information Interchange (ASCII, pronounced "ASS KEY") is shown in Figure 4.35. This is typically used on computer terminals where a keyboard inputs information to a digital system. Each key generates a unique 7-bit code that corresponds to the character or letter that was pressed. Similarly, the display presents characters to the operator of the terminal. The digital computer also supplies these characters in an ASCII format, and the display electronics converts each ASCII character into the proper character or control for the display. ASCII is also used for printers.

The least-significant bits of the ASCII code appear on the horizontal rows, and the most-significant bits specify the vertical columns of the

7-bit ASCII code ($b_6 \leftarrow b_0$)			MSB b_6	0	0	0	0	1	1	1	1
			b_5	0	0	1	1	0	0	1	1
			b_4	0	1	0	1	0	1	0	1
b_3	b_2	b_1	LSB b_0	Control characters		Printable characters					
0	0	0	0	NUL	DLE	SPACE	0	@	P	`	p
0	0	0	1	SOH	DC1	!	1	A	Q	a	q
0	0	1	0	STX	DC2	"	2	B	R	b	r
0	0	1	1	ETX	DC3	#	3	C	S	c	s
0	1	0	0	EDT	DC4	$	4	D	T	d	t
0	1	0	1	ENQ	NAK	%	5	E	U	e	m
0	1	1	0	ACK	SYN	&	6	F	V	f	v
0	1	1	1	BEL	ETB	'	7	G	W	g	w
1	0	0	0	BS	CAN	(	8	H	X	h	x
1	0	0	1	HT	EM	)	9	I	Y	i	y
1	0	1	0	LF	SUB	*	:	J	Z	j	z
1	0	1	1	VT	ESC	+	;	K	[	k	{
1	1	0	0	FF	FS	,	<	L	\	l		
1	1	0	1	CR	GS	-	=	M	]	m	}
1	1	1	0	SO	RS	.	>	N	^	n	~
1	1	1	1	SI	US	/	?	O	_	o	DEL

Figure 4.35 The American Standard Code for Information Interchange.

chart in Figure 4.35. It is important that the codes for the decimal numbers have a binary value that corresponds to the decimal number. Also, to make it easier for a computer to arrange items in an alphabetic order, the letters should also be in an ordered sequence in their ASCII coding (so A precedes B, etc.).

In addition to ASCII, there is another standard code used in most of the IBM equipment, Extended Binary Coded Decimal Interchange Code, EBCDIC (pronounced "eb C dic").

Encoding an analog voltage. Another possible use for binary bits is to represent an analog voltage. This is typically used in circuits that are called "analog-to-digital (A/D) converters." An analog voltage can be encoded and thereby converted to a digital number. A/D converters are used at the input to a digital system.

Figure 4-36 shows the digital output codes that result from analog input voltages for a simple 3-bit A/D converter. The vertical scale of this plot is the digital output code that results for a given analog input voltage, which is shown on the horizontal scale. The major divisions (the 0 through 8 on the horizontal analog input voltage scale) are representations of the analog input voltage expressed in least-significant bits (LSBs). For example, the analog input voltage ranges from 0 to 5 V. But this A/D has only a 3-bit digital output code. Therefore there

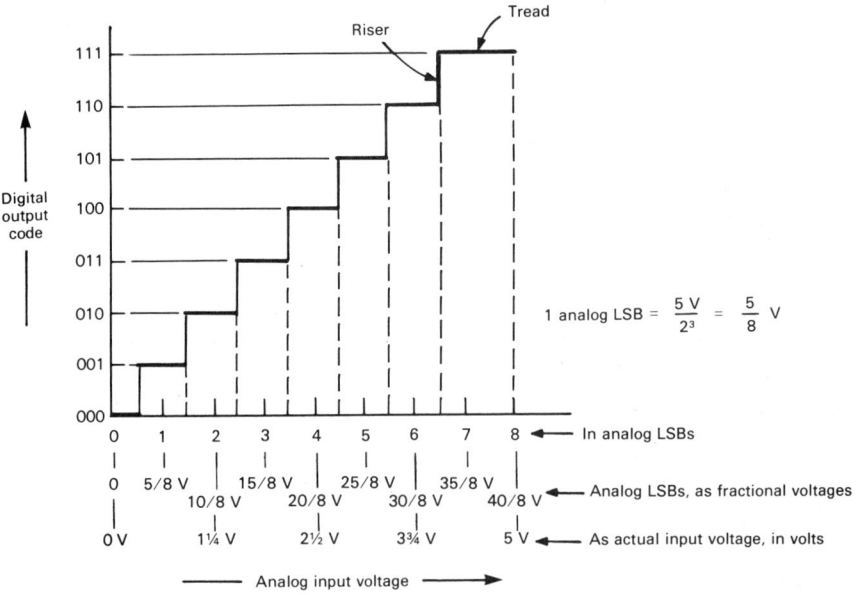

Figure 4.36 A 3-bit A/D quantizing an analog input voltage.

are only eight boxes (the width of each box is 1 analog LSB) that will be used to represent this analog input voltage "span" of 0 to 5 V. The size of each digital "box" is the 5-V full-scale voltage divided by the eight digital output codes. This provides ⅝ V as the value of 1 analog LSB.

An A/D "quantizes" a continuous analog input voltage. Analog voltages are smooth; they can have any values over the complete range from 0 V to the maximum voltage. The purpose of an A/D converter is to find the best fit, to encode each analog input voltage into the closest-fitting digital output code. Each analog input voltage is "placed" into one of the available boxes because that is all the "resolution" there is. This 3-bit A/D does the best fit that it can in converting each analog input voltage into only one of the eight possible digital output codes. Therefore, information is lost with an A/D conversion because as long as the analog input voltage is appropriate for one digital box (say its value places it in the middle of a box) this input voltage can wander around within that box and the digital output code will not change.

Starting with an analog input voltage of 0 (the lower-left corner of this graph), the A/D would give a digital output code of all 0s. This output of all 0s will remain until the analog input voltage increases to one-half of an analog LSB (½ of ⅝ V, or ⁵⁄₁₆ V). Just after this voltage, the A/D converter will indicate the 001 output code.

The analog LSBs are converted into actual fractional voltage values under the horizontal scale of this graph. These fractions are left in an unsimplified form to indicate how they were derived (by multiplying the number of analog LSBs by ⅝ V).

The "staircase" nature of this transfer curve has made people refer to the vertical portions as "risers" and the horizontal portions as "treads" (the words carpenters would use). The tread represents a constant digital output code over a range of analog input voltages. The center of each one of these treads is at a whole number of analog LSBs (all of these are shown as actual input voltages, in volts). In fact, the tread representing the digital code 010 centers on 2 analog LSBs or 2 × ⅝ V = ¹⁰⁄₈ V = 1¼ V. If 1¼ V was the analog input voltage to this A/D converter, the digital output code of 010 would be provided. But the analog input voltage could wiggle back and forth around this 1¼-volt value, and the digital output code would not change. This creates a loss of knowledge about the exact value of the analog input voltage called "quantization uncertainty." The analog input voltage would have to increase by one-half of an LSB before the next riser would be reached to provide the next higher digital output code of 011.

Rarely are only 3 bits used. The smallest resolution A/D converters are more typically 8 bits, and A/Ds are available with as high as 20 bits (where over one million digital output codes are provided).

Decoding: To find out what was meant

We've just described a number of encoding techniques; now we'll look at some "decoding" schemes. Decoding is the opposite of encoding; and, in addition to deciphering the above codes, a few specific decoders will be discussed.

One-of-N decoders. A 1-of-8 decoder, shown in Figure 4.37, allows three inputs (A, B, and C) to select only one of eight possible outputs. For example, if A, B, and C were all 0, the lower output would be in the 1 state and the other seven outputs would be in the 0 state. A 3-bit binary input has therefore been decoded into one of eight individual outputs. In general, 1-of-N decoders exist; this example is a 1-of-8 decoder.

As an example of a practical application for a 1-of-8 decoder, a personal computer, operating in a home lighting control mode, could use 3 bits to turn on or off (using a separate code for each function) any one of four lights located, for example, in the bathroom, front porch, hallway, and garage.

A 1-of-64 decoder is shown in Figure 4.38. This is making use of a decoding "matrix." In higher levels of decoders, this type of matrix decoding is used. For example, the inputs A, B, and C control the horizontal lines, and the inputs D, E, and F control the vertical lines. It takes 64 AND gates "looking" at each pair of the intersecting lines to detect the coincidence of two 1s and to then provide a logic 1 output. The AND gate that is shown on the figure is decoding the 101000 input

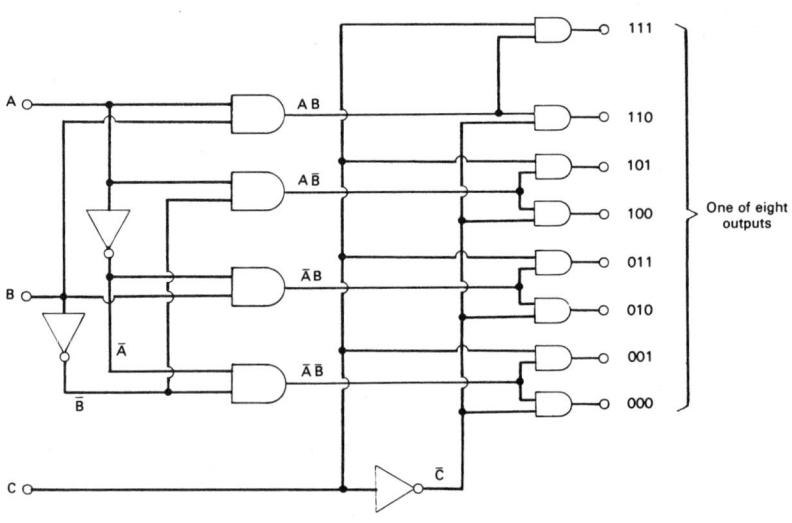

Figure 4.37 A 1-of-8 decoder.

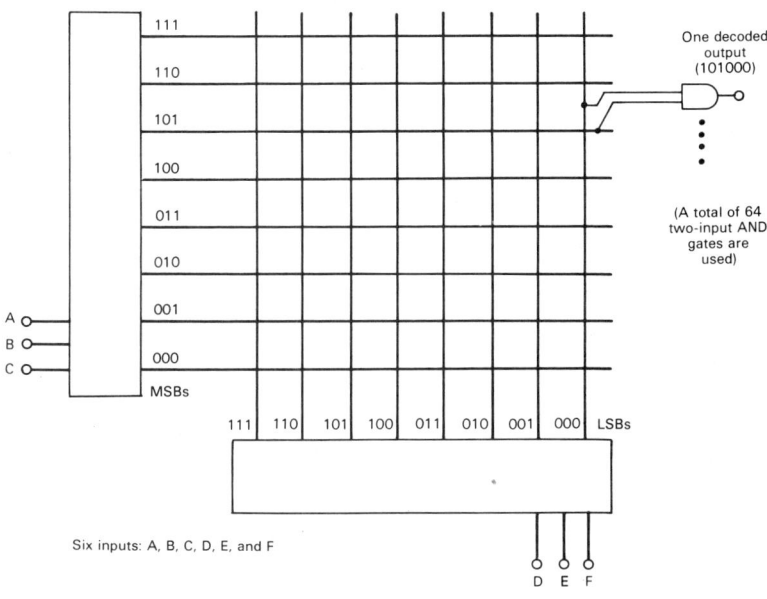

Figure 4.38 A 1-of-64 decoder.

combination. Only for this particular state of the input variables will the output of this AND gate be true. It would be the only one of the 64-output gates that would be in the 1 state.

Decoding to provide an analog voltage. In some digital systems, digital numbers have to be converted into analog voltages. A "digital-to-analog converter" (DAC) is used whenever an analog voltage is required as an output from a digital computer.

The analog output voltages that are supplied by a 3-bit DAC are shown in Figure 4.39. Again, for simplicity, only a 3-bit DAC is used. This implies that eight unique output voltages can be provided. These output voltages are shown along the vertical axis of this graph. The output voltage that is provided for the all-0s input code is 0 V. For an input code of 001, 1 analog LSB (⅝ V) is the output voltage. The maximum input code of 111 would produce an output of 3⅝ V (4⅜ V, not 5 V; it is 1 analog LSB short).

A DAC provides output voltages that are the center values of the treads of an A/D converter. Because of the lack of resolution that is implied with the 3-bit DAC shown here (only eight different output voltages exist), they are evenly spread over the range 0 to 5 V. A DAC cannot provide intermediate output voltage values. If values in between

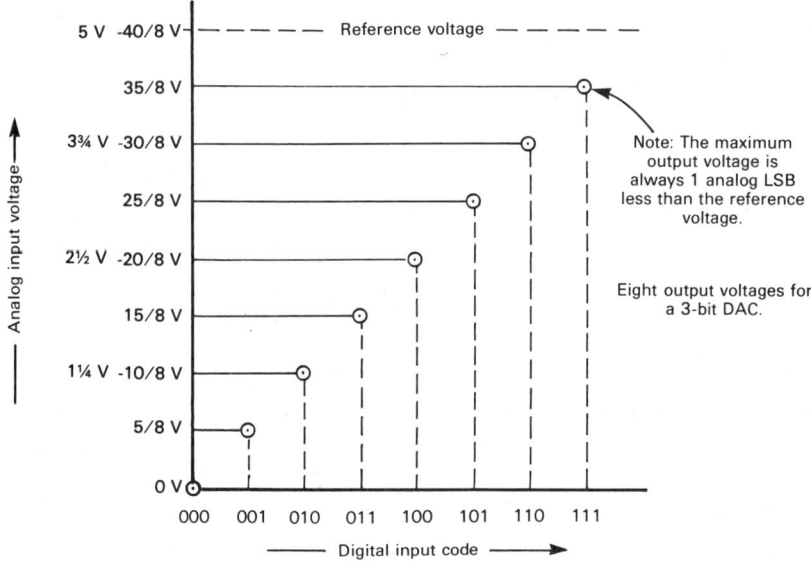

Figure 4.39 The analog output voltages of a 3-bit digital-to-analog converter.

are needed, more resolution must be used such as a 10-, 12-, 14-, or 16-bit DAC.

Some Logic Circuits

Logic circuits have undergone a continuous evolution since they first incorporated transistors. Transistorized logic is an improvement over the simpler diode logic circuits that were discussed in Chapter 3, because transistors have voltage gain and can therefore restore the logic voltage levels.

A very successful family of logic uses bipolar transistors, the transistor-transistor logic, T^2L. This will be discussed because this family has been very popular.

A simulated T²L NAND gate

Figure 4.40 shows a diagram of a simulated T^2L circuit that can be built using the components available in the lab kit. This is a two-input NAND gate and embodies the major ideas of the actual T^2L circuit shown in Figure 4.41.

Some changes to the T^2L circuit were made. The single input transistor (Q_1) in a conventional T^2L circuit (Figure 4.41) has multiple emitters. In the simulated circuit of Figure 4.40, an additional input is sup-

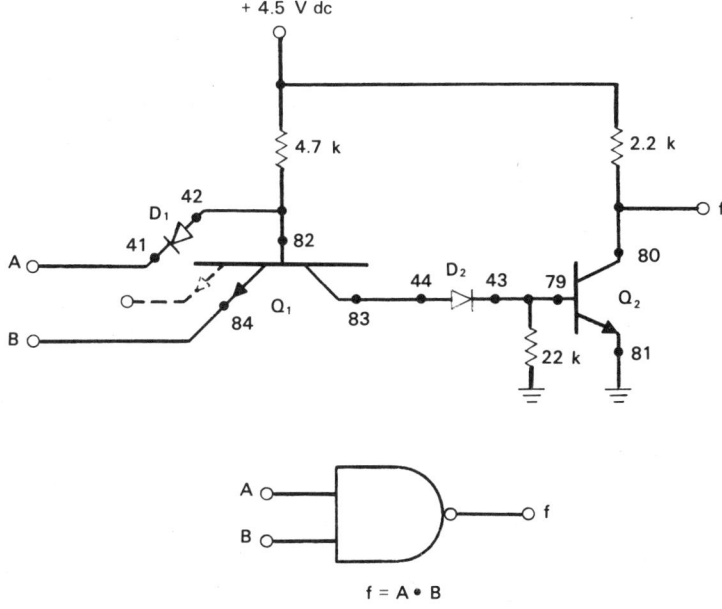

Figure 4.40 A simulated T²L 2-input NAND gate.

plied with the diode D_1 because multiple input transistors are not available in the lab kit. This will functionally serve as a second input.

There is a second diode (D_2 in Figure 4.40) that is used to raise the trigger voltage of this logic circuit. The trigger voltage of a logic circuit is defined as the voltage that can simultaneously exist at both the input and the output. This represents the point of decision. If an input voltage is below the trigger voltage, it is interpreted as a logical 0; above the trigger voltage it is a logical 1 input.

This simulated T²L circuit gives the same functional relationships that exist in an actual T²L gate, although this circuit has been changed a little bit so that it can be built out of the components in the lab kit. The essential circuit ideas are still represented here.

Notice that if either input A or B is held low, the current available through the 4.7-kΩ base resistor of transistor Q_1 is diverted to ground. This current is therefore not available to flow through the base-collector diode of Q_1 to eventually turn on the output transistor (Q_2). So, with either input low, the output transistor is off and the 2.2-kΩ collector load resistor (called a "pull-up resistor") of this output transistor "pulls the output voltage up" to the high state. Both inputs have to be in a high state in order for the current through the 4.7-kΩ resistor to be diverted through the base-collector junction of Q_1 to become base cur-

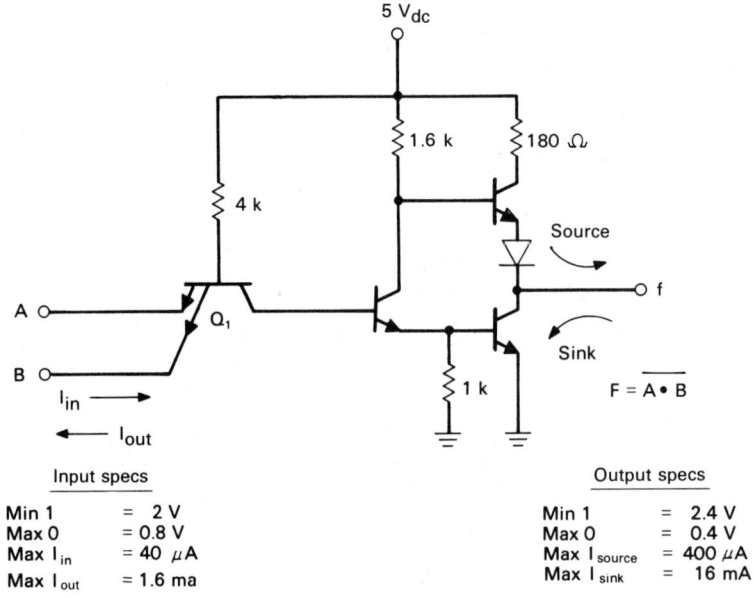

Figure 4.41 An actual T²L 2-input NAND gate.

rent for the output transistor (Q_2) and turn the output transistor on. This is the basic circuit functioning of a T²L NAND gate.

Measure the trigger voltage, as shown in the test setup of Figure 4.42. Simply leave the A input open to simulate the logical 1 state, and connect the B input to the wiper of the Control potentiometer. The top of the potentiometer is tied to a positive 3-V tap in the battery section of the lab kit. Adjust the Control for a dc output voltage of about

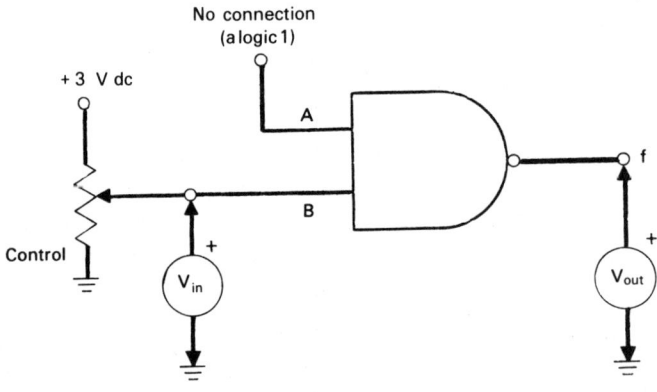

Figure 4.42 Measuring the trigger voltage.

1.2 V. Then move the meter over to the B input. This input voltage should also be very close to 1.2 V (the trigger voltage of this logic circuit). As the Control is adjusted to provide a slightly higher voltage level on the input, the output will drop toward the low state. If the Control is adjusted for a slightly lower voltage level at the B input, the output will go high.

The basis of Schottky logic

One problem with T^2L logic circuits is that the output transistor is driven into "saturation." The extra current into the base of the output transistor (provided to guarantee that the collector voltage of the output transistor will be at a very low voltage level) causes the collector-base diode of the output transistor to conduct current. This collector-base-diode current flow floods the internal regions of the transistor with excess electrons. When the transistor is turned off, extra time is needed to clear out these excess electrons before the transistor can go to the OFF state. Therefore, to achieve the highest switching speed, saturation of transistors in logic circuits is not desirable.

Many years ago, a man named Baker came up with an idea that would prevent a transistor from entering saturation. This Baker clamp is a circuit technique that is used to increase the transistor switching speed.

A version of Baker's clamp, shown in Figure 4.43, uses a silicon diode and a germanium diode at the input to the transistor. The silicon diode diverts the excess base current over into the collector lead. Notice that as the collector voltage falls toward ground, the silicon diode will turn on and divert the excess current (after the base current is provided)

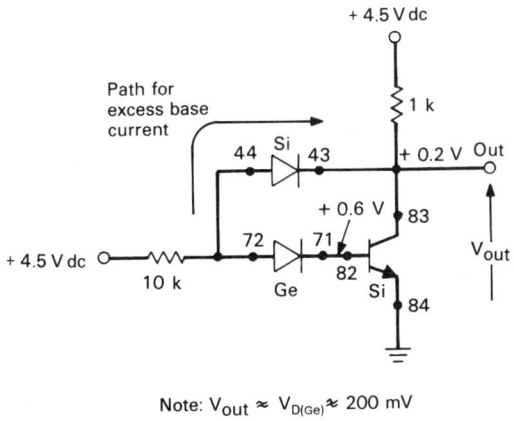

Note: $V_{out} \approx V_{D(Ge)} \approx 200$ mV

Figure 4.43 The basic idea of the Baker clamp.

that is available from the 10-kΩ resistor over into the collector lead. This circuit keeps the forward voltage across the base-collector diode of the NPN transistor small enough so that this diode will not conduct. Therefore, the transistor is not driven into saturation.

A modern equivalent of the Baker clamp is shown in Figure 4.44. This is making use of a "Schottky diode" that is shown with the special symbol that incorporates an "S." Only one Schottky diode is used between the base and the collector lead. A Schottky diode has a very low forward voltage drop and therefore keeps the collector-base diode of the transistor from conducting. This Schottky diode can be fabricated within the transistor structure. This merged diode-transistor structure is given the S-type of transistor symbol shown in Figure 4.44b.

Low-power Schottky logic can achieve the same speed as T^2L with a power drain that is less by a factor of 10:1. Schottky logic has been a very successful improvement on the basic T^2L circuitry and therefore most modern bipolar logic ICs use Schottky transistors.

CMOS logic circuits

Complementary metal-oxide silicon (CMOS) logic circuit designs are quite different from those that have been used with bipolar transistors. The "complementary" nature of this MOS technology provides both

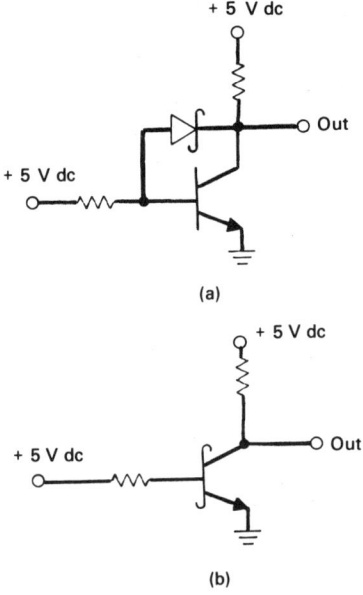

Figure 4.44 The Schottky clamp. (a) Actual circuit and (b) symbol.

"N-channel" and "P-channel" transistors. The IC logic circuit designers use both of these transistor structures to achieve high-performance logic circuits. CMOS logic circuits are emphasized because CMOS is rapidly becoming the most popular digital IC technology.

The basic operation of CMOS transistors is indicated in Figure 4.45. These transistors no longer have collector, base, and emitter leads. Instead, they have a "drain," a "gate," and a "source." These are the MOS terms for the functional equivalents of the three leads of a bipolar transistor.

In this figure, arrows are drawn on the source leads (like the emitter arrows on bipolar transistors). This type of a symbol is not universally used. Some people will leave arrows off the MOS transistor symbols, but this makes it difficult to distinguish the drain from the source.

The N-channel transistor is functionally similar to an NPN transistor. If the gate is grounded, as shown in Figure 4.45a, an N-channel transistor will be in the off state. This is similar to an NPN transistor with the emitter at ground and with the base also grounded. The bipolar transistor would then also be in a nonconducting or off state.

The new thing about the N-channel MOS transistor is that the gate voltage can be raised clear up to 5 V. Recall that a bipolar transistor has a diode at the input (the base-emitter diode) and 5 V should not be directly connected to a diode (with no current limit, it would burn out).

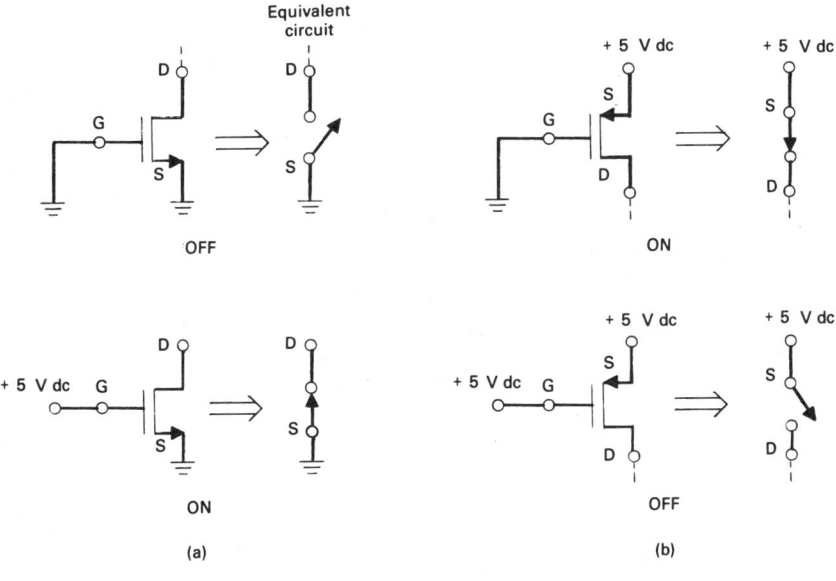

Figure 4.45 Turning CMOS transistors on and off. (*a*) The N-channel transistor and (*b*) the P-channel transistor.

A MOS transistor can accept this voltage on the gate to turn it on, and it is equivalent to having this transistor switch closed (because the drain-source path of the transistor becomes a low resistance). N-channel transistors are therefore used to cause circuit nodes within a logic circuit to go to ground (0 V).

The P-channel MOS transistor (also shown in this figure) is functionally similar to a PNP transistor. In most logic circuits, the sources of the P-channel transistors are connected to the 5-V power supply. The response to the gate voltage is opposite from that of an N-channel transistor. When the gate is grounded, a 5-V gate-source drive exists. This turns the P-channel transistor on and provides a switch that can be used to cause circuit nodes within a logic circuit to go to 5 V.

If the gate voltage were lifted up to 5 V, there would be 5 V on the gate and also 5 V on the source. There is then no difference between the gate and source voltages, so there is no voltage to turn on the transistor. The transistor is therefore off; the switch is open. This basic opening and closing of these MOS transistor switches takes place in logic circuits. Input voltages as well as output voltages in CMOS logic circuits typically range from 0 to 5 V.

A CMOS logic inverter. In CMOS logic circuits, resistors and diodes are only used at the inputs and outputs to guard against accidental electrostatic discharge voltages. CMOS logic circuitry is made using only two types of components, N-channel and P-channel transistors. This is unique and very different from bipolar logic circuits.

A simulated CMOS logic inverter, shown in Figure 4.46a, is composed of an upper P-channel transistor and a lower N-channel transistor. This is the simplest of the CMOS logic circuits. If the input is at 0 V, the N-channel transistor will be off, but the P-channel transistor is turned on. An input of 0 V will therefore cause the output voltage to rise to 5 V, a logic inversion.

Similarly, if the input is at +5 V, there is no source-gate voltage drive for the P-channel transistor, so it is off; but the N-channel transistor is on. This causes the output voltage to go to 0 V.

A bipolar simulation of a CMOS logic inverter can be made by making use of the PNP and the NPN bipolar transistors that are available in the lab kit, as shown in Figure 4.46b. (MOS transistors are difficult to use in experiments because they can easily be destroyed by electrostatic voltages that you are not even aware of. MOS IC circuit designers use computer circuit simulations; no circuits are actually built.) The N-channel MOS transistor is functionally similar to the bipolar NPN, and the P-channel MOS transistor is functionally similar to the bipolar PNP. Therefore a PNP is used on the upper side and an NPN

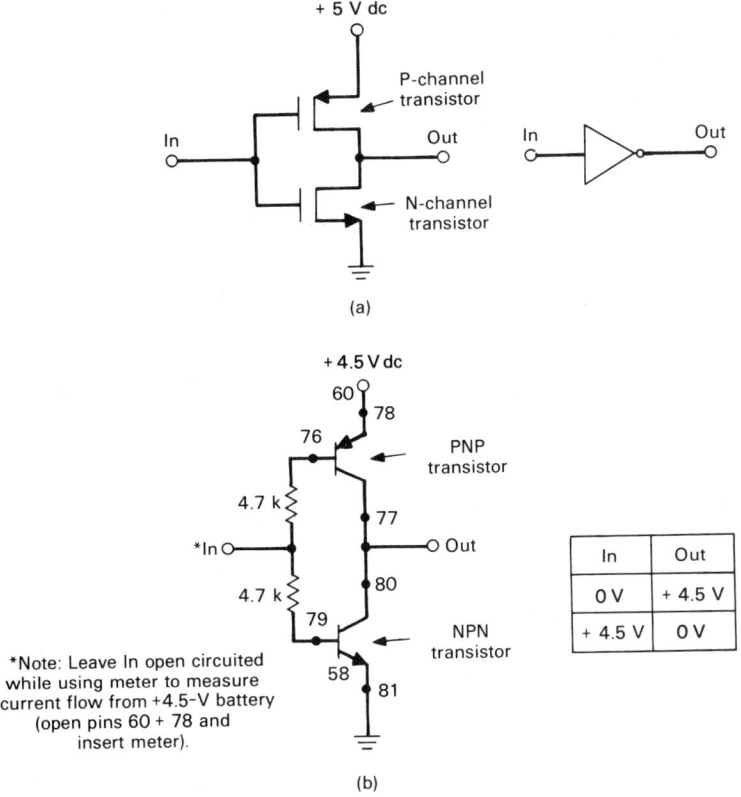

Figure 4.46 A bipolar simulation of a CMOS logic inverter. (*a*) The CMOS logic inverter and (*b*) a bipolar simulation.

on the lower side of this simulated CMOS logic inverter. Input resistors are placed in series with the bases of these transistors to limit the current flow.

Connect the input to ground (to turn off the lower NPN and turn on the upper PNP), and notice that the output voltage will be very close to 4.5 V. When the input is connected to the 4.5-V power supply, the NPN will be turned on and the PNP transistor will be held off. Now the output voltage will be very close to 0 V.

The key idea of CMOS logic circuit design is that there is no path for dc current flow from the power supply to ground. The P-channel and N-channel transistors that are connected between the power-supply voltage alternately conduct. This property of no dc current flow is the reason for the very low power drain in CMOS logic circuits. When the input is in a high state, the lower transistor conducts. When the input is in a low state, the upper transistor conducts. Both transistors should never be turned on at the same time. This means that current is only taken from the power supply to charge the stray output capacitance to raise the output voltage. On the next logic change at the input, that output stray capacitance is discharged (this charge is now dumped to ground).

Both transistors will be conducting as the input voltage gets near the middle of the swing. The circuit of Figure 4.46b can be used to demonstrate this by just floating the input (do not tie the input lead to anything). Both transistors will now be conducting, and a very large current can flow from the power supply to ground. To measure this current, open the connection from the emitter of the PNP transistor to the power supply and insert the milliampmeter (do not leave this input floating very long because of the large current flow that results).

This demonstrates the problem that exists with all CMOS logic circuits when an input is left floating. The rule in CMOS logic is: *Do not leave unused inputs unconnected.* Always connect them to ground or to the positive power-supply voltage, whichever will properly disable each unused input.

In bipolar logic, it is also poor practice to let inputs float, but the performance of a bipolar logic circuit is not nearly as drastically affected. Leaving the input of a T²L gate floating is similar to tying it high. Also, a T²L input should not be directly connected to the power-supply voltage. To properly bias unused inputs at the high state, they should be tied to the output of a T²L circuit that is permanently wired at its inputs so that this output will be in the high state (at a voltage that is less than the power-supply voltage).

CMOS logic voltage levels. The voltage levels of CMOS logic circuits are shown in Figure 4.47. Notice that the outputs of these circuits are

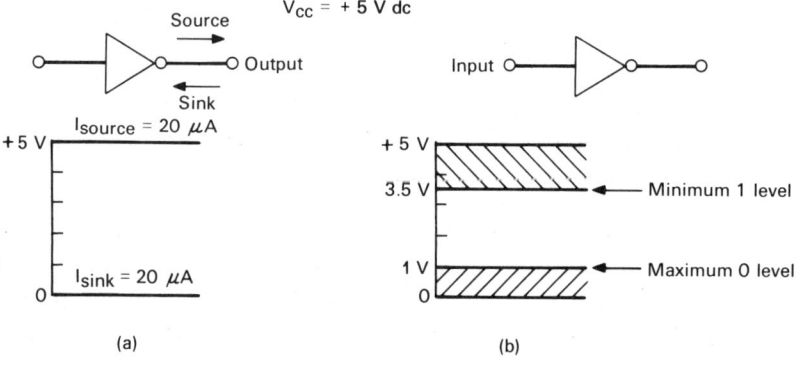

Figure 4.47 Typical CMOS logic levels. (a) Output specs and (b) input specs.

specified to source 20 μA when they are at 5 V and to sink 20 μA when they are at 0 V. This shows that the output of one logic gate can provide the leakage current that may be needed by other logic gates that are tied to it without significantly degrading the logic voltage levels.

The input specification is that the maximum 0 level can be 1 V. Voltages of 1 V or less will therefore be recognized at the input as a valid 0 level. The minimum 1 level is 3.5 V. To be recognized as a valid 1 at the input of CMOS logic, the voltage needs to be 3.5 V or larger. This indicates that there is a difference of 2.5 V between these logic voltage levels. It is very difficult to have an input low level degrade to the point at which it is raised clear up to 3.5 V. The bipolar logic problem of dc input current flow (that tends to raise the low-state output-voltage level) does not exist with CMOS logic. This absence of dc input current allows CMOS logic circuits to switch closer to both ground and the 5-V power-supply voltage.

A CMOS NAND gate. CMOS logic circuits achieve complex logic functions by making use of only N-channel and P-channel transistors. For example, the circuit diagram for a CMOS NAND gate is shown in Figure 4.48. The P-channel transistors on the upper side are connected in parallel; the N-channel transistors on the lower side are connected in series.

The truth table shows that the only time the output is in the low-voltage state is when both inputs are high. With both inputs high, both P-channel transistors are held off and both N-channel transistors are turned on. This causes the output voltage to be 0 V. A practical thing about this NAND gate is that the upper paralleled P-channel transis-

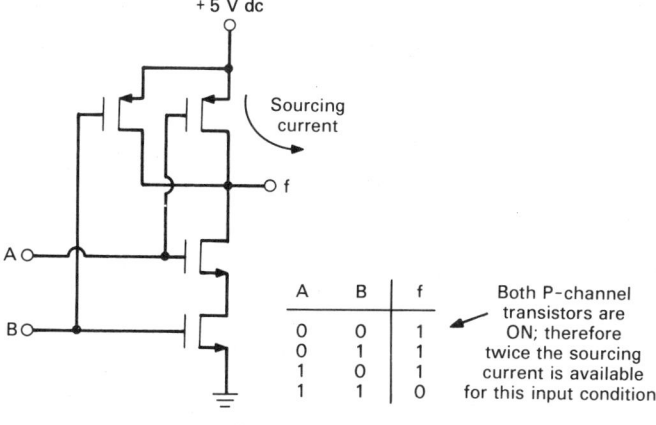

Figure 4.48 The CMOS NAND gate.

tors will source twice the output current of a standard CMOS logic gate. A CMOS NAND gate is therefore often used when larger currents must be supplied to a load.

A CMOS NOR gate. A CMOS NOR circuit is shown in Figure 4.49. Notice that the same basic idea is used, but the transistors have been interchanged. The N-channel transistors are now in parallel, and the P-channel transistors are in series. In order to get the output high, both inputs must be in the low-voltage state. If either input is high, one of the N-channel transistors on the lower side would be conducting, and one of the P-channel transistors on the upper side would be off. This would disconnect the output from the positive power supply. The two parallel N-channel transistors allow a CMOS NOR circuit to "sink" twice the current of a standard CMOS gate.

Obtaining a tri-state output. The inputs of many different logic circuits can all be wired in parallel. Problems can occur when the outputs of many gates are connected together. If one output is high and the other is low, it is not clear which output circuit will win this battle. Will the output at the high state overwhelm the output at the low state, or vice versa?

It is very convenient in a communication path to have the outputs of many digital circuits connected in parallel to the same communication wire. This is the basic idea of a "bus structure" in digital systems (there will be more about buses later on).

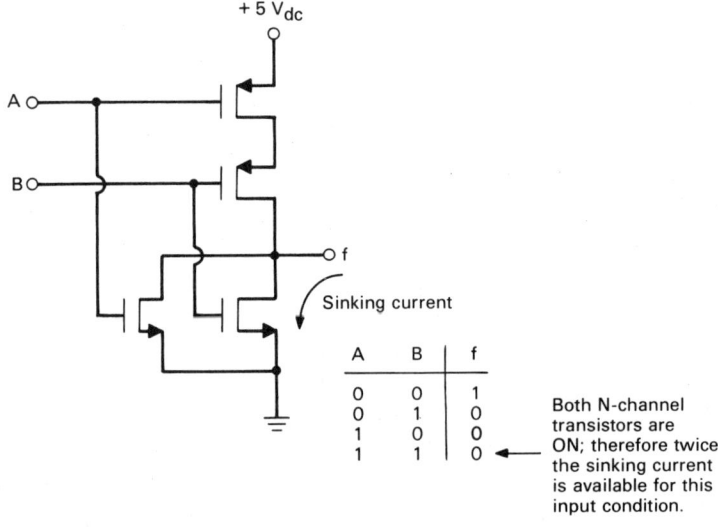

Figure 4.49 The CMOS NOR gate.

The name for a general class of logic circuits that allow many outputs to be wired in parallel is a "tri-state" logic circuit. This sounds strange because a tri-state output seems to suggest *three* output voltage levels or that three "logical" states exist at the output. Neither of these possibilities is correct. The third state is actually a "high-impedance" output state. That is, all of the output transistors are off, and therefore a high output impedance (or a high output resistance) condition results. The disconnected outputs, being in a high-impedance state, will not force any voltages on the common wire. Only a slight amount of output capacitance loading exists. Tri-state is therefore a way to electronically disconnect the outputs of logic gates from a common communication wire. Only one of the outputs is allowed to be active at any given time. Multiple tri-state logic gates can be wired in parallel, and only one of these gates will be allowed to take control of the common output wire.

The symbol for a tri-state buffer is shown in Figure 4.50. This is a noninverting buffer so there is no inversion ball used at the input or output. The logic input at A will therefore be replicated at f.

The tri-state Control is shown coming in on the side of this symbol. This is another input to this gate, the Control (or C input). With C a logical 0, this gate will be in tri-state; the output will be in a high-impedance state. With C a logical 1, the output will be "enabled," and the noninverting buffer is then active. Therefore, there are four input combinations (as shown in the truth table). When C is 0, the output is

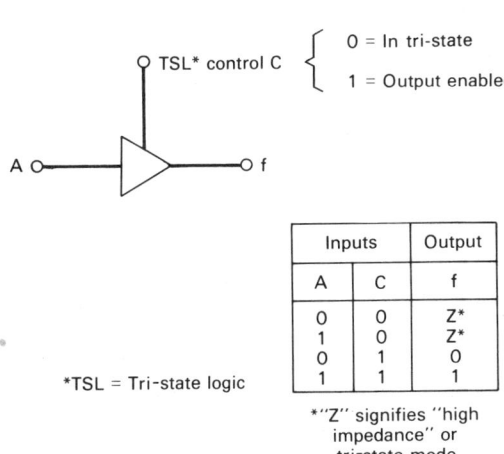

Figure 4.50 A tri-state buffer.

in the Z or high-impedance state (independent of the A input). When C is 1, the output follows the input.

The logic that is necessary to provide this tri-state feature is shown in Figure 4.51. Notice that a NAND gate and a NOR gate are used to drive the output P-channel and N-channel transistors, respectively. The second input to each of these gates is derived from the tri-state Control signal. With this Control in the logic 0 state (as shown here), this buffer circuit is in the tri-state (or high-impedance) mode.

Let's chase this logic through to see how this high-impedance state is achieved. With the Control at 0, one of the inputs to the upper NAND gate is 0. Therefore, the output of this NAND gate will be in the high state (independent of the logic state of the data input). With this NAND gate output at a 1 level, the P-channel transistor is kept off.

Notice that the Control signal is also inverted to produce a 1 level. This logical 1 is an input to the NOR circuit shown driving the N-channel output transistor. The output of this NOR circuit is therefore forced to be a logical 0, independent of the logic state of the data input. This logical 0 at the output of the NOR gate forces the N-channel output transistor to also be off. Therefore, neither output transistor is conducting in this tri-state buffer. There are only the stray capacitances and the dc leakage currents of these output transistors connected to the output.

If the Control signal were to change to the logic 1 level, this buffer would be enabled. The data at the input would then flow through to the output.

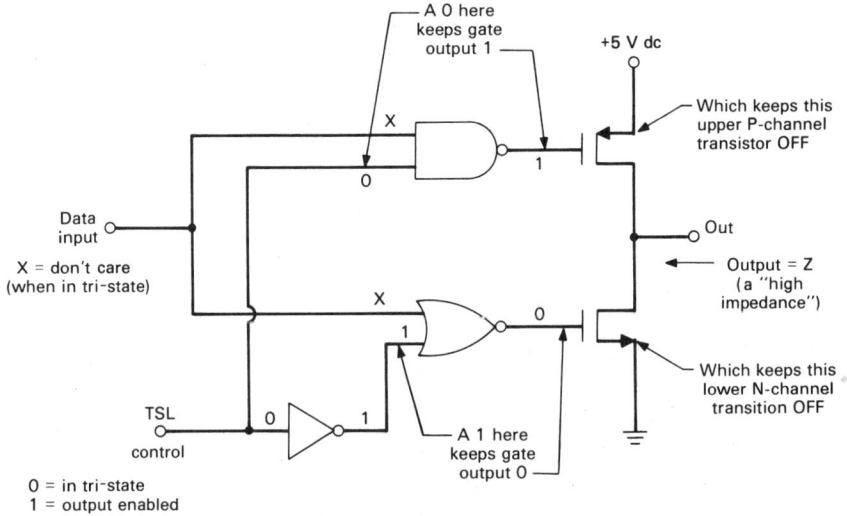

Figure 4.51 The logic needed to make a tri-state, noninverting buffer.

Some examples of commercially available, CMOS, tri-state buffers are shown in Figure 4.52. Notice that both types of Control polarity are provided. For example, in Figure 4.54a the tri-state Control input (C) enables the output when it is in the low state. When C is in the high state, the output is in the high-impedance state. This Control input has a little inverting ball drawn next to the buffer symbol to imply that the gate is enabled when the Control is low.

A different type of Control polarity is indicated in Figure 4.54b. For this circuit, when the Control is high, the gate is enabled. Both of these circuits are tri-state quad buffers with individual tri-state Controls.

Logic gates with built-in Schmitt triggers. Problems exist in digital circuits and systems when logic waveforms do not abruptly change states. If the rise and fall times become excessive, troubles can arise. Special circuits are used to "regenerate" logic voltage waveforms, to make them abruptly change from one state to another. These circuits involve positive feedback (regeneration) in order to speed up a slowly changing logic input-voltage waveform.

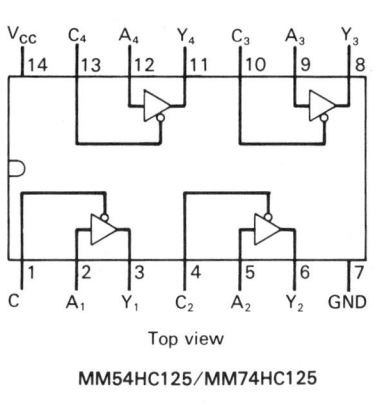

MM54HC125/MM74HC125

Truth Tables

Inputs		Output
A	C	Y
H	L	N
L	L	L
X	H	Z

(a)

MM54HC126/MM74MC126

Inputs		Output
A	C	Y
H	H	H
L	H	L
X	L	Z

(b)

Figure 4.52 Examples of tristate buffer ICs. (a) TSL control low enables output "active low" and (b) TSL control high enables output "active high."

Many years ago, one of the early regenerative circuits was invented by a man named Schmitt. Any circuit that uses positive feedback in order to regenerate a voltage waveform is therefore called a "Schmitt trigger."

Some commercially available Schmitt-trigger logic gates are shown in Figure 4.53. The hex inverting Schmitt trigger of Figure 4.55a has been one of the most popular CMOS logic circuits. It is used not only to clean up degraded logic voltage waveforms but also to provide many unique circuit applications.

A quad two-input NAND Schmitt trigger (shown in Figure 4.55b) is also available. One of these inputs can serve as an ON-OFF control in a "gated" oscillator application (there will be more on this later).

This basic operation of cleaning up a degraded input voltage waveform is shown in Figure 4.54. An input voltage waveform is shown that has very slow rise and fall times. A Schmitt trigger has two internal voltage trigger levels that are established by the circuit design. When the input voltage is low, an upper trigger level is activated (V_{T+}). As the input voltage increases and crosses V_{T+} (about 2.9 V), the output is rapidly regeneratively driven to the low-level state. With the output in the low state, the trigger level is internally changed from 2.9 to 1.8 V (the V_{T-} level). Now the input voltage has to drop down to 1.8 V before the next triggering action takes place to regeneratively drive the output to the 5-V level.

Some other useful applications of Schmitt trigger logic circuits are shown in Figure 4.55. By connecting a resistor and a capacitor around an inverting Schmitt trigger buffer, a very simple oscillator results. If the input is low, the output is high. The resistor charges the capacitor (when the output voltage is high) until the input voltage reaches the upper trip voltage. This causes the output to switch low. The resistor now discharges the capacitor until the lower trip voltage is reached, and then the cycle repeats.

Substituting the dual-input NAND gate adds logic control to this oscillator, as shown in Figure 4.57b. If the Control is in the logic 1

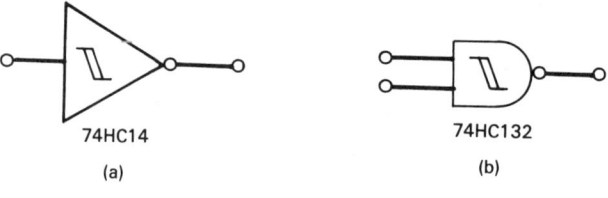

Figure 4.53 The useful Schmitt-trigger logic gates. (a) Hex inverting Schmitt trigger and (b) quad two-input NAND Schmitt trigger.

state, the oscillation will take place. The oscillation is stopped if the Control input goes to the logic 0 state.

Another use for Schmitt triggers is to introduce a time delay in a logic signal path. This time delay is derived by an RC network. A resistor is placed in series with the input to the Schmitt circuit and a capacitor is placed from this input to ground. The Schmitt trigger will "resquare" the resulting exponential voltage waveform that is generated by this RC network so that the output is a desired abruptly changing logic voltage that has been delayed because of the relatively slow charging and discharging of the input capacitor.

Flip-Flops: The Circuits that Remember

Flip-flops and latches provide memory in a logic system. These circuits will hold on to or "remember" a logic level for as long as the power is applied to the circuit. A latch is differentiated from a flip-flop in that a latch does not have a clock input. Flip-flops establish control of the exact time that output voltage changes are made via a clock input.

The logic gates that have previously been discussed are called "combinational logic circuits" because the outputs are directly related to the combination of the inputs at every instant of time. Flip-flops and

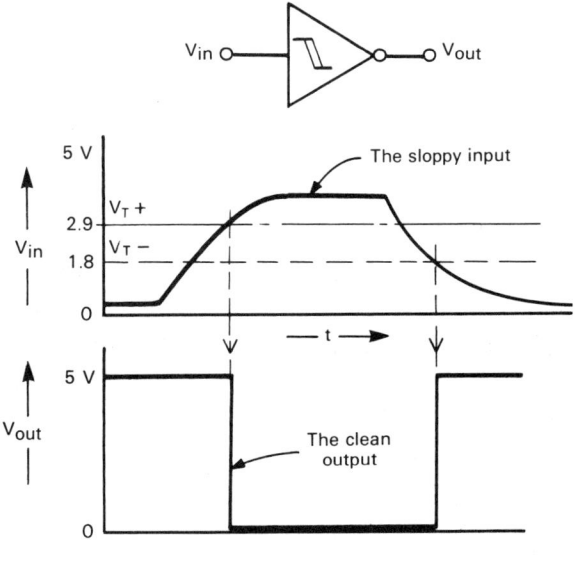

Figure 4.54 A Schmitt circuit "cleaning up" a sloppy input voltage.

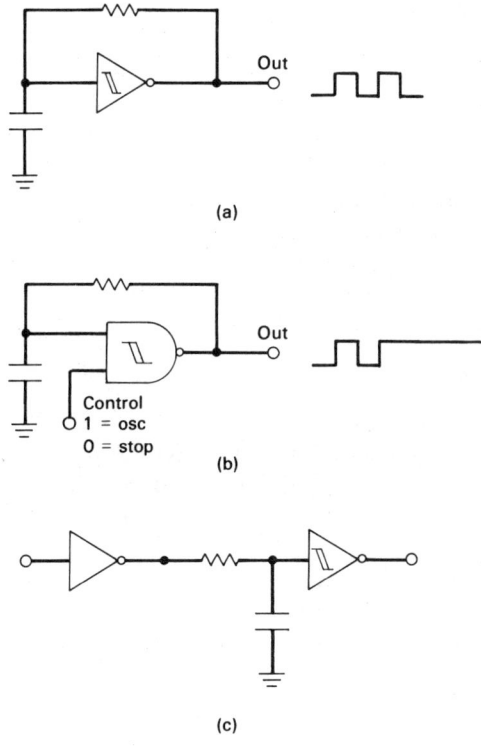

Figure 4.55 Some other uses for Schmitt-trigger logic circuits. (a) Simple oscillator, (b) gated oscillator, and (c) delaying a signal.

latches are used in "sequential logic circuits" because they have the ability to store a logic state and thereby can affect the subsequent sequence of logic state changes within a digital system.

RS latch circuits

Standard logic gates can be cross coupled to provide what are known as RS (Reset-Set) "latch" circuits, as shown in Figure 4.56. Cross coupling of the gates provides the regeneration that is needed to hold onto the logic state and to thereby provide memory.

Applying a Set input will drive the Q output of a latch to the high level. Applying a Reset will drive the Q output to the low level. In either case, the Q and $\bar{Q}$ outputs are always complementary. If the Q output is a 1, the $\bar{Q}$ output will be a 0, and vice versa.

Both NAND gates and NOR gates can be used to make an RS latch. The major difference is in the level of the active state of the Control signals. With NAND gates, both the Set and Reset controls are active

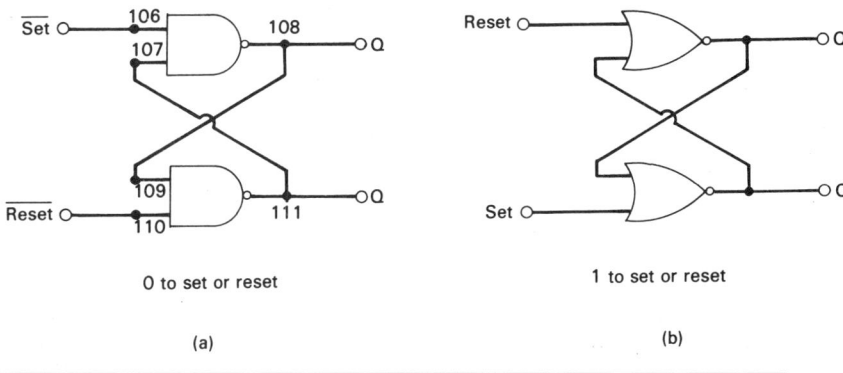

Figure 4.56 Assembling RS latches using logic circuits. (*a*) Using NAND gates and (*b*) using NOR gates.

when they are in the low state. With NOR gates, both the Set and Reset controls are active when in the high state. The Set and Reset inputs only need to be momentarily pulsed to change the logic state of a latch. When not active, these inputs should be disabled. For the NAND gates, the high state disables; for the NOR gates, the low state disables.

The operation of a NOR gate RS latch is shown in Figure 4.57*a*. This circuit can be more easily understood if the functional logic equivalent of the NOR gate is used, as shown in Figure 4.57*b* (this is easier than trying to recall the details of how a NOR gate responds to all of the combinations of its inputs). The assumed 0 at the Q output and the 0 at the Set pin force $\bar{Q}$ to a 1. This 1 is also input to the upper logic gate and forces the Q output to 0. This is the regeneration mechanism that takes place in this circuit.

While the Set input is high (Figure 4.57*c*), the $\bar{Q}$ output is forced to a 0. This 0 also forces the output of the upper logic gate (Q) to a 1. When the Set input returns to the inactive 0 state, the 1 at the Q output forces the $\bar{Q}$ output to 0. This 0 forces the output of the upper logic gate (Q) to a 1. Once set, additional Set inputs will have no affect on the output. As an exercise, go through the setups that are necessary to reset the latch.

These RS latch circuits will not operate properly if the Set and Reset inputs are both active at the same time. Only one of these inputs should be active at any given time; otherwise the circuit response will not be predictable. This is called a "race condition." With both the Set and Reset inputs simultaneously active, it is not clear which Control signal will win this race because the final state of the latch will depend on the relative timing as the Control signals return to their inactive states. The uncertainty that results from race conditions must be avoided in digital systems and many logic design approaches are used to ensure that race conditions will never happen.

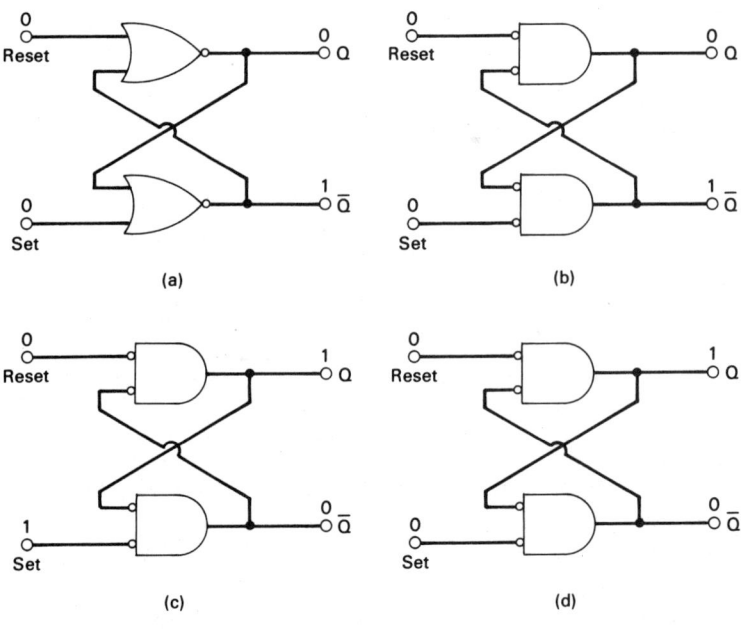

Figure 4.57 Operation of the NOR gate RS latch. (a) Initially assumed in the reset state, (b) redrawn using functional equivalent logic, (c) while the set input is active, and (d) after set returns to inactive state.

An application of an RS latch (using the two input NAND gates) is shown in Figure 4.58. This will "debounce" the switch (SW_1) shown on the left side of this diagram. Mechanical switches rapidly make and break contact a number of times following each change in the switch position. Although this multiple triggering is relatively rapid, logic circuits can easily follow these changes and the circuits can get confused by these bouncing switch contacts. Switches, whether on a keyboard or simply an on-off toggle switch, exhibit this undesired bouncing.

Some electronic or other means is needed to eliminate the detrimental effects of this bouncing. For example, a latch circuit can be tied around a switch so that the initial switch closure will change the state of the latch and any additional bouncing is disregarded (because the latch is already in the new state). Although bouncing is still happening directly at the switch contacts, the Q and the $\bar{Q}$ outputs will not change state. There will just be one clean logic transition at the output of this latch circuit for each change in the switch position.

The CMOS transmission gate

The circuit design techniques that are used for CMOS logic circuits are quite different from those used for bipolar circuits. This difference

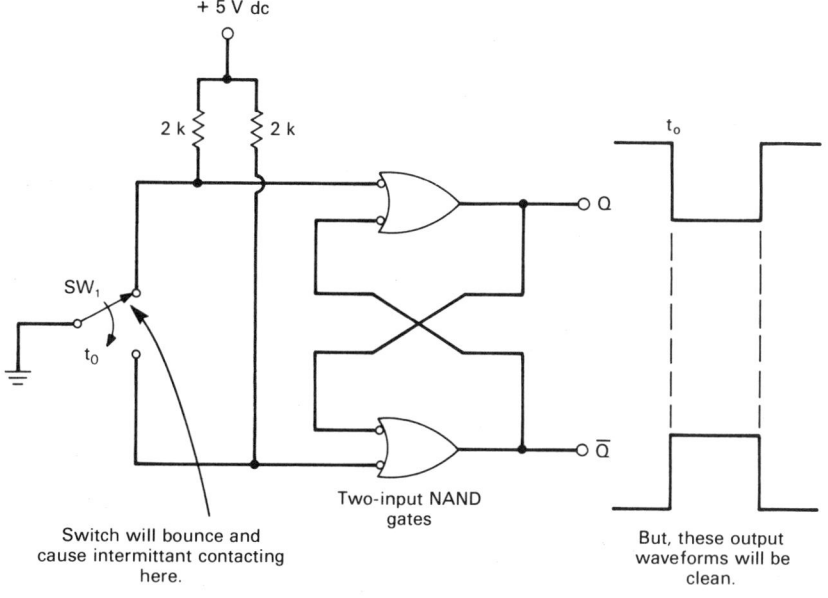

Figure 4.58 Using an *RS* latch to debounce a switch.

is based on the use of MOS transistors as "analog switches": electronic switches that will allow a voltage to pass through when closed or block the voltage when opened.

The digital designers' name for this analog switch (Figure 4.59) is a CMOS "transmission gate." This switch is composed of a P-channel transistor connected in parallel with an N-channel transistor. There is a Control input, a Signal input, and an Output. A logic 0 on the Control input opens the switch, Figure 4.59a. This Control input of 0 V ties directly to the gate of the N-channel transistor and keeps this transistor off. The inverter in the Control line provides a 1 level that goes to the P-channel transistor. This high voltage at the gate of the P-channel transistor also keeps this transistor off. Both transistors are therefore held off when the Control is at a 0 level. The 2-V signal at the input therefore will not propagate to the output because the switch is open.

The switch is shown closed in Figure 4.59b. Notice that the logic 1 level on the Control input now turns on the N-channel transistor. The inverter in the Control line to the P-channel device changes this 1 to a 0, which also turns on the P-channel transistor. With both transistors on, the 2-V input signal is allowed to propagate through the switch and will appear at the output. This analog switch (or transmission gate) is unique to CMOS logic circuits and is very useful to CMOS logic circuit designers.

166 Chapter Four

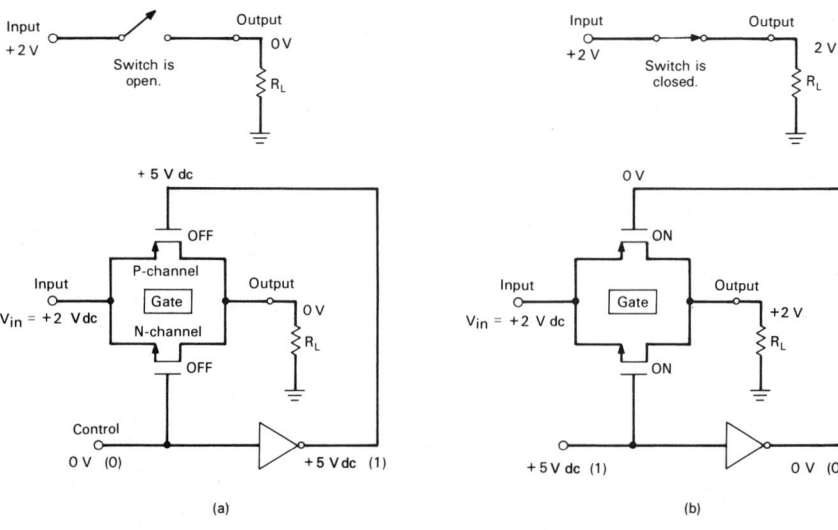

Figure 4.59 The CMOS transmission gate. (a) Gate open—no signal transmission and (b) gate closed—signal transmission.

The internal operation of a CMOS transmission gate can be demonstrated by a simulation that uses the bipolar transistors that are available in the lab kit. A circuit connection that accomplishes this is shown in Figure 4.60. Again, notice that the P-channel transistor is simulated

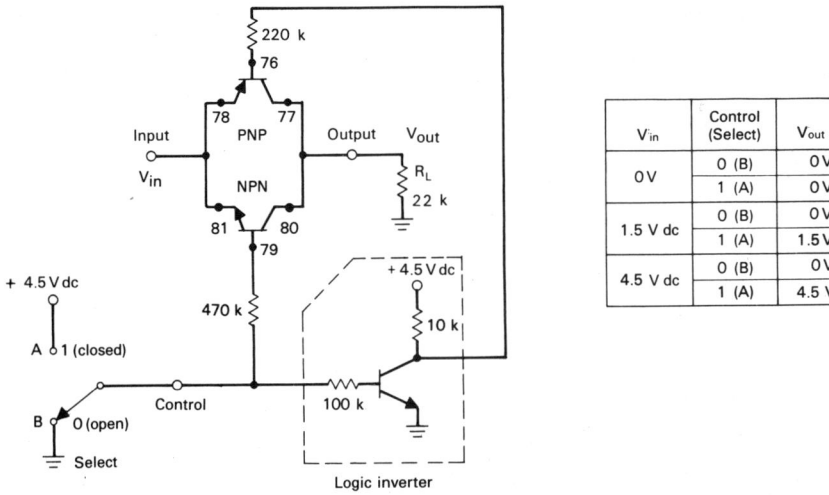

Figure 4.60 Simulating a CMOS transmission gate.

with a PNP transistor at the top of the drawing. The N-channel transistor at the lower side is simulated with an NPN transistor. The inverter for the Control line that leads to the PNP device is provided by the additional NPN transistor.

The CMOS flow-through latch

Two transmission gates and two logic inverters can be interconnected to make a CMOS "flow-through latch," as shown in Figure 4.61. This latch circuit has two operating modes, flow through or latched. In the flow-through mode (shown in Figure 4.63a), any logic state at the input is allowed to flow through and will provide an inverted state at the output. In the latched state (Figure 4.63b), the output remembers the logic state that existed at the time the latch condition was enforced.

To help the understanding of this flow-through latch, the transmission gates are simply represented as switches. In the flow-through mode (Figure 4.63a), the first transmission gate (TG$_1$) is closed and the second transmission gate (TG$_2$) is open. This open gate (TG$_2$) and also the lower logic inverter can be eliminated from consideration (because they are disconnected and therefore have no effect on the circuit operation). The data (D) is simply flowing through a logic inverter to provide the $\bar{Q}$ output.

The Control on the transmission gate can change at any time to establish the latched state. This will interchange the states of the switches, as shown in Figure 4.63b. The upper transmission gate (TG$_1$) is open, so there is no longer a response to the data input. The lower transmission gate (TG$_2$) is closed. The resulting loop interconnection of the two logic inverters provides a flip-flop. This circuit will hold onto the logic state that existed at the time just prior to the opening of TG$_1$.

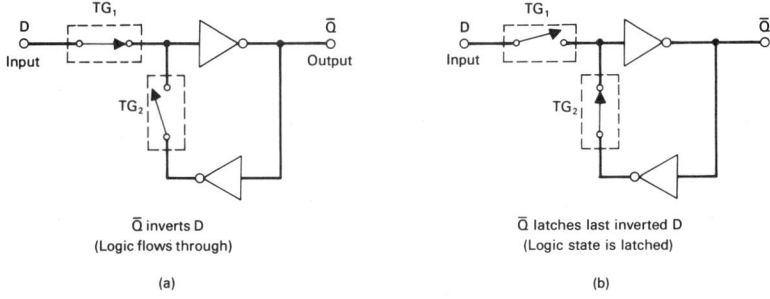

Figure 4.61 Using the CMOS transmission gate in a latch circuit. (*a*) In flow-through state and (*b*) in latched state.

A CMOS D-type flip-flop

Two of these latch circuits can be cascaded (connected in series) to provide the very useful edge-triggered D-type flip-flop shown in Figure 4.62. Four transmission gates are now used. They are activated in pairs: TG_1 and TG_4, and TG_2 and TG_3. The first latch circuit involves TG_1 and TG_2 and the second latch circuit involves TG_3 and TG_4.

The clock input (which controls the states of these transmission gates) is shown in the timing waveform that is located along the bottom of the figure. In the first time interval of the clock (region 1) the switches are as shown in the figure. The first latch is in flow through and the second latch is latched. On the rising edge of the clock (region 2) the latch states interchange (the details of this will be considered next). While the Control stays at the high level, there is no further change.

It is important to notice that the latching action took place on the *rising edge* of the clock signal. This is why this circuit is called "edge triggered" (or more completely, positive-edge triggered). The output of this flip-flop depends on the logic states at the time of the occurrence of the positive edge of the clock voltage waveform. When the clock voltage returns to the low-level state, the transmission gates will return to their previous states.

The conditions at the positive edge of the clock are shown in Figure 4.63. The first latch is in the latched mode and the second latch is in the flow-through mode. Memory is provided by the first latch. The sec-

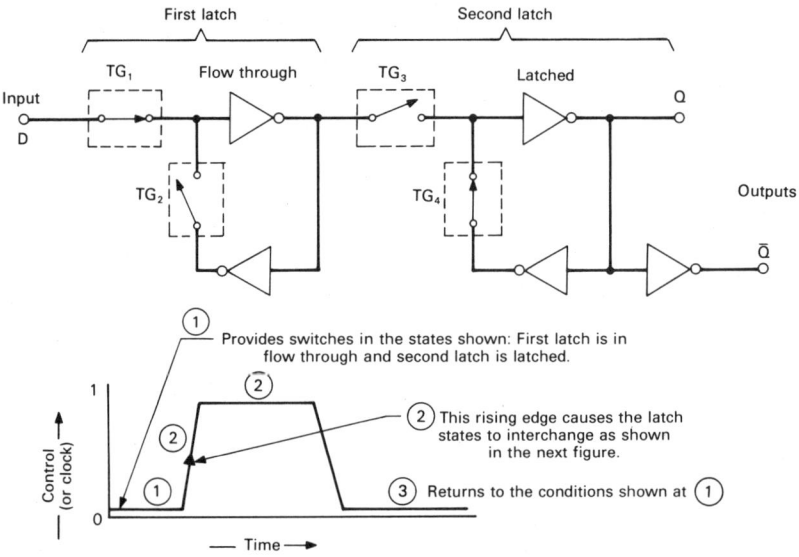

Figure 4.62 Transmission gates in a D-type edge-triggered flip-flop.

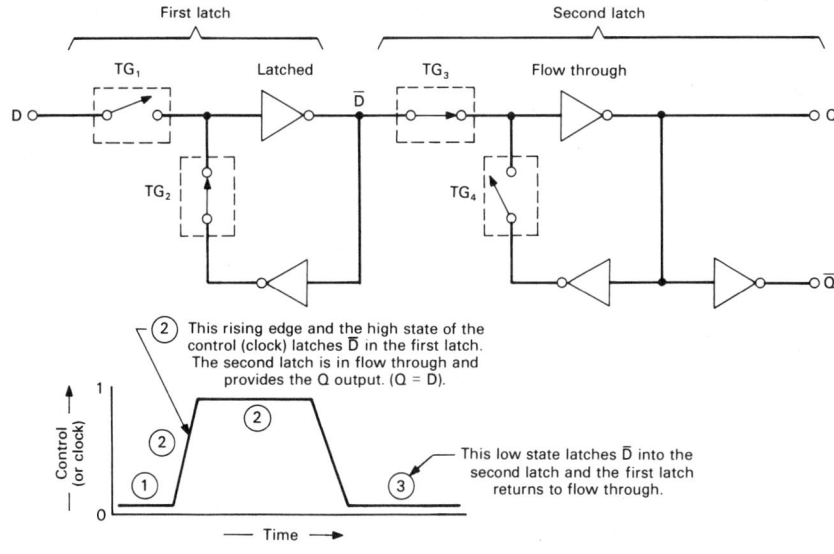

Figure 4.63 The previous flip-flop with the clock high.

ond latch, operating in the flow-through mode, allows the output of the first latch to flow through the inverter to provide the overall output.

When the clock returns to 0 (at time 3) the latched state transfers to the second latch and the first latch enters the flow-through mode. This first latch will keep up with the input signal and will be ready to freeze or capture this input signal on the next positive edge of the clock.

Many times a D-type flip-flop is provided with a "Clear input" to allow forcing the Q output to the low state. This is implemented as shown in Figure 4.64. One of the inverters in each latch is replaced with a two-input NAND gate so it can be used as a gated inverter. In this case the gating control is provided by the Clear input.

Independent of which latch circuit is providing the memory and independent of the stored logic states, when the Clear line goes to 0, there is an unconditional forcing of the Q output to the logic 0 state. The Clear input is independent of the clock and can be asserted at any time to immediately bring the Q output to 0. This resets or clears the flip-flop.

The operation of a D-type flip-flop with Clear is shown in Figure 4.65. In the symbol on this figure, the clock input is shown with a little triangle-shaped indication inside the overall symbol. This triangle symbol is used to indicate edge triggering. This example represents positive-edge triggering. Another way to represent positive-edge triggering is to show an arrowhead on the rising part of a waveform next to the clock input (this convention is also shown in this figure).

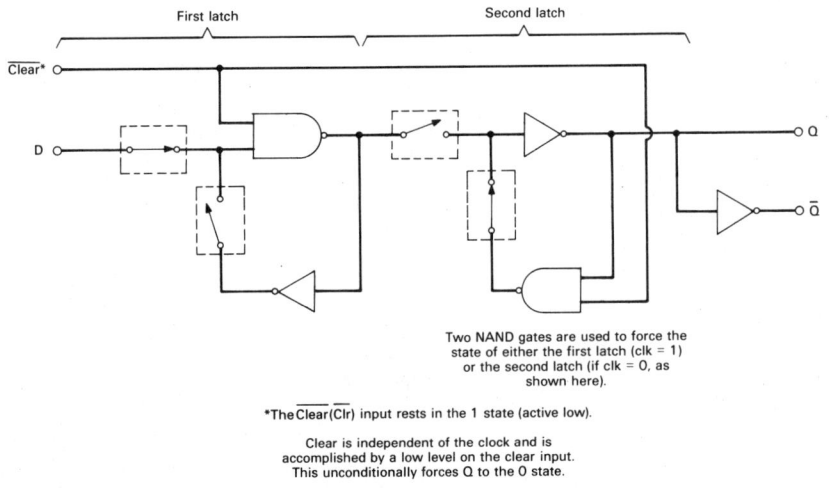

Figure 4.64 Adding a clearing function to a D-type flip-flop.

Circuits are also available with negative-edge triggering. These either show the falling part of a waveform with the arrowhead pointing down, or a small inverting ball is added where the clock line meets the flip-flop symbol.

In the truth table on this figure, the data input, the clock input, and the Clear input are shown. As long as the Clear input is held high, the Clear function is disabled. The Clear operation will only take place

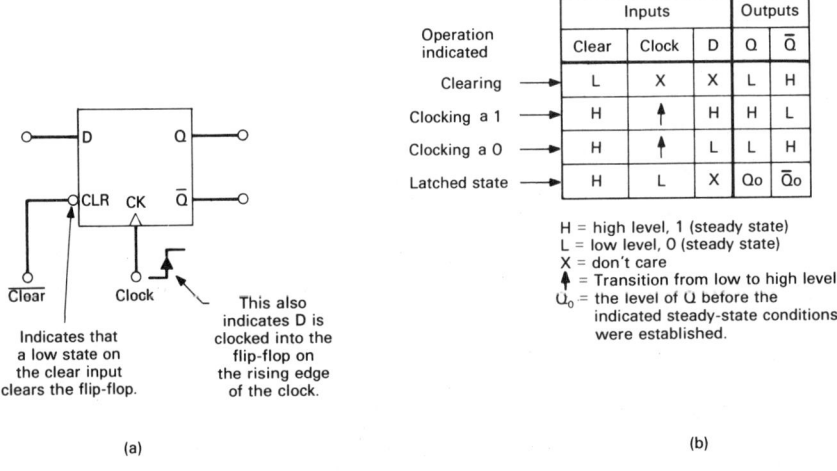

Figure 4.65 Symbol and truth table for a D-type flip-flop with clear. (a) Symbol, and (b) truth table.

when Clear is pulled low. The first row of the truth table shows that if Clear is low, a "don't care" (X) condition exists with the clock. As far as the circuit is concerned, it "don't care" if the clock is high or low, and it also "don't care" what is taking place at the D input. If the Clear input is low, the Q output will be low, and the $\overline{Q}$ output will be the complement, high.

Triggering a flip-flop

Positive-edge triggering and negative-edge triggering have both been discussed. In addition, there is "level triggering." You will hear this distinction between edge-triggered and level-triggered circuits. The previously discussed RS latches were level-triggered circuits. The D-type flip-flop just described is edge triggered. Both types of circuits are used in logic systems.

These triggering possibilities are shown in Figure 4.66. There are four regions available on a pulse waveform that can be used as a triggering signal: the rising edge, the 1 level, the falling edge, or the 0 level.

In level triggering or level clocking, a race condition is possible because the inputs may change many times during the total clock enable time. In bipolar logic families, two cascaded "master-slave" flip-flops are used to prevent this race condition. The master flip-flop accepts inputs only during one clock phase and then transfers this logic to the slave flip-flop during the opposite clock phase. This circuit complexity is avoided with less complex CMOS edge-triggered circuits.

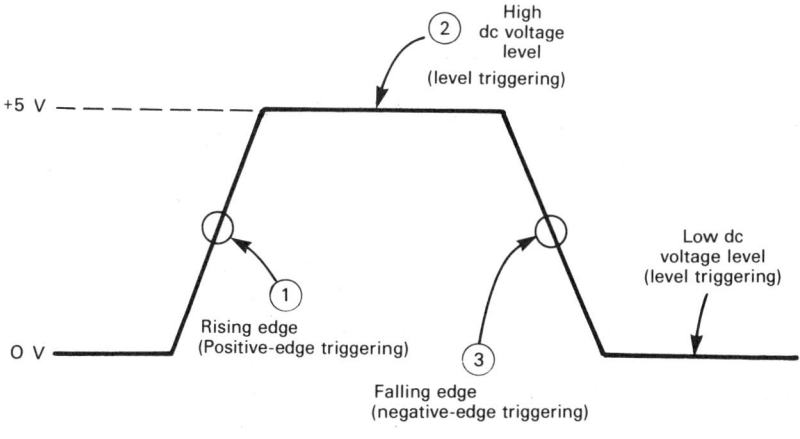

Figure 4.66 The triggering possibilities available on a pulse waveform.

Set-up and hold times

The D-type flip-flop will acquire the input data at the rising edge of the clock signal. To prevent ambiguity, the signal presented to the D input has to exist for a slight time interval *prior to the rising edge of the clock* in order to be properly recognized by the flip-flop circuitry. This earlier appearance of the D input signal is called the "set-up time," and is indicated in Figure 4.67. For example, a set-up time of 12 ns means that the voltage at the D has to exist as a valid logic signal for 12 ns *prior* to the occurrence of the rising edge of the clock in order to be properly recognized, either as a 1 or a 0.

In addition to the set-up time requirement, the logic level has to be maintained at the D input for a specified time following the rising edge of the clock signal. This is the "hold time" requirement for the flip-flop. A typical hold time is 1 ns. If the set-up and hold time specifications are met, the flip-flop will properly respond to the D input.

Levels of logic

Logic gates operate with inputs that are provided by either flip-flops or other logic gates. Logic gates also provide the inputs to other flip-flops. In a digital system, logic propagates out of flip-flops, through a

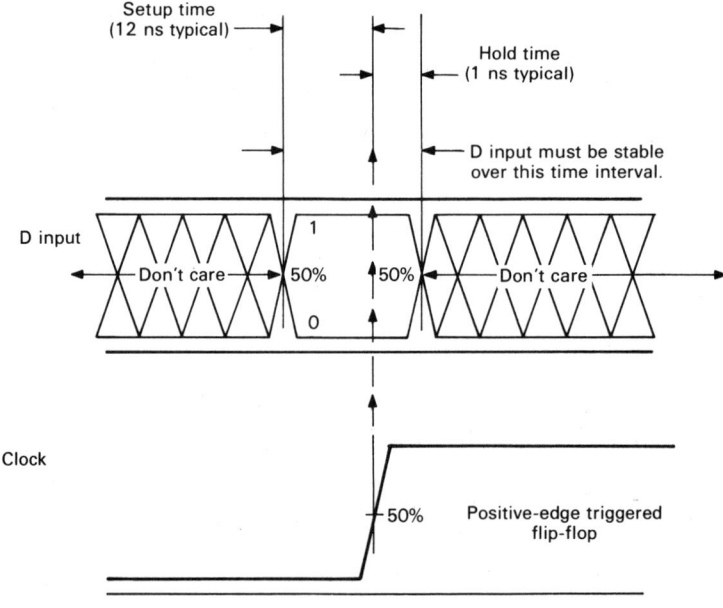

Figure 4.67 The set-up and hold times of a D-type flip-flop.

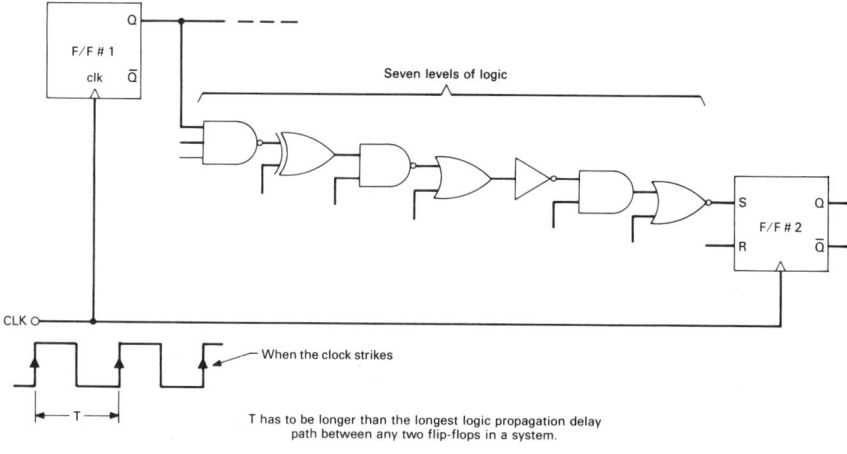

Figure 4.68 One limit on the minimum clock period.

number of logic gates, and eventually provides the control inputs for other flip-flops, as shown in Figure 4.68.

Notice, in this figure, that the logic signals must propagate through seven different logic circuits or seven levels of logic from the output of flip-flop No. 1 to the input of flip-flop No. 2. The clock period therefore has to be long enough so the logic has time to propagate out of flip-flop No. 1, through seven levels of logic gates, and be properly set up at the input of flip-flop No. 2 before the next clock strikes. The number of logic levels between flip-flops sets a limit on the maximum clocking rate of a digital system. The period of the clock (T) has to be longer than the longest propagation delay path between any two flip-flops in a system.

Four basic flip-flops

Just as there are a number of useful logic gates that are available to digital system designers, there are also a number of useful flip-flops. These flip-flops will now be described. For simplicity, the Preset and Clear controls will be eliminated from these examples. Commercially available flip-flops can have a Preset, Clear, neither, or both controls.

An *RS* flip-flop is shown in Figure 4.69. This is similar to the *RS* latch, except a clock input now exists (remember that the distinction between a latch and a flip-flop is that a flip-flop has a clock input). This is a positive-edge-triggered flip-flop. The truth table shows the functional relationships between the inputs and the output of the flip-flop. Just as the *RS* latch could not allow the Set and Reset inputs to be simultaneously asserted, the *RS* flip-flop also has this constraint. This is an illegal state because a race condition is established and the

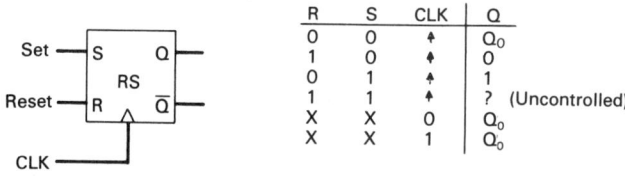

Figure 4.69 The RS flip-flop.

flip-flop is out of control. When operating with an RS flip-flop, it is up to the designer to guarantee that R and S will never be simultaneously asserted.

This race problem of the RS flip-flop is solved with the JK flip-flop shown in Figure 4.70. This example is a negative-edge-triggered JK flip-flop. The function of a JK flip-flop is almost identical to an RS flip-flop. The J input sets the flip-flop; the K input resets the flip-flop. The difference is, if J and K are both simultaneously true, the flip-flop will change state. There is no longer the problem of a race condition.

The data or D-type flip-flop (previously discussed) is a very popular circuit in CMOS logic. This D-type flip-flop is again shown in Figure 4.71.

The last flip-flop type that will be mentioned is the toggle flip-flop (the T flip-flop) shown in Figure 4.72. This is similar to the D flip-flop, except that when the T input is true and the clock strikes, the output changes state (it toggles).

A 2-bit ripple counter

A 2-bit asynchronous counter can be assembled using the flip-flop ICs that are available in the lab kit. This is also called a "ripple" counter because, during the counting sequence, the carries ripple to the next most-significant flip-flops. This rippling of the carries results because each flip-flop "clocks" the next most-significant flip-flop. Therefore the clocks do not occur simultaneously; they ripple down the cascade of flip-

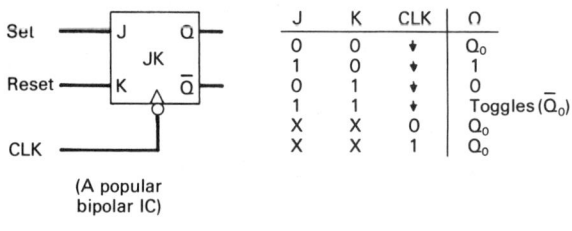

Figure 4.70 The JK flip-flop.

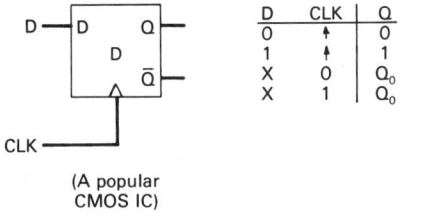

Figure 4.71 The D flip-flop.

flops. Counters can also be synchronous, where all of the flip-flops change state at the same time, when the clock "strikes" (logic gates are used to insure that these flip-flops count in the proper manner).

The schematic diagram for this ripple counter is shown in Figure 4.73. The two flip-flops that are available in the lab kit are T^2L bipolar flip-flops of the JK variety. This particular interconnection provides a 2-bit counter; so four output states exist. This number of possible output states is called the "modulus" of the counter. A counter of mod 10 or modulo 10 is also called a "decade counter" because it can count up to (or divide by) 10.

The T^2L quad two-input NAND gate that is available in the lab kit can be used to decode these four separate output states. These NAND gate outputs are then used to drive the LED display. Just a few of the segments will be used, segments A, B, G, and F. When the key is pressed to advance the count, notice that the segment that is lit will rotate in a clockwise direction, indicating that the counter is properly changing states. This is a very useful circuit to build and spend some time with because it shows a useful application of how flip-flops can be used to make a counter circuit.

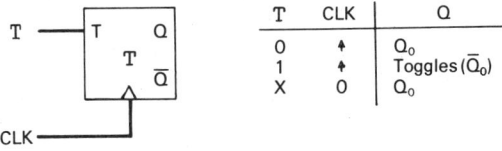

Figure 4.72 The T flip-flop.

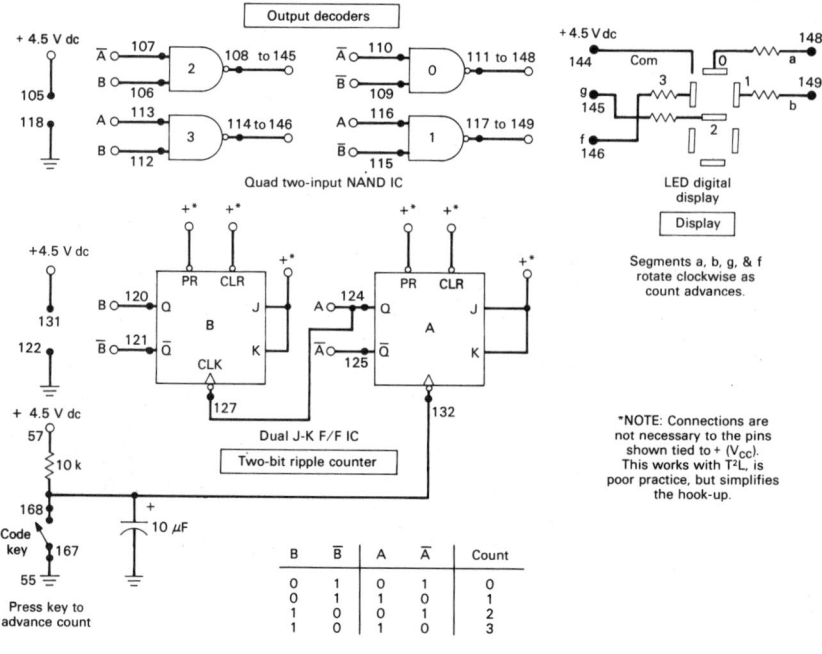

Figure 4.73 A 2-bit ripple counter with output decoders.

The Key switch advances the count, and the 10-μF capacitor is used in an attempt to prevent contact bounce problems. Key bounce problems still exist with this simple circuit, but there are not enough logic circuits available to provide a better debounce function.

The contact bounce problem can be demonstrated with this circuit. Remove the 10-μF capacitor and notice that the contact bounce problem makes this counter essentially inoperative. The 10-μF capacitor is a help, but it does not completely eliminate the bounce problem.

Frequency division by 2,147,483,648 to 1

Counters are often provided as a complete subsystem in one integrated circuit package. For example, Figure 4.74 shows an IC (in a 16-pin package) that is a programmable frequency divider (a counter that can divide by values up to 2,147,483,648 to 1). This very high ratio requires 31 flip-flops. By programming five of the inputs to the IC (A through E), a system designer can control the division that is obtained. For example, a 1 megahertz (MHz) clock (that is, 1 million clock cycles per second) can be used to provide a number of different, lower frequencies. The highest division ratio would provide an output frequency of 0.000466 Hz, a very, very low-frequency square wave. This frequency is so low that rather than talk about cycles per second, it is better to

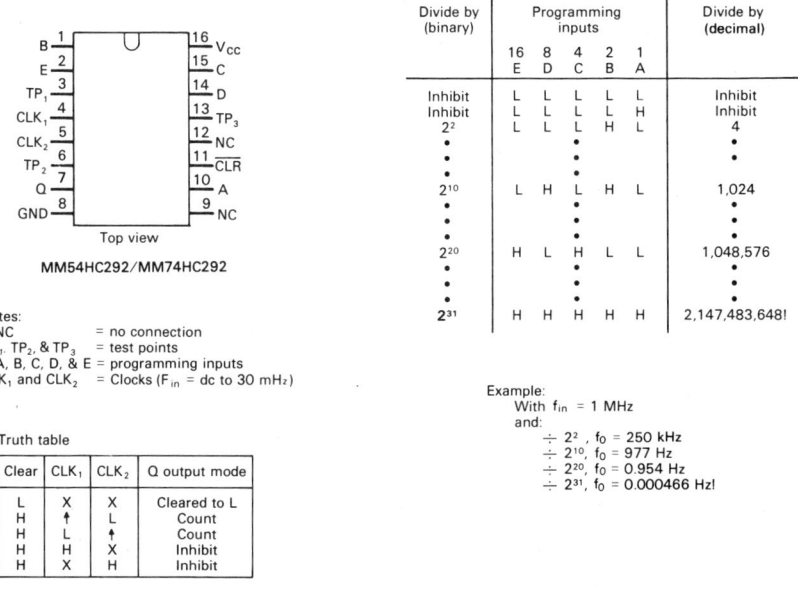

Figure 4.74 A programmable frequency divider/digital timer.

talk about seconds per cycle (2,145.9 s per cycle). Each state of this output square wave will last for more than half an hour (2,145.9 s/2, or 36 min). The period of a 1-MHz input frequency is 1 μs. Therefore the period coming in is one-millionth of a second, and the period coming out is a little over 1 hour (h). This IC is only a partial indication of the logic complexity that is available on a single chip.

Communicating in Digitalese

Digital systems need to communicate between individual circuits, subsystems, and major systems. This communication takes place using a digital format, a grouping of 1s and 0s that can exist on just a few wires or on a parallel array of many wires. We will now take a look at some of the communication techniques that are used.

Nibbles, bytes, words, and long words

Groupings of 1s and 0s are called many things. A group of 4 bits is called a "nibble;" 8 bits are a "byte." A byte is very common because ASCII encoding uses 1 byte per character. Therefore many computers that are handling text make use of either 8 bits or some multiple of 8 bits as the basic number of bits that they work with so that they can efficiently handle ASCII characters.

The number of bits that a digital system works with is called the "word size." The capability of doubling this basic word size by placing two words together makes what are called "long words." Two long words then make up a "quad word." These names for the word groups make it much easier to talk about them.

Protocols and handshakes: The rules of the game

In every digital system, the designer has to establish a communications "protocol." This is all of the rules that have to be followed so the circuits, subsystems, and systems can communicate with each other. This communication has to be done according to a prearranged protocol.

A "handshake" is used to initiate a working relationship between two digital circuits, subsystems, or systems. This handshake takes place prior to the exchange of information or data and consists of getting the attention of the other party, requesting what is wanted, and then obtaining the "go-ahead" from the other party. Handshakes are important when there is competition for the same equipment because a proper handshake prevents simultaneous *requests* for service and also prevents simultaneous *grants* to proceed.

Serial communication

Serial communication of digital information can take place on only a few wires. Therefore, serial data communication is used over long distances to eliminate the cost of using a large number of interconnecting wires.

On your wire. Timing synchronization is needed for serial communication in order to define exactly when to examine the signaling voltage levels that are transmitted over these wires. There are "synchronous communication" schemes in which both the transmiting and receiving ends have access to the same clock. This clocking signal is transmitted to the receiving unit. There are also digital codes in which the clocking signal is embedded within the code. These "self-clocking" encoding schemes allow the receiver to recover the clock signal from the data stream and do not require the separate transmission of the clock signal.

For low-speed communications on a minimum number of wires, use is often made of an "asynchronous communication" technique. This does not require clock recovery from the encoded data or the use of a common clock. An example of an asynchronous communication scheme is shown in Figure 4.75 in which it is desired to transmit the capital letter H in ASCII code.

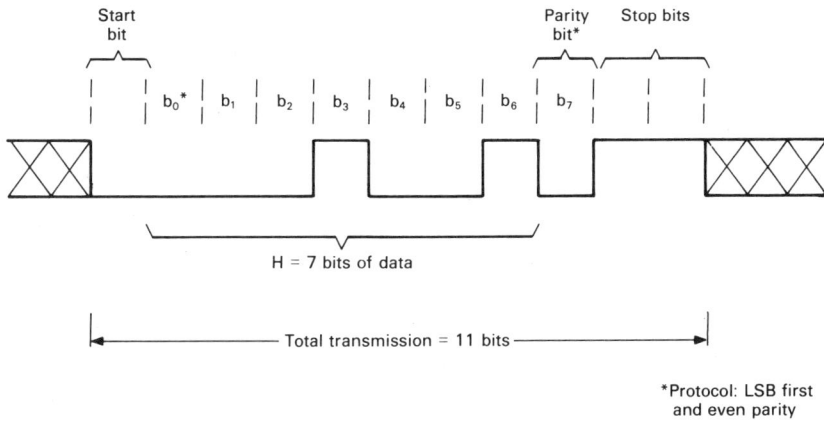

Figure 4.75 "H" in ASCII.

Negative logic is specified in a standardized protocol known as RS-232C. This was one of the first serial standards and has the title, "Interface between Data Terminal Equipment and Data Communication Equipment Employing Serial Binary Data Interchange." Data Terminal Equipment (DTE) refers to any device that transmits or receives information (like a computer). Data Communication Equipment (DCE) refers to any device that only passes on or relays information (like a modem that is used to pass digital information over the telephone lines; there will be more on this later).

With RS-232C, a logical 0 (also called a "space") is specified as a voltage level from +3 to +25 V dc, and a logical 1 (also called a "mark") is specified as a voltage level from −3 to −25 V dc. Special line-driver and line-receiver circuits are necessary to handle these unusual voltage levels.

The ASCII encoding of the letter H requires 7 bits. With the use of an 8-bit group (a byte) there is room for an extra bit (a *parity bit*) that is automatically generated by circuitry that "looks" at the 7-data bits. "Even parity" means that the parity bit is chosen to provide an even number of 1s in the 8-bit group (data plus parity). "Odd parity" means that an odd number of 1s will appear in each data byte. Parity is a relatively simple way to verify that the received data does not contain a single bit in error (2 bits or more in error may not be detected).

In the 7-bit ASCII code for an H, there are two 1s (all the other bits are 0s). Two is an even number, so in this case of even parity the parity bit will be 0. (An odd number of 1s in the 7 data bits would require a true parity bit to make an even overall total number of 1s.)

The receiving station does a parity check on each byte and verifies that an even number of 1s was received. If this is the case, the assumption is made that there are no errors. If an odd number of 1s appears, the receiving station will ask for a repeat of the transmission.

There are also some additional "overhead bits" placed around each transmitted data group. The parity bit is one of these overhead bits. There is also a "start bit," always a 0, that initiates the transmission of each data group. This start bit is an alerting signal that tells the receiving station that information will be coming. Similarly, at the end of the transmission, the last 2 bits are always held in the 1 state; these are the "stop bits."

One of the problems of serial data transmission is the requirement for these overhead bits. There are only 7 bits of information, but 11 bits must be transmitted. This reduces the efficiency of communication of an asynchronous serial link. A synchronous serial link greatly reduces this problem because the position of the data words is known. Start and stop bits are therefore not needed for each byte.

The serial protocol shown in Figure 4.75 is that the least-significant bit will be transmitted first and even parity will be used.

The receiving station uses a crystal as a frequency (and therefore a timing) reference that is very close to the same frequency as the crystal used by the transmitting station. It is important that nearly the same transmitting and receiving crystal-controlled frequencies be used so that timing errors do not accumulate within the total time span needed for the transmission of the 11 bits. A timing reference is derived from a crystal-controlled oscillator so that the locations of the centers of each one of the bit-time intervals can be determined. By reading the data at these mid points, deteriorated voltage waveforms with large values of rise and fall times can be tolerated.

Over the telephone. The telephone system within any country is a vast network of wires that can be interconnected to allow communication between any two points. It is convenient to also transmit digital data over this existing network. One way this is done is to convert from the high-low voltage levels of a digital bit stream into one of two transmitted audio tones, a process called "modulation." These audible tones are then easily handled by the telephone system and are sent to the receiving destination, where they are "demodulated" to return them to digital voltage levels. Computers on both ends can originate and answer calls automatically.

An example of transmitting digital data over the telephone line is the standard low-speed, 300-baud modem shown in Figure 4.76. Modem is an acronym derived from *MO*dulator (uses the incoming digital data stream to modulate or control the transmit frequency going out on the telephone lines) and *DEM*odulator (the conversion of the received audio frequencies back into digital voltage levels).

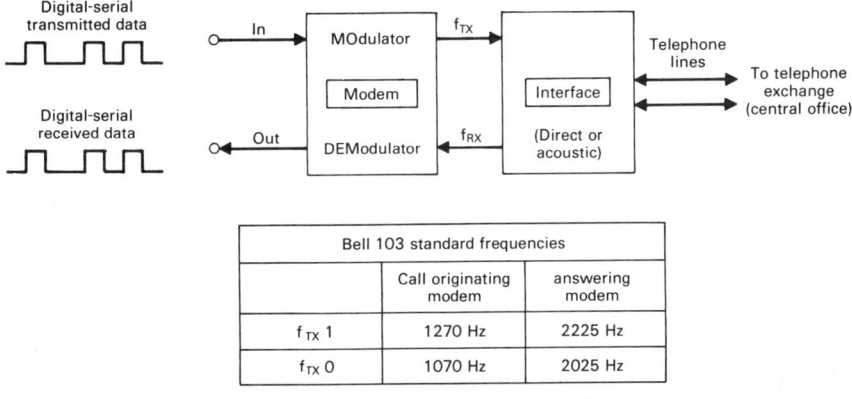

Figure 4.76 A basic low-speed modem.

The "baud rate," named in honor of the early data communication pioneer Emile Baudot, is an indication of the signaling rate that is used. The presence of overhead bits makes the information rate typically less than the baud rate, although there are complicated modulation schemes that have high efficiencies.

A standard voice-grade telephone line has been called a "2400-baud line." "Adaptive equalizers" (special electronic compensation for the signal distortion that results from transmission over the conventional telephone lines) have raised this to 9600 baud without requiring special modifications to a standard voice-grade line. To preserve compatibility with the switching equipment of the telephone company, even multiples of 2400 baud have been standardized: 2400, 4800, 7200, and 9600 baud. Special wide-band higher-cost channels are also available from the telephone companies that permit transmitting at higher baud rates.

A modem standard, called the "Bell 103 Standard," prescribes a protocol which specifies the transmitting and receiving frequencies. The modem that originates a call will transmit a 1 as a short burst of 1270 Hz. The answering modem will use a higher frequency, 2225 Hz to transmit a 1. A 0 will be transmitted using a lower frequency in both cases.

A modem has to interface with the telephone lines. This interface can be a direct connection, but the telephone system must not be disturbed, and the large voltage transients that can exist directly on telephone lines (as a result of lightning strikes) must not damage the modem.

The interface from the modem to the telephone lines can also take place via an "acoustical-coupling network." For this interface, the standard telephone handset is placed in an acoustically coupled cradle that allows an easy way to get the information-bearing tones onto and off of the telephone lines.

An acoustic-coupled modem is diagrammed in Figure 4.77. The handset picks up the tones that are to be transmitted from a small loudspeaker. A small microphone picks up the received audio tones at the other end of the handset. The received audio signals then go to the modem to be converted into a digital data stream.

A bus speeds things up

There is a basic speed limitation with serial communication because each bit must be transmitted in sequence. If extra wires can be used, faster "parallel communication" can be used. With parallel communication, all the bits of a digital word are transmitted simultaneously (each bit uses a separate wire).

Parallel communication lines are called a "bus." Buses are used over short distances but are too costly if long distances exist between the communicating systems. For example, buses are used in and immediately around a computer.

Thanks for the Memory

Digital systems make use of a number of different types of memory. Memory is basic to digital computation. The type, speed, cost per bit, physical size, and storage capacity of a memory are all important considerations.

A memory hierarchy exists. Memories are classified within this hierarchy as "primary memory" (which is used to directly support a computer in current operations), "secondary memory" (a higher-storage-capacity memory that is used to load and offload the primary memory), and "backup memory" (used to offload the secondary memory to guarantee that information is not lost).

We will now take a look at these memories.

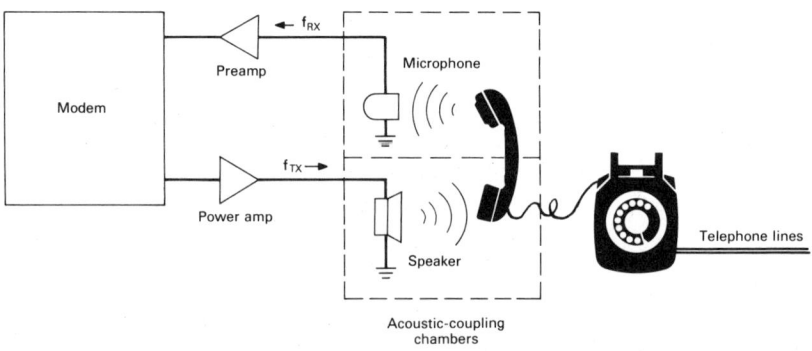

Figure 4.77 An acoustically coupled modem.

Primary memory

There are various forms of primary memory. In general, primary memory has the highest cost per bit. Fast "access time" is needed so as not to slow down the processing speed of a digital computer. A large separation exists between primary memories that is based on whether a computer can write new information to the memory or is only allowed to read the contents of the memory.

Remember what I tell you (R/W or RAM). There are uses for memory that can be read from as well as written to by the computer. The best name for this type of memory is a "read/write memory" (or R/W memory). Unfortunately, this is also known as a "random access memory," or a RAM. The nomenclature "random access" is not a clear indication of the memory function because a ROM memory (considered next) can also be accessed in a random manner. It is more precise to speak of RAM as a R/W memory, but tradition has made RAM the more popular designation.

RAMs are divided into those that store digital data with flip-flops (called "static RAMs," SRAMS) and those that store digital data as voltage levels on small internal capacitors (called "dynamic RAMs," DRAMs, because these stored voltage levels must be periodically restored, called "refreshing" the DRAM). The basic advantage of SRAM over DRAM is that it is easier to use because it does not have to be refreshed, but it is more costly because of larger IC chip sizes. Also, there are "integrated RAMs" (iRAMs) that are DRAMs which internally have circuitry that combines the best features of SRAM and DRAM.

Computer systems make use of R/W memory for storing any type of data that is subject to change. For flexibility, a general-purpose computer must have as much R/W memory as possible to allow storing both programs and the data for these programs.

Never forget this (ROM). A particular type of memory that is initially programmed (and is never changed) is the "read only memory" (ROM). The popularity of ROMs was enhanced when microprocessors became popular. Microprocessors (the processing units for miniature digital computers) are often used in small dedicated computers that are used to solve a specific problem (such as in a control application). A small digital computer that is dedicated to a specific control function will use a ROM to store the sequence of control statements (the program) that are necessary to repetitively execute to provide the desired control action. In addition, ROMs have been used to store look-up tables and also to store relatively small fixed programs that are frequently used by a computer. In fact, most of the personal computers use ROM to store the monitor system and the BASIC interpreter (there will be more on this in Chapter 5). When a personal computer is first turned on, there is a substantial program already in place (the program is said to "reside" within the computer or is resident within the computer) because of the use of built-in ROM memory.

There are "programmable ROMs" (PROMs) that can be programmed by the system designer (using fusible links) and placed in service until a factory-programmed ROM can be made available by an IC supplier. There are also "erasable programmable ROMs" (EPROMs). This type of memory can be identified because it has a small clear quartz window that is positioned over the chip. The internal IC chip can be seen by looking through this window. Ultraviolet light can be directed through this window and onto the IC chip to erase an existing program and put the memory in a state for accepting a different program. EPROMs are very useful in developing an initial system and have also been used for small quantity runs for systems in production.

Remember these, my dying words (E^2PROM). A relatively recent addition to memory alternatives is an "electrically erasable and electrically programmable read-only memory." These E^2PROMs are finding many uses in systems. It is very convenient to have the capability for an electronic system to automatically write information into a memory device that will not lose this information if the power should fail. This ability to hold onto the information is called "nonvolatile storage." Most semiconductor memories lose information if the power fails; they are "volatile memories."

One example of the benefits of nonvolatile E^2PROM is that at the onset of a power loss, information within the volatile memories of a computer can be automatically written into an E^2PROM so that data will not be lost. In addition, E^2PROMs can also provide for alterable system options. At the time circuit boards for a system are assembled, particular system configurations or options can be selected by making use of an E^2PROM. At a later date, if a change is required, it is a relatively simple matter for the user to change the code in the E^2PROM to adapt the system to a new requirement.

E^2PROM memory can also be used as a part of an IC chip to provide the capability for changes so that the IC chip is not rendered obsolete if a slight change is required. If certain changes can be anticipated, they can be allowed for by the use of a small E^2PROM as a part of a complex IC chip.

Register your memory. Registers (collections of flip-flops) are also used as a form of memory in digital systems. Registers are very high speed and are therefore a very valuable type of memory.

Computers and microprocessors have internal "working registers" that are used to temporarily store data as part of the solution of a problem. These "scratch pad" registers are handy; they provide the same function that a scratch pad does for someone who is working at a desk.

Cache memory. A "cache memory" is a memory that can hold a block of information and can be accessed rapidly. The idea is to load data into a cache memory from a slow-access high-capacity secondary memory. The computer can then randomly access data within this cache memory much more rapidly than it could have accessed the bulk storage memory device (such as a tape or a disk). Bulk memory devices are slow to access, but once accessed, they can rapidly transfer a block of data.

Virtual memory. "Virtual memory" is a software technique that relieves the programmer of the detailed concerns of exactly where a program is located in memory. The concept of virtual memory allows the programmer complete freedom to operate with a virtually unlimited memory size. The computer system automatically swaps the data between the secondary and primary memories.

For example, the memory of a computer might be large enough to simultaneously store a number of programs that are all waiting to be run. When a computer system starts operating on multiple programs, it will run the first program until some slow operation comes up, like outputting data. When this happens, the computer system will then rapidly transfer this block of output data into a local buffer memory. The computer system will also allow a buffer memory to be loaded by input data from some slow-responding peripheral device. The computer system then will not have to shut down and wait until these slow operations are completed; the computer is free to execute the next program. Execution will continue until this next program reaches some relatively slow-speed operation. In this way, one computer system can solve many more problems in a given time interval. This is a much more efficient utilization of the computer resources.

If these programs were fixed in the exact space in memory where they had to be located, there would be problems because the programs might overlap in some memory locations. There also might be a "fragmentation problem," in which there is enough total unused space available within memory to hold an additional program, but this new program may be longer than any one of the individual spaces that is currently available. It is desirable to have the computer automatically rearrange existing programs and data to make a large-enough contiguous (adjoining) space available for the next program.

Multiprogramming creates additional problems because a software monitor must get new programs into the RAM of the computer and also must dump previously used programs back out to the secondary memory. All of these problems of swapping programs in and out of primary memory are solved by making use of the concept of virtual memory.

Content addressable memories. Most memories are first addressed and then data is read out or written into the memory. This is called a "coordinate-addressed memory." A "content-addressable memory" has the property that if the contents of a predetermined part of the stored data (called the "tag," or content address) are presented, the data will be retrieved. The exact addresses for these data do not have to be known.

Associative memories. An "associative memory," when presented with an item of information, delivers one or more associated items of information. This is similar to the way a human memory operates.

Secondary memory

"Secondary memories" provide low cost per bit and high storage capacity but suffer because of relatively slow access times. This form of memory is not used for the current information that the computer works with (the function of primary memory) but serves to support the primary memory and is therefore called secondary memory. Because immediate access is not required, a lower-cost-per-bit memory can be used. A computer system loads small "chunks" of data from secondary memory into primary memory for processing by the computer and also off-loads data back to the secondary memory.

To appreciate the need for large amounts of secondary memory in a computer, the example of storing the textual information contained in a book will be used. With 74 spaces for characters within each line of print and 43 print lines to a full page of text, $74 \times 43 = 3182$ total possible characters can be placed on a single page. (Each line of text is not always completely full of characters, but this will be used as an estimate.) Therefore, approximately 3K of storage are needed per page. The text of a 300-page book (excluding illustrations) would therefore require approximately 900K of memory space.

Disk memories. "Disk memories" are generally used for secondary storage. These magnetic devices are sequentially accessed (as opposed to random access) because the data are obtained in a sequential order as the disk passes under a read/write head. Large computer systems have many disk drives simultaneously online to allow accessing a large amount of data.

Digital disk memory consists of rigid (also called "hard," usually an aluminum disk) or flexible (called "floppy," a thin plastic film) disks.

Both of these basic types of disks have a thin magnetic coating (usually on both sides of the disk) for data storage. These magnetic memory devices are nonvolatile and have a faster access time than a tape system (but have less storage capacity).

Data is stored along a number of tracks that form a series of concentric circles around the disk. (This is different from the continuous spiral that is used in audio recording on phonograph records.) In hard disk drives, many disks (also called "platters") are used to increase the storage capacity. The high cost of read/write heads and their associated amplifiers usually forces one set of heads to read from several tracks. Therefore, these heads must be moved to the proper track in what is called the "seek time": An additional time allowance of one-half revolution of the disk, called the "latency time," must then be made (on the average) to get the desired segment of a track under the heads.

Relatively low-cost small-diameter hard disks have been successfully introduced for the personal and small business computer markets. Large increases in the storage capacity of hard disks have been made by making use of techniques used in semiconductor processing, including an extremely small spacing between the head and the magnetic surface coating.

It is important to keep the read/write (R/W) head close to the magnetic recording surface to prevent lateral space-consuming spreading of the magnetized surface area. Sophisticated approaches that make use of what IBM introduced as "Winchester disk technology" allow the R/W head to be "flown" on an air cushion at a spacing of less than 1 micrometer (μm) (a micrometer is one-millionth of a meter or 0.039 mils; typing paper is approximately 1.5 mils thick), which is less than the "feature sizes" (minimum spacings) that are used by the high-technology IC industry. To allow operation with such small head-to-surface spacings, Winchester hard disk systems must be housed within an ultraclean, sealed, filtered environment. These disk drives are achieving unbelievable performance. Much like the story that aeronautical engineers can calculate that a bumblebee should not be able to fly, it also is amazing (from the mechanical standpoint and also the electronic standpoint) that modern hard-disk systems actually work!

Most of the hard disks are not removable from the drive unit. A removable hard disk is a major design problem. The general approach that is used keeps the disk within its sealed enclosure so the complete drive assembly is removed rather than just the disk.

Floppy-disk systems were originally introduced by IBM as a replacement for punched cards as a way to enter data into a computer. The first floppies were 8 in in diameter, but continued development brought out the 5¼- and later the 3½-in-diameter floppies. All of these can store approximately 1 Mbyte of data.

Floppies are very convenient storage devices. For this reason alone they will probably continue to be used (especially for the smaller computer systems). Other advantages of floppies are that they provide low-cost removable data storage.

Magnetic tape. Large reels of magnetic tape are used for secondary storage in large computer systems; tape cassettes are used in smaller computers. Magnetic tape has been around for a long time and has proven to be a very reliable and relatively low-cost storage medium.

Information is stored on magnetic tape in blocks with short interrecord gaps that are long enough (¾ in) so that they can be electronically detected and yet still allow enough time to not only stop the tape drive but also to later restart the drive and get it up to speed before the next block of data (¾ in away from the last) comes under the heads.

Tape for digital data storage has to be of high quality to prevent bad spots in the magnetic coating that will cause "drop-out" errors (lost bits) or "drop-in" errors (added bits) in the recovered data. Reels of 2400 ft of tape are recorded using many parallel data tracks. These reels of tape are stored in special temperature- and humidity-controlled fireproof vaults.

Optical storage. A newer technology for both secondary and back-up storage is "optical memory". The simplest optical storage technique uses a laser beam to burn very small holes in a coating that is supported by a disk. These earlier optical ROMs are being replaced with R/W memories that are based on advanced optical techniques which are challenging the Winchester disk for the high-capacity storage applications.

Back-up memory

"Back-up memory" is used to save data in the event of a catastrophic failure or to save data that is obtained from a volatile memory that would otherwise lose data when the power is removed. Floppy disks and magnetic tape (discussed in the previous section) are also used for backup memory.

Streamers. A recent tape storage device, known as a "streamer," uses a low-cost tape drive mechanism that is not sophisticated enough to provide rapid starts and stops. A streamer is a low-cost way to store large quantities of data for which subsequent rapid access is not required. Streamers are used to off-load the contents of a hard disk within a computer (for example all of the accumulated data at the end of each day). Nearly 100 Mbytes of data can be stored on a single reel of tape.

Disk memories. Floppy disks and removable hard disks also find application as back-up storage devices.

Looking at the Output of a Computer

Computers can provide electronic output signals for controlling other electronic systems or they can provide outputs intended for human observers via displays, printers, and plotters. We will now consider some of the display devices that are used in digital systems and computers.

Displays

A wide variety of display devices is used in modern electronic equipment. These range from the simplest panel light to the large, sophisticated, multicolored cathode-ray-tube displays that are used in high-cost systems and also in video games.

Displays are often divided into either "segmental" displays or "dot-matrix" displays. Some examples of segmental displays are shown in Figure 4.78. Figure 4.78a is the very popular 7-segment display that is used for numbers only. Figure 4.78b is a very complex 16-segment display (often known as the "British flag" display) that will provide "alphanumeric" (both letters and numbers) characters.

Examples of a few dot-matrix displays are shown in Figure 4.79. The simplest of these (the 3 by 5 display) is only capable of displaying numbers. Both the 4 by 6 and the 5 by 7 provide alphanumeric displays. Characters have a better appearance with the higher number of dots that are available in the 5 by 7 display.

Cathode-ray tubes (CRTs). A very common display device for a computer is the "cathode-ray tube." CRTs are used in digital computer terminals to provide the display of typed words and computer graphics.

The two basic types of CRT scanning that are commonly used are shown in Figure 4.80. Figure 4.80a shows the "raster scan" (the scan-

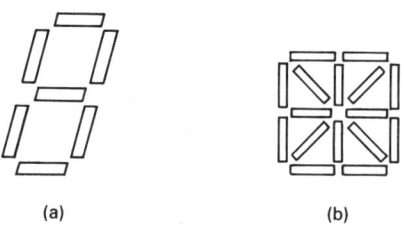

Figure 4.78 Segmental displays. (a) Seven segments (numerical only) and (b) "British flag" sixteen segments (alphanumeric).

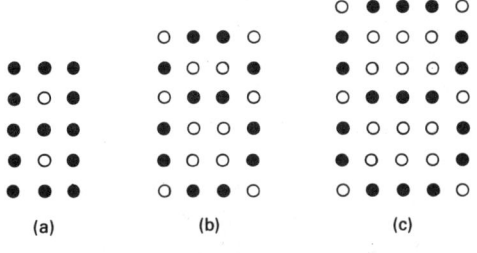

Figure 4.79 Dot-matrix displays. (a) 3 by 5 (numeric only), (b) 4 by 6 (alphanumeric), and (c) 5 by 7 (alphanumeric).

ning technique used in television sets). This can be interlaced (as used in television, and shown here), where the first field or scanning of the screen is indicated by the heavy lines and the interlaced second field is indicated by the dashed trace. Interlacing reduces "flicker" and allows slower updating of the CRT image. Noninterlaced scanning is usually used in computer graphics and this type of scan must be operated at a higher scanning rate to prevent flicker.

In contrast to raster scanning, "vector scanning" (shown in Figure 4.80b) is used if a high-quality picture must be displayed. Vector scans are more costly because analog circuitry is used to provide smooth continuous changes in deflection voltages that are necessary to make the beam move in smooth continuous paths.

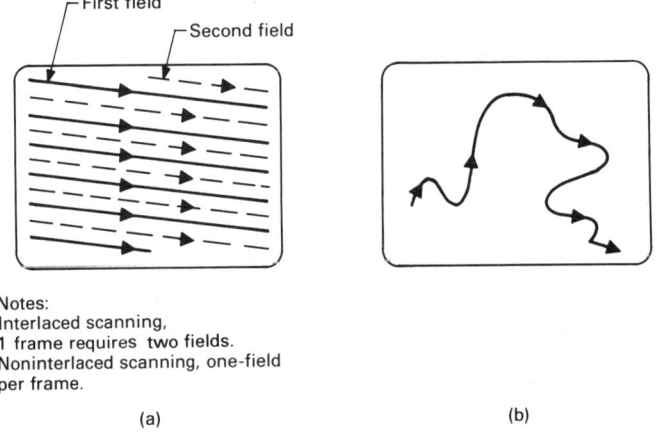

Figure 4.80 Cathode-ray-tube displays. (a) Raster scan and (b) rector scan.

When discussing CRT displays, you will hear reference to a "pixel," a *PIC*ture *EL*ement (the smallest dot the screen can display). The total number of pixels is an indication of the resolution or the quality of the image. The more pixels or individual dots that are capable of being presented on the screen, the better the picture resolution. This is very similar to the effects of grain size in photographic film.

Computer graphics is rapidly advancing to satisfy the large market for large, full-color, very-high-resolution, affordable displays. The move to color increases the memory requirements because information for red, green, and blue must be provided. High-speed screen updating must be used because of the large amount of information that must be transmitted to the screen.

Light-emitting diodes (LEDs). A few of the popular devices that are used to display letters and numbers on the front panel of electronic equipment are shown in Figure 4.81. Figure 4.81a shows a light-emitting diode. LEDs operate on relatively low voltages but require relatively high currents. LEDs were popular in wristwatches and hand-held calculators, but the high current drain of an LED display has reduced its popularity in battery-powered equipment. LEDs are still used in non-battery-powered displays, like microwave oven panels (where they are a popular display device).

Liquid crystal displays (LCDs). A "liquid crystal display" is shown in Figure 4.81b. There is no light generation involved in a liquid crystal display. Applying voltage to LCDs changes the polarization of the incident light that strikes the surface of the display and produces dark

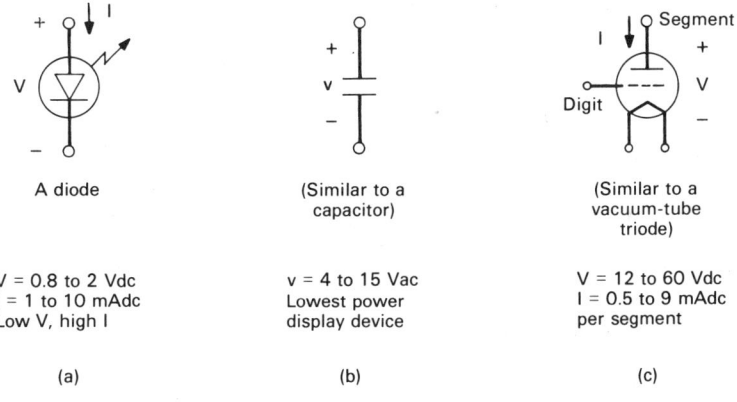

Figure 4.81 Popular display devices. (*a*) Light-emitting diodes (LEDs), (*h*) liquid crystal displays (LCDs), and (*c*) vacuum fluorescent (V-F) display.

regions that create the displayed characters. LCDs are therefore very low in power drain because they make use of the ambient light.

The electrical equivalent of an LCD is a capacitor. The voltage is changed on this "capacitor" to make the display dark or light. LCDs operate with relatively low ac voltages and require very low power. They are the lowest-power-drain electronic display device currently available and are therefore popular for battery-powered electronics. For example, an LCD is used for the digital multimeter that is used with this book. LCDs are also widely used in wristwatches and calculators, and relatively large flat-panel LCD displays for computers are even challenging the CRT as the display device of the future. When full-color LCD displays become available at low cost, the CRT may lose the dominant position it has held as the most popular display device for a computer.

Vacuum fluorescent (VF) displays. A "vacuum fluorescent" display is shown in Figure 4.81c. VF displays provide very nice-looking characters, but they are more complex and require relatively high operating voltages (20 to 40 V). VF displays are very similar to the old vacuum-tube triode except they use a phosphor-coated plate. They also have a filament that has to be powered in order to provide electron emission. VF displays are a little higher in overall cost, produce very pleasing characters, and are in high-volume usage as a result of their adoption for dashboard displays in automobiles.

Printers

Printers can be generally divided into "impact" and "nonimpact" categories depending on whether or not a hammer mechanism is used. There are many additional ways to provide a printed output for a computer.

Impact printers. Impact printers are available that use a rotating plastic wheel that contains multiple formed-type faces (called a "daisy wheel"), a hammer, and a ribbon to produce "letter-quality" characters. For highest printing rates, line printers are used that have a print wheel for every column across the page (higher-cost ink jet and laser line printers are also available). All of the print wheels are rapidly positioned and then a complete line of 132 characters is printed in one impact at rates ranging from a few hundred lines per minute to 1000 or 1500 lines per minute.

In addition to daisy wheel printers, higher printing speeds and lower cost can be obtained with dot-matrix printers. Dot-matrix printers use multiple dot hammers that strike a ribbon against a sheet of paper to create a matrix of closely spaced round dots that form the characters.

Large numbers of dots (and other tricks such as slightly shifting the platten position during printing) are used to achieve "near-letter-quality" characters (usually at a slower printing speed) from lower-cost dot-matrix printers. An additional benefit of the dot-matrix printers is that they can be used to print in many type fonts with various type sizes, and also they can provide a graphics capability that consists of making images with the dots.

Nonimpact printers. Ribbonless nonimpact printers also exist. Most nonimpact printers use specially treated heat-sensitive paper. These are called "thermal printers." Specially formed small filament heaters (like small branding irons) create hot regions that change the color of the specially treated paper to produce the characters.

"Ink jet" printers are also nonimpact. An electrically charged ink spray is electronically deflected to form a character that is "spray painted" onto the paper.

Very-high-resolution "laser printers" are also available. These relatively expensive nonimpact printers are used to replace typesetting and also to create high-resolution graphics for many jobs that used to require the services of a graphics artist and a printer. A laser printer electronically sets up a complete page and then uses an internal office-copier technique to print out a complete page of information at a time. Multiple copies of the same page are then available at a higher rate, limited only by the capability of the internal copier that is used.

Plotters

"Plotters" are devices that have movable pens that draw out patterns on paper. These are useful for producing graphs and line drawings. They are not well suited to providing the standard characters used for text.

A Computer for All Reasons

A number of years ago, computers were large expensive systems that were housed in special rooms and were accessible only by the people in large government agencies or major universities. Today, computers exist in various sizes; There are even the small special-purpose computers that control the operation of the engine in an automobile.

All computers operate in a similar manner, whether the smallest control-oriented processors or the largest highest-speed computers. Fundamental principles change very little. The biggest changes are the circuit and architectural innovations that are necessary to achieve high speed. The largest market for ICs today is in computer products and computer-based systems.

The introduction of the microprocessor has caused computing techniques to be used in all types of electronic systems. There has been a move away from the traditional logic solutions which used only collections of logic gates and flip-flops to the new alternative: programming. Even mechanical systems are using computer control. For example, the automotive industry is a large consumer of microprocessors that are used in a number of systems for electronic engine control, dashboard instrumentation, trip computers, monitoring and display of maintenance information, and in-car diagnostics.

Control-oriented processors

Control-oriented processors are very small digital controllers that are dedicated to a specific function. They are not intended for the general-purpose uses that computers are designed to handle. These control functions can be as simple as controlling the water sprinkler for the yard in a private residence. There are even controller-oriented processors built into small kitchen appliances such as food blenders. These are all used in simple control applications and are characterized by having the program stored in a ROM. The processor repetitively cycles through and executes this same program.

Eight-bit microprocessors and microcomputers

The microprocessor revolution really got started with the 8-bit microprocessors. These were the heart of fairly capable computer systems and allowed this new digital systems approach to be used in a wide range of applications.

There has been a continuing improvement in the capabilities of 8-bit microprocessors. Microprocessors are available that have memory (both ROM and RAM) on the chip, as well as additional control outputs and inputs. These single-chip "microcomputer" systems can be very capable and, yet, are quite low in cost. Each one of these microcomputer IC chips has to have a custom program tailored for its specific application.

Sixteen- and thirty-two-bit microprocessors

IC microprocessors are available for 16- and 32-bit computers. The increasing circuit density on IC chips is allowing very sophisticated computer systems to be provided by just a few IC chips.

The appearance of these high-performance microprocessors has caused another revolution in the applications for computers. There is an ever-increasing tendency to provide higher performance and additional capability. It is a problem for anybody who buys a digital system to suddenly discover that within 1 or 2 years that system is obsolete. For less money, systems with higher speed and more performance are available in a very short time following the purchase of any digital system. There continues to be a very rapid evolution in the whole computer area, and it is not over yet.

The mainframes

The largest of the computer systems are referred to as "mainframes." These computers are shrinking in size because the physical size of a computer system limits the ultimate speed that can be obtained. In fact, some of the highest-speed modern computers tend to be built in a cylindrical container to reduce the path length between the circuit components. There is even research today to put the major part of the silicon electronics for a sophisticated mainframe computer on one large chip of silicon as a means to reduce the time delays in the intercircuit communications.

Mainframe computers are also moving to extremely high speeds, support enormously large memories, and execute instructions at a very high speed. In the past, brute force circuit performance and parallel operation ("concurrent operation") were the two main ways to provide an advanced computer. Techniques today take advantage of the increased amount of circuitry that now can be placed on a single IC chip.

All of the traditional computer classifications are moving to higher and higher performance. Today, a midrange computer (a minicomputer) is as capable as a large mainframe was just a few years ago. It is very difficult to put labels on computers: these labels change as a function of time. The performance of computers is evolving so rapidly that even the technical descriptive words are obsolete every few years.

New fifth generation computers are operating simultaneously on large blocks of data. These machines are getting away from the idea of simply processing a sequential list of instructions, and the simultaneous processing can make 100-fold increases in the computational speed.

The multiuser environment

The increasing demand for computer support is partially solved by "timesharing" a number of users onto a single computer system. A "scheduler" is used to insure that each user periodically receives the attention of the computer.

This multiuser environment creates interest in protection because each user must be protected from the other users. If one program runs wild, it can convert other memory contents into garbage; so programs must not be allowed to interfere with each other.

One solution to this problem has been to assign each user a block of memory and then constrain that user to read and write only within this assigned memory space. Interest in maintaining privacy also forces each user to be allowed to read only certain memory blocks. For example, "key registers," used as memory access registers, contain a special code for privacy. If you know this code, you can have access to this block of memory.

There are always interesting stories about someone "getting into" a computer and starting wars, stealing secrets, giving himself or herself good grades in college, or stealing money. This is one of the most popularized problems in a multiuser environment.

With this background in digital techniques and computer basics, we'll now take a look inside a computer to find out how these techniques and circuits can be used to create something as awesome as a computer.

Chapter

5

The Techniques of Digital Computers

The fact that digital circuits can be somehow grouped together and made to calculate or create a computer seems very strange. The purpose of this chapter is to introduce some basic ideas that will make it easier to understand some of the internal ways that computers work. The intent is not to describe any given system but to use the simplest examples possible (not necessarily the most popular techniques) to indicate the internal operations of a computer. The motivation here is to try to make computers seem more real and to make it easier to understand the basic operations that are necessary for computers to accomplish some of their tasks.

How to Make Logic Circuits Compute

We will now consider some of the basic digital computational circuits to indicate how mathematical operations can be performed with interconnected logic circuits. We start with a description of a shift register because a shift register is often used within the internal circuitry of a computer.

A 4-bit shift register, shown in Figure 5.1, is assembled out of D-type flip-flops. This shift register is initialized by momentarily pulling the Clear line low. This loads 0's into all of the flip-flops. Then, the D input (shown to the left) brings in a serial bit stream of digital information. For every rising edge of the clock, the D input to each flip-flop will be clocked in.

For example, consider the shift register that is initially cleared and then the D input to the first flip-flop is brought high. At the first low-

198 Chapter Five

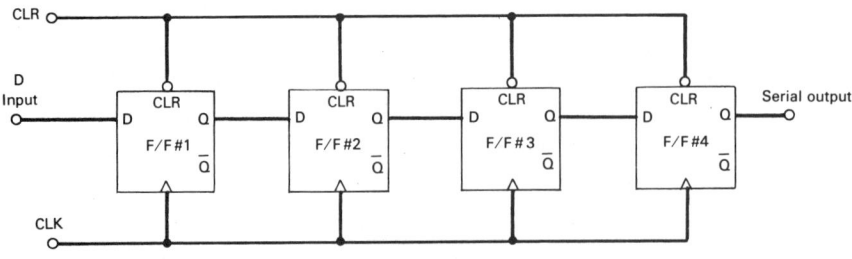

Figure 5.1 A shift register using D flops.

to-high transition of the clock, this 1 would be clocked into the first flip-flop (0s would be clocked into all of the other flip-flops). So a 1 would exist in the first flip-flop and 0s would remain in the other three. If the D input to the first flip-flop was then returned low, the next rising edge of the clock would clock the 1 output of the first flip-flop into the second flip-flop (and a 0 would be clocked into the first flip-flop). In subsequent clock cycles, this 1 would "walk through" and finally appear at the output of the fourth flip-flop.

A shift register can be used to accept a serial input data stream, capture it in flip-flops, and then provide that same word in a parallel format: a serial-to-parallel converter. Additionally, data can be loaded into a shift register in parallel and then shifted out in serial. Other uses for shift registers will be indicated in some of the circuitry that will now be considered.

A logic circuit that adds

A serial adder is used as an example to develop an understanding of how logic gates and shift registers can be interconnected to add two binary numbers.

To make a serial adder, two shift registers are used as shown on the left side of Figure 5.2. These registers hold the two binary numbers (A and B) that are to be added. The sum output will be loaded into the register to the right (labeled S) each bit in turn. The sum of the two inputs A and B will therefore be provided in this register at the end of the shifting sequence.

In the center of this figure is special logic to do the addition. A "carry flip-flop" is shown in the upper right-hand corner. The carry function has to be done with a flip-flop to provide memory, because a carry that may be generated in each bit position does not take effect until the next bit time. A memory element for the carry is therefore used so that the carry can be added in with the next-more-significant bits that are provided by the A and B registers.

The Techniques of Digital Computers   199

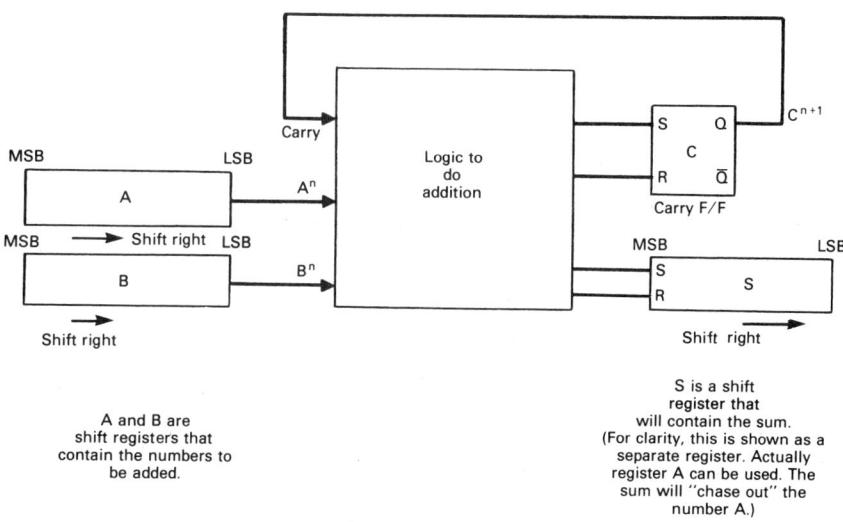

A and B are shift registers that contain the numbers to be added.

S is a shift register that will contain the sum. (For clarity, this is shown as a separate register. Actually register A can be used. The sum will "chase out" the number A.)

Figure 5.2 A block diagram of a serial adder.

Addition starts from the least-significant outputs of the A and B shift registers. The carry flip-flop for this first operation is initialized to provide a 0 carry (there is never a carry *into* the least-significant-bit position). If a carry is generated from the sum of the first two bits of each number, that carry will appear 1-bit time delayed and is then added into the second least-significant-bit digits.

The logic that is needed to provide for the serial adder is shown in the truth table of Figure 5.3. There are three inputs: A, B, and also the carry C. Two outputs are provided, one of which goes to the sum shift-register (S) and the other one goes to the carry flip-flop (C). All of the eight possible states of these three inputs are indicated, and the resulting states that are needed at the sum and carry outputs are shown.

At time $t = n$			At time $t = 2n + 1$	
A^n	B^n	C^n	S^{n+1}	C^{n+1}
0	0	0	0	0
0	0	1	1	0
0	1	0	1	0
0	1	1	0	1
1	0	0	1	0
1	0	1	0	1
1	1	0	0	1
1	1	1	1	1

Figure 5.3 Specifying the logic for the serial adder.

$S_s = \overline{A}\overline{B}C + \overline{A}B\overline{C} + A\overline{B}\overline{C} + ABC$

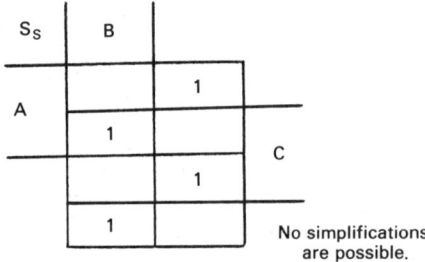

No simplifications are possible.

$R_s = AB\overline{C} + A\overline{B}C + \overline{A}BC + \overline{A}\overline{B}\overline{C}$

Note: $R_s = \overline{S}_s$

No simplifications are possible.

Figure 5.4 Looking for simplified logic for the sum flip-flop.

This logic is implemented with standard logic circuits (after being simplified by making use of the logic reduction technique that was described in Chapter 4).

Figure 5.4 shows the four-input combinations that create a 1 in the sum output, set sum (S_s). When these four minterms are plotted, it can be seen that there is no simplification possible (because the occupied squares are not adjacent). Therefore all of the logic shown for S_s has to be provided. The other four conditions on the inputs require the sum to be reset (R_s), so a 0 has to be shifted into the sum shift register.

The conditions that require the carry flip-flop to be set (S_c) are shown at the top of Figure 5.5. Again, there are four conditions of the inputs that require S_c. These four minterms have been plotted. Notice that three of these already have the carry previously set. It is not necessary to again set the carry because the carry flip-flop will remain in the set condition. So the four positions in the middle of this diagram (where the carry was previously true) are don't care (X) entries. Only the one minterm in the upper left-hand corner has to be picked up, and that one can be grouped with the adjacent minterm below it so the logic to set the carry flip-flop is simplified to A AND B. Reset carry is the complement of the set carry.

This logic to do serial addition is shown in Figure 5.6. With 8-bit words, in eight clock periods the sum would appear in the S register.

This is the basic logic needed for performing serial addition. Additional control circuitry has to be added to initialize this system and to clock it eight times. The main purpose in presenting this is to tie

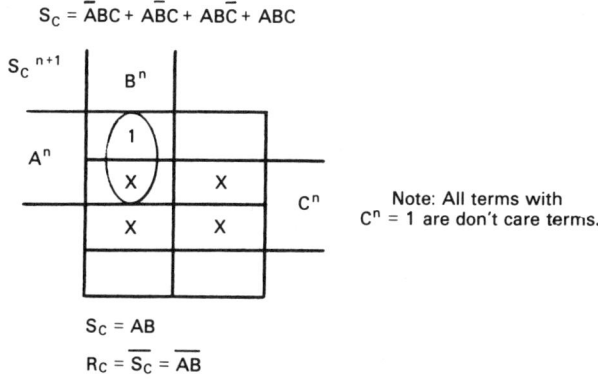

Figure 5.5 Looking for simplified logic for the carry flip-flop.

together some of the previous ideas and to show how logic gates and flip-flops can be interconnected to accomplish a mathematical operation.

An algorithm that multiplies

Multiplication of two numbers is difficult, whether in decimal or binary. The more familiar decimal multiplication of 45 × 32, shown in Figure 5.7a, is accomplished in a conventional way. First, consider the units digit (2) of the multiplier (32). The rules for multiplication provide the first entry (45 × 2 = 90). Then, move over to the 10's digit (3) of the multiplier (32). The rules for multiplication provide 45 × 3 = 135, but this product is also shifted over one place to the left (multiplying it by 10) before it is written under the previous product (90). These two numbers (90 and 1350) are then added to provide the answer (1440).

Multiplication can be accomplished by using simple rules, as computers like to do. Multiplication tables won't be needed. This different approach, shown in Figure 5.7b, is called "multiplication by successive addition."

The procedure starts by first looking at the units digit (2) of the multiplier (32). This 2 indicates to add the multiplicand (45) to itself twice. The 10's digit (3) of the multiplier (32) is next considered. This 3 indicates to add 10 × 45 (= 450) to the previous sum three times, to provide the answer of 1440.

A successive-addition multiplication algorithm (a sequence of rules to follow) for the decimal system is shown in Figure 5.8. A register called the "accumulator" (A) is where the answer accumulates. Assume the problem is to multiply 45 × 32. The multiplicand is 45 and the multiplier is 32.

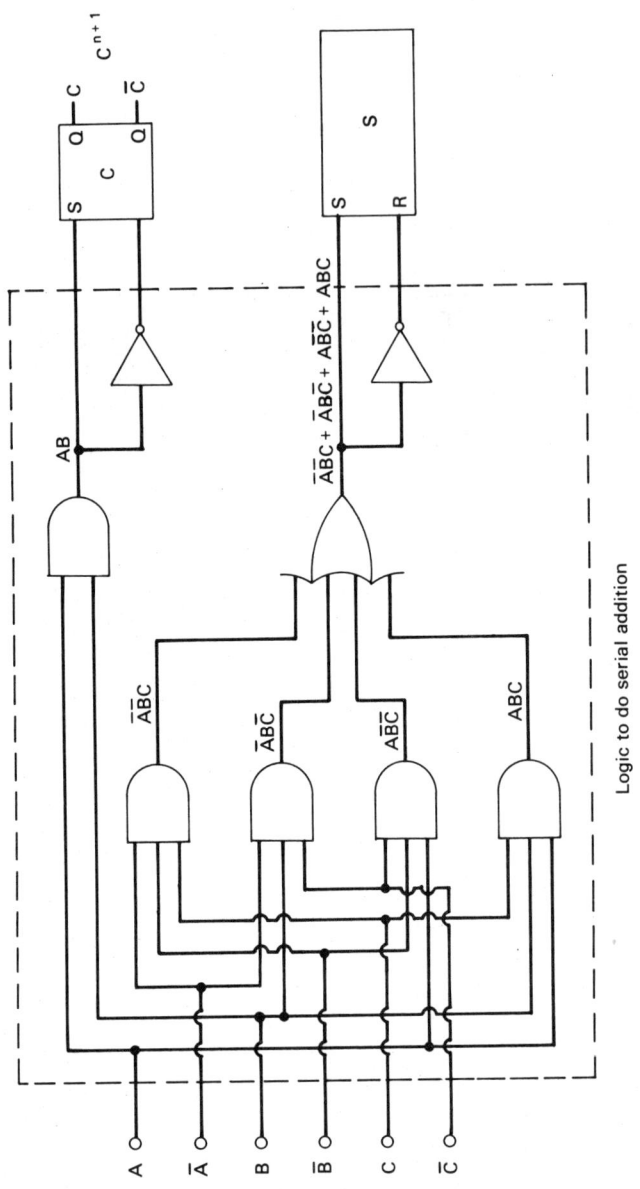

Figure 5.6 The logic to implement a serial adder.

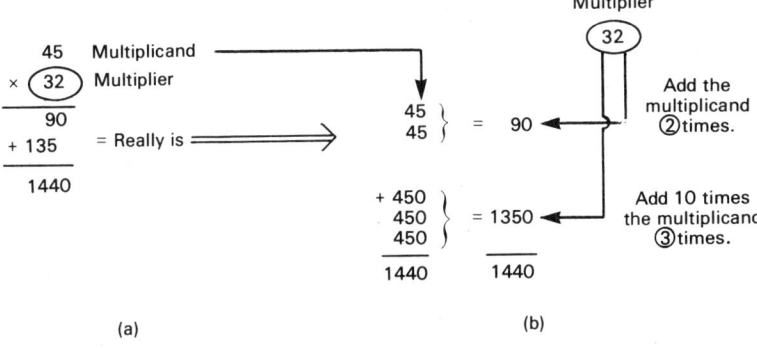

Figure 5.7 Another way to look at multiplication. (a) Conventional multiplication and (b) multiplication by successive addition.

This sequence of eight steps is the algorithmic solution to this multiplication problem. The technique of this algorithm is to notice that the units digit of the multiplier is 2, and this means to add the multiplicand to itself twice. Next, the 10's digit of the multiplier is considered. The multiplicand is shifted one place to the left, making it 450

The problem: 45 × 32 = product
　　　　　　　↑　　↑
　　Multiplicand　Multiplier

An algorithmic solution:	Accum. (A)	Multiplier
1. Clear the accumulator (A) and look at units digit of multiplier (U).	00	32 ←u
2. U > 0, so add multiplicand (M) to A and decrement (dec) U.	+ 45 (M) 45	31
3. U > 0, so add M and dec U.	+ 45 90	30 ←T
4. U = 0, so now look at 10's digit (T).		30
5. T > 0, so now shift M one digit to left and add to A and dec T.	+ 450 540	20
6. T > 0, so add shifted M and dec T.	+ 450 990	10
7. T > 0, so add shifted M and dec T.	+ 450 1440	00
8. T = 0, and all digits of multiplier = 0; therefore end. A = product.	1440 = product	

Figure 5.8 Decimal multiplication by a successive addition algorithm.

instead of 45 (this is multiplying by 10). Then, because the 10's digit of the multiplier is 3, 450 is added three times to the previous contents of the accumulator.

If each one of the steps of the algorithm is followed, the proper product ends up in the accumulator. Notice that 45 was not added to itself 32 times. The multiplicand (45) was added to itself twice because the units digit of the multiplier is 2. Then 450 was added to this sum a total of three times because the 10's digit of the multiplier is 3. This type of multiplication algorithm can also be used for binary numbers.

The binary multiplication algorithm is shown in Figure 5.9. Notice that the multiplicand is the binary number 1011, and the multiplier is 0011. In a similar manner, the least-significant bit of the multiplier is first considered: it is a 1. So the multiplicand is added to the accumulator once. That takes care of the least-significant bit (LSB) of the multiplier.

The next bit of the multiplier is then considered. Notice that it is also a 1. The multiplicand is shifted one place to the left, and a 0 is filled into the least-significant-bit position (this multiplies the multiplicand by 2). This is then added to the previous contents of the accumulator. Because the rest of the bits of the multiplier are both 0s, no more additions are needed. Only two additions were needed to achieve

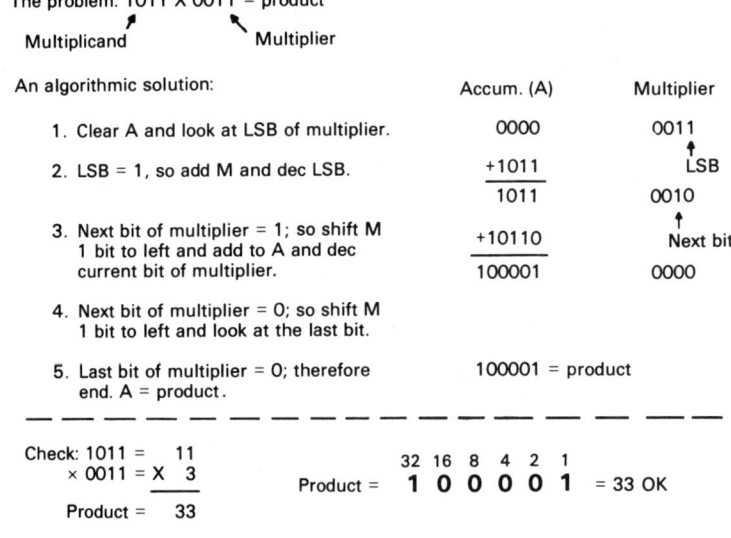

Figure 5.9 Binary multiplication by a successive-addition algorithm.

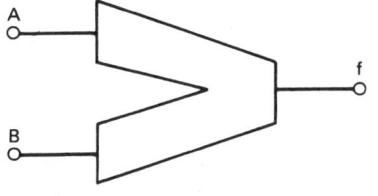

Figure 5.10 Symbol for the arithmetic and logic unit.

this multiplication. The check of this answer is also shown on the figure. This successive-addition multiplication algorithm is relatively simple in the case of binary numbers.

The arithmetic and logic unit (ALU)

Within every digital computer there exists circuitry that is collectively called the "arithmetic and logic unit." This ALU accomplishes all of the primitive logical and arithmetic operations for the computer. The symbol for an ALU is shown in Figure 5.10. There are two inputs (*A* and *B*) and these represent the binary numbers that are used in the operations. All possible outputs (shown here only as *f*) are simultaneously made available. Only one of these outputs will be passed to a particular register within the computer.

A few of the typical operations that are performed by an ALU are shown in Figure 5.11. More complex operations are realized by sequentially going through a number of these primitive ALU operations. In this manner, more complicated instructions can be executed by a computer.

In the "logic functions" that are provided are things called "shifts" and "rotates," which can be in either direction (right or left). The difference between these operations can be seen by considering the "logical right shift" shown in Figure 5.12. The main register shifts its contents

Logic functions	Arithmetic functions
AND	Add
OR	Subtract
XOR	Increment
Compare	Decrement
Set bit	Arithmetic left or
Reset bit	right shifts or
Test bit	rotates
Logical left or right shifts or rotates	

Figure 5.11 Some typical operations performed by the arithmetic and logic unit.

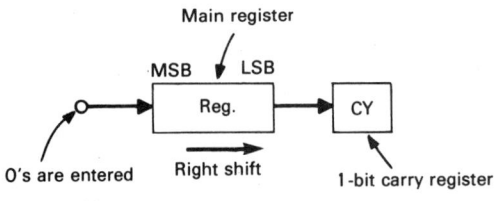

Figure 5.12 A logical right shift.

out the least-significant-bit end into the 1-bit carry register. This carry register is very useful because computer instructions can test the state of this register and respond differently if the carry is a logical 0 or a logical 1.

As part of the shift-right operation, 0s are entered at the most-significant-bit end of the main register. Therefore, after shifting eight times with an 8-bit register, the contents will have been removed (0s will fill all positions of the main register).

In contrast to shifts, there are also rotates. Figure 5.13 shows the logical right rotate. Notice that the rotation can be through the carry register, as shown in Figure 5.13a, in which first the least-significant bit is shifted out of the main register, into the carry register. The previous carry bit is simultaneously shifted into the most-significant-bit position of the main register. This exchange operation continues for a prespecified number of shifts. Because each bit is going through the carry register, it can be tested.

A right rotate with copy to the carry is shown in Figure 5.13b. This is an end-around exchange. The least-significant bit is tied back to become the input to the most-significant bit of the main register. In addition, as each bit comes out of the main register, it is also copied into the carry register. Again, tests can then be made on the carry bit.

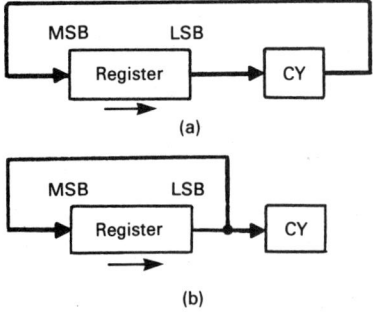

Figure 5.13 Logical right rotates. (a) Right rotate through carry and (b) right rotate, copy to carry.

In addition to the logical shifts, "arithmetic shifts" are also provided, as shown in Figure 5.14. A single arithmetic right shift divides a binary number by 2. Data enters the carry register from the least-significant-bit end. The original sign bit (the most-significant bit) is remembered and is repeatedly entered into the most-significant-bit position for each of the shifting operations. In this way the sign bit is not lost.

A single arithmetic left shift, Figure 5.16b, causes a multiplication by 2. Notice the difference here: 0s are entered into the least-significant-bit position, and the sign bit remains unchanged. The second most-significant bit is output into the carry register.

A Basic Computer

A basic computer consists of a set of working or scratch-pad registers, an ALU, control circuitry (to allow all of these subsystems to work together), memory, and input/output (I/O) devices. If the memory for the program is fixed in a ROM, the computer is called a "fixed-program computer," or a "controller." If a RAM is used for the program storage, it becomes a flexible "stored-program computer."

Conceptually, a computer has a data section and a control section. The data section contains the registers, functional units, and the interconnecting buses. The control section decodes machine-language instructions to provide a sequence of control signals that manipulate the data section in order to execute each instruction. Computers are compared based upon the rate at which they can execute instructions. This instruction-execution rate is usually given in units of a million instructions per second (MIPS, pronounced as it appears). Therefore you will hear of a 0.5- or a 1.5-MIPS computer.

The control section of a computer can also use a stored program (a microprogram) to decode the machine-language instructions. If this

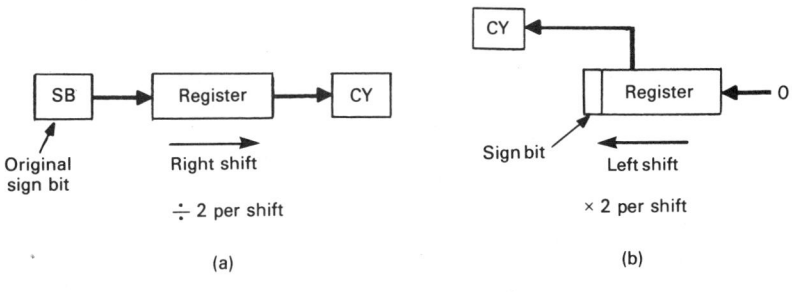

Figure 5.14 Arithmetic shifts. (a) Right shift and (b) left shift.

208   Chapter Five

microprogram can be modified by the user so that a customized instruction set can be provided, it is called a "microprogrammable computer."

The block diagram of a microprocessor

A microprocessor, together with external memory and other supporting peripheral equipment, makes up a computer system. The microprocessor consists of the central processing unit (CPU, which will be discussed later) and the ALU.

When microprocessors first were used to replace discrete logic, digital system designers were forced to expand their knowledge beyond hardware to also include programming and even the techniques of interfacing various I/O devices to a computer.

A successful 8-bit microprocessor is the Z80. Figure 5.15 shows a block diagram of the internal functioning of the Z80. These are the major functions for any microprocessor.

The first things to notice about this block diagram are the signals that enter and leave this basic processor. Notice that I/O lines are collected in three areas. At the top there is an 8-bit-wide parallel "Data

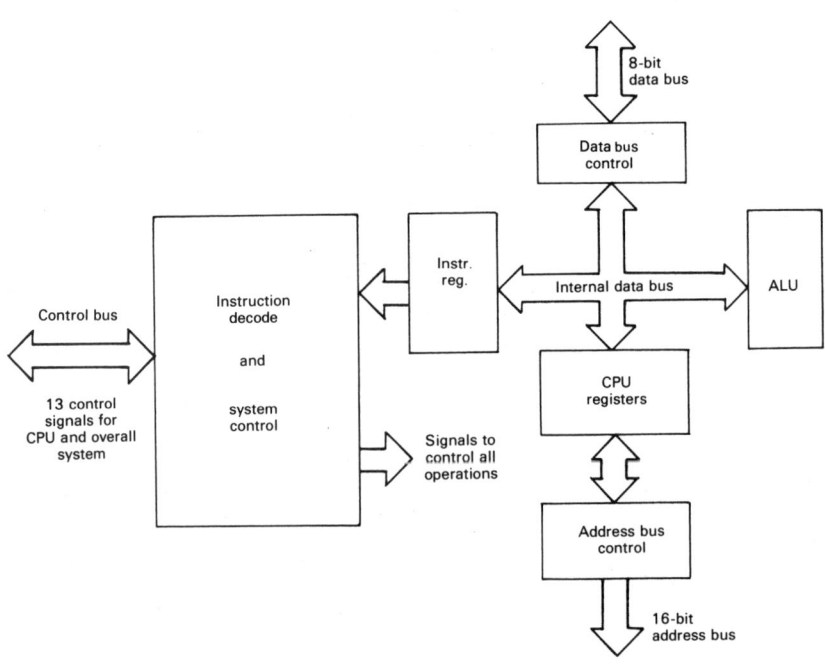

Figure 5.15 The Z80 CPU block diagram.

Bus." This is where data will be output by the processor or input to the processor. It is a parallel communication bus; therefore all 8 bits are simultaneously provided.

Immediately below this (at the bottom of the block diagram) is shown a 16-bit "Address Bus." This Address Bus is primarily used to address memory. Each location in memory will correspond to a particular bit pattern on this 16-bit Address Bus. In addition, if the processor is communicating with an input-output device (an external device other than memory), the address for that external device will also be provided on this Address Bus.

On the left side of this diagram, notice that there are 13 signals associated with the "Control Bus" that are used to control the overall computer system.

The central processing unit (CPU) is the name given to that particular processor (in the event that there is more than one) that is serving as the basic control for the computer system. The CPU controls, sequences, and coordinates all the activities of a computer. There is a tendency to use more than one processor in a given computer system to speed things up. Over the years, additional I/O processors have been added to efficiently get the data in and out of the main processor. The CPU is then freed from these chores and can more rapidly execute code and solve problems. As time goes on, more and more processors are being used in the same computer system. "Multiprocessing" is becoming common.

The largest block on the diagram of Figure 5.15 is the "Instruction Decode and System Control." The Instruction Decode is the logic circuitry that is used to interpret each instruction of a program. An instruction inherently specifies which specific events should take place. Once an instruction is obtained from memory, it is placed in the Instruction Register (shown near the center of this diagram, feeding the Instruction Decode and System Control Block).

Based on the bit pattern of the instruction, specific signals are generated to control operations within the CPU chip. This is indicated in the lower right-hand part of the Instruction Decode and System Control Block, where CPU Control Signals access registers, transfer the contents of certain registers to the ALU, and take a result from the ALU and put it back into a prespecified register.

All of the control for the computer is derived from instructions. To execute a given instruction, the System Control has to provide a number of sequential steps that involve many of the internal registers on the CPU chip. These internal registers act as temporary storage areas. Data are written into these registers, and the contents of these registers can be combined in logical and arithmetic ways by the ALU. Results from the ALU will return to these registers and also to primary memory.

In addition, special signals are generated that control the external functioning of the computer system. Data has to be written to and read from the data bus. Addressing information also has to be written to the address bus. Special control signals must be provided to external memory and I/O chips to indicate the particular operation the CPU is requesting and also the timing for that operation. For example, a signal is needed to indicate exactly when the memory should read the data that is made available on the data bus.

A data bus is usually the only way to get information into and out of a computer; all data flows on the data bus. The address bus is used to address the proper memory location to either read data from or write data to a prespecified memory location. The data bus and the address bus are both constantly busy handling information; therefore it is necessary that the external circuits be given timing signals (read and write strobes) so that the information can be picked off these buses at the correct time.

A hypothetical processor (which will be used to explain some of the basic operations that are involved) is shown in Figure 5.16. This figure has a little bit more detail. Internal registers, specifically called the "accumulator" and two general-purpose registers (GP_1 and GP_2), are shown. In addition, the "Internal Bus" is shown accessing the registers and the ALU.

Also shown on this diagram is the Program Counter (PC) (some other names for this are the Instruction Location Counter and the Instruction Pointer). The Program Counter is a register that keeps track of the sequence of addresses to the memory. The PC is incremented to read the contents of the next sequential memory location in order to execute all of the code (stored in memory) that is involved in a program.

The external Address Bus is shown at the top of this diagram. There is an Address Bus Control and a Memory Address Register (MAR) associated with the Address Bus. The MAR holds the address. The Address Bus Control then transfers this address to the external wires that make up the Address Bus. The memory address is therefore first moved into a holding register (the MAR), and when the time is right, this address is moved from the MAR out onto the external bus lines. In a similar manner, a Data Bus Control and a Memory Buffer Register are associated with the external Data Bus.

The Instruction Register is shown in the lower left-hand corner. This register will contain the current instruction that has been fetched from memory. This instruction will specify a particular operation to be performed by the computer.

When the instruction is loaded into the Instruction Register, all of the bits of the instruction are fed into decoding circuitry (called Control and Timing). This decode section determines what each instruc-

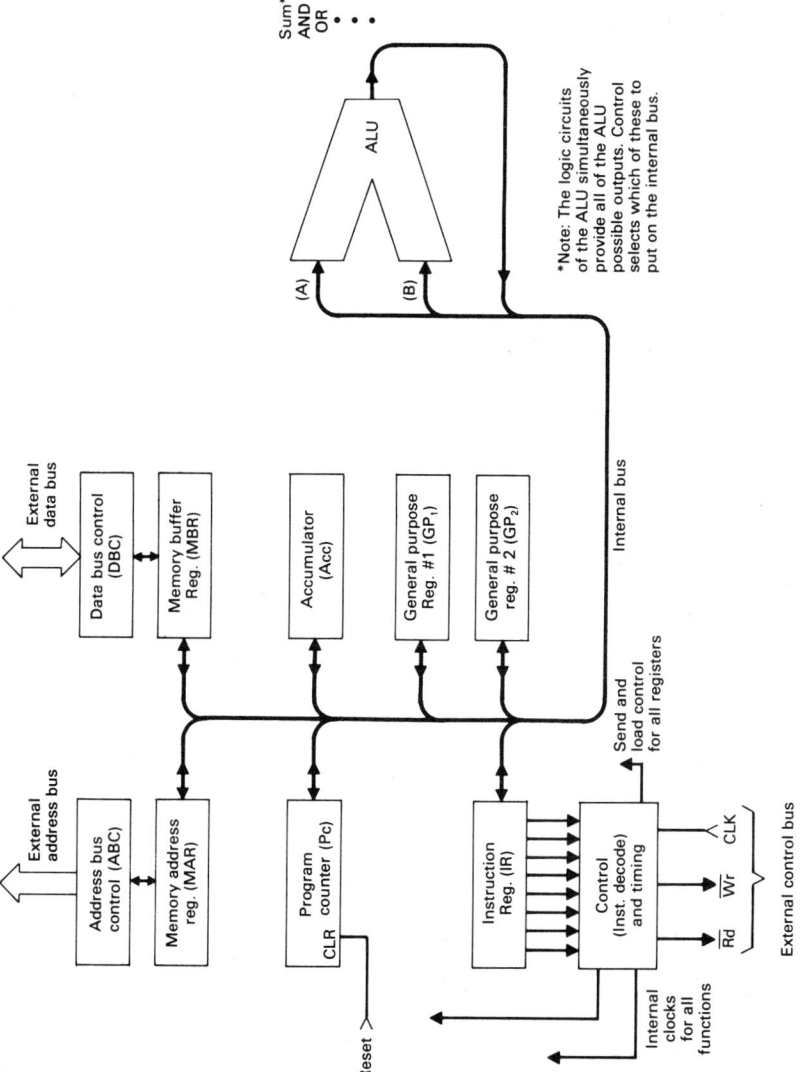

Figure 5.16 The major blocks of a simplified processor.

tion is requesting and generates the internal clocking and control that are needed to move the data around so that the instruction will be properly executed.

The outputs of the Control and Timing block are internal clocks for all of the operations that take place on the CPU chip such as the Send and Load control signals for all of the internal registers. A Send control means that a selected register is designated to output data to the Internal Bus. A Load signal implies that a selected register is designated to receive data from the Internal Bus. In this way data can be moved from one register to another, from registers to the ALU, or from the output of the ALU back into a prespecified register.

In addition, across the bottom of this block diagram are a couple of signals called "$\overline{Rd}$" and "$\overline{Wr}$." These are the read strobe and the write strobe, respectively. The bar over the symbol implies that the strobe is active when it is in the low state. These strobes specify the direction of the data flow from the CPU (all of the directional referencing is from the standpoint of the CPU). When the CPU wants data from memory (a memory read operation), the read strobe falls low. These strobes specify the type of operation (whether it is a read or a write), and the rising edge of these strobes also specifies the precise time that the data is valid. At the time of this rising edge, either the memory will read the data (if the data originated at the CPU) or the CPU will read the data (if the data originated from memory). The external clock input (CLK) is the main timing signal that keeps the system synchronized.

Some operating concepts

There are many unique circuits and operating concepts used in computer systems. A number of these will be presented in this section to serve as background material to aid the overall understanding of the internal operation of a computer.

Addressing memory. With 16 address bits available on the address bus, there is a possibility of 64K (2^{16}, or 65,536) unique memory addresses. One way of addressing 64K of memory is shown in Figure 5.17. The two most-significant bits of the address bus (A_{14} and A_{15}) separately feed a 1-of-4 decoder to provide four outputs that are called "Page-Select Lines." These select signals go to four separate modules of memory that are called pages of memory. Each page contains 16K (2^{14}, or 16,384) bytes of memory. The low-order bits of the address bus (A_0 through A_{13}) are simultaneously provided to every chip in memory. If 32K IC memory chips were used, there would be only two pages of memory (selected by A_{15}), and A_0 through A_{14} would then be provided to each chip in memory.

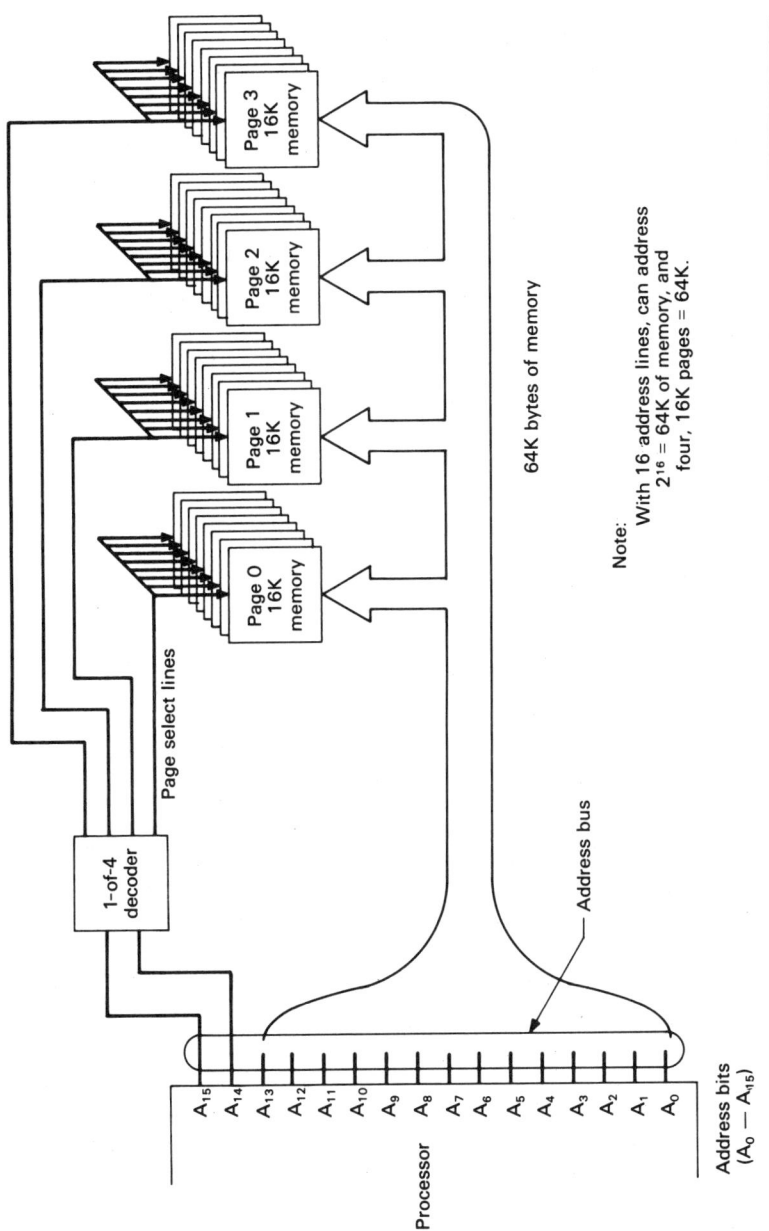

Figure 5.17 Addressing memory in 16K pages.

The organization of the IC memory chips shown here is 16K by 1. Notice that each page has to have eight separate memory chips to store the 8 bits of data. There is another possible organization for a 16K memory: 2K by 8.

The two most-significant bits of the address select the page in memory. The 14 lower-ordered bits then select the memory locations within each page. In this way, 64K of memory can be addressed by the processor.

A major part of a computer program has to do with obtaining the "operand," the data that will be operated on by the instruction. A number of different ways of obtaining this data have been derived: from the next memory location following the instruction (immediate), from an internal register, or from memory (a memory address must then be determined).

"Immediate addressing" is shown in Figure 5.18. With immediate addressing, the byte of data immediately follows the instruction in the next sequential memory address. In this mode, the instruction will indicate to the CPU to read the memory again; the next byte will be the operand. This is called immediate addressing because the operand immediately follows the instruction in memory.

"Immediate, extended addressing" is shown in Figure 5.18b. This is very similar to immediate addressing and is a way to provide a long word. The next 2 bytes in memory will now contain the 16-bit operand.

In other memory addressing techniques, ways are provided to generate or compute the memory address that will locate the operand. A couple of these, shown in Figure 5.19, derive the memory address by adding a signed data-byte "displacement" to the contents of a CPU register.

For example, in Figure 5.19a, "relative addressing" is shown that makes use of the Program Counter. The Program Counter is always pointing to the next instruction to be fetched out of memory; so the Program Counter provides a local memory for this next address. In relative addressing the next memory location following the instruction contains a signed data byte that will be added to (or subtracted from)

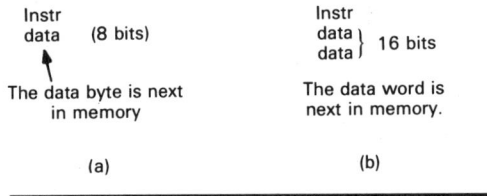

Figure 5.18 (a) Immediate addressing and (b) immediate extended addressing.

```
INSTR                              INSTR
coded data address (an 8-bit       coded data address (an 8-bit
   signed 2's complement              signed 2's complement displacement
   displacement from program          from an index register)
   counter)
          (a)                                  (b)
```

Figure 5.19 Addressing using a displacement. (*a*) Relative addressing and (*b*) indexed addressing.

the contents of the Program Counter. This computed memory address will provide the operand that is needed by the current instruction.

Another example, shown in Figure 5.19*b*, is called "indexed addressing." This is similar to relative addressing. The difference is simply that the data byte, instead of being added to the contents of the Program Counter, is added to a separate 16-bit register. This separate register is called an "Index Register." Indexed addressing is very handy for accessing data from a table that has been set up in memory. The Index Register then contains the starting address of the table. The displacement is added to this starting address and, in this manner, can easily address the complete contents of the table.

Some additional memory-addressing modes are shown in Figure 5.20. "Extended addressing" is shown in Figure 5.20*a*. The next 2 bytes following the instruction in memory are the memory address for the operand. This provides 16 bits of memory-address information and can therefore access the operand from any desired location within memory. Relative addressing and indexed addressing (which were previously described) make use of an 8-bit signed number to calculate the memory address. This restricts the total addressing capability to be within -128 to $+127$ memory addresses in relation to the contents of the Index Register or the Program Counter. In contrast to this, extended addressing provides complete freedom to go anywhere in memory.

"Register indirect addressing" is shown in Figure 5.20*b*. This implies that two of the internal 8-bit registers or one 16-bit register contains the memory address of the operand. As the instruction is decoded, the control logic will grab the 16-bit data from the prespecified registers

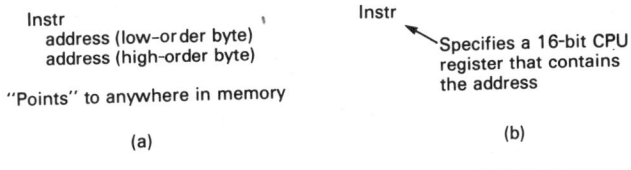

Figure 5.20 Some additional memory addressing modes. (*a*) Extended addressing and (*b*) register indirect.

and load this data into the Program Counter so that the operand can be fetched from any part of memory.

The data bus. Figure 5.21 shows how the data bus is physically connected to one of the pages of memory. This is an 8-bit data bus, so the data bit positions on the bus range from D_0 to D_7. The memory organization is 16K by 1; therefore each of the eight chips within the memory page ties to a different one of the bit lines of the data bus.

The read and write strobes are shown entering each memory chip to provide two-way information flow. Information can come from the memory to the CPU or from the CPU to the memory. Remember that reading or writing is always based on the CPU; so, for example, if the CPU is providing information to the memory this is called a "write" operation.

The control signals that are supplied to the memory for a read operation are shown in Figure 5.22. The upper strobe is called the "chip select" ($\overline{CS}$), which is active low. The chip select for our example of four 16K memory modules is derived from the most-significant 2 bits of the address bus. The 1-of-4 decoder will generate a chip select for all of the memory chips within the selected page.

The read strobe will fall within the active low portion of the chip-select signal. This is another signal that is active low, so it is specified

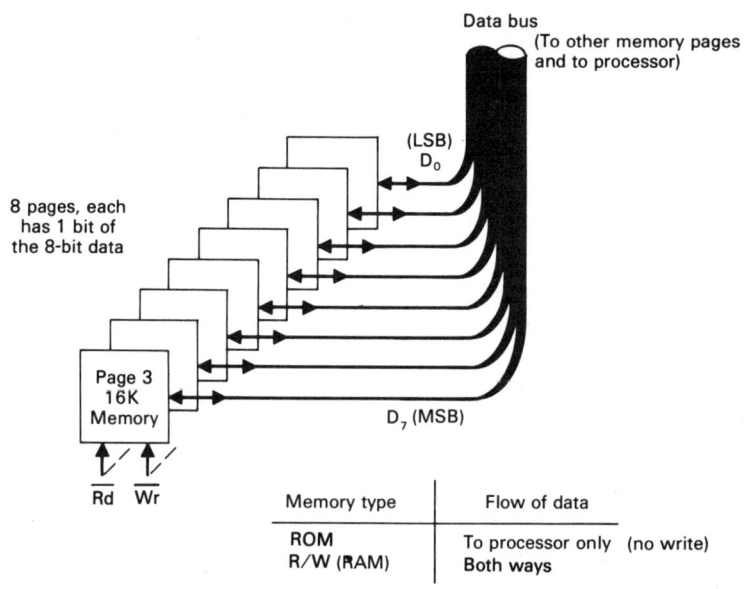

Figure 5.21 Data bus access to memory.

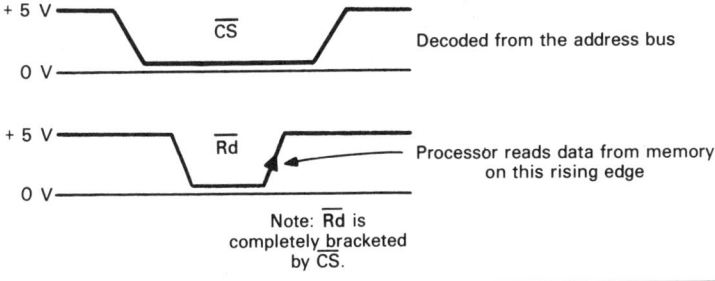

Figure 5.22 The control signals for a read operation.

as $\overline{Rd}$. Not only does this indicate a read operation, but also the time that the memory should read the data bus is established by the rising edge (the trailing edge) of this strobe.

The control signals for a write operation are shown in Figure 5.23. Notice again that the chip-select signal must be provided so that a definite memory location is being specified. The write strobe again fits inside of the chip-select pulse. The rising edge of the write strobe specifies the time when the memory should read the data from the data bus.

Register transfers on the internal bus. Most CPUs make use of an internal bus structure to allow register-to-register transfers and also register-to-ALU transfers (and vice versa). The circuitry to allow tying a number of registers to common wires is shown in Figure 5.24. This example shows three registers, A, B, and C. For simplicity, only the two least-significant bits of each register are shown. A register of 8 or 16 bits would be just a continuation of the type of circuitry shown here.

Notice the use of the D flip-flops and also the tri-state bus drivers that are used on the outputs of each one of these flip-flops. The rising edge of a Load command will allow all of the flip-flops associated with that register to pick up data from the bus. To put data onto the bus,

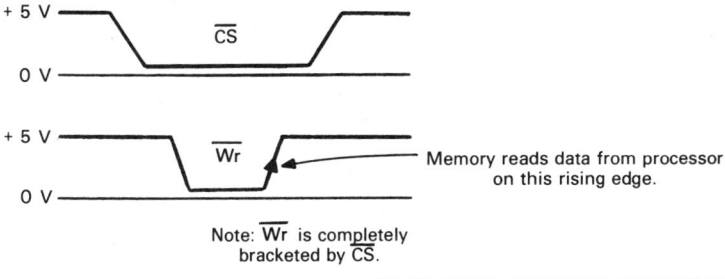

Figure 5.23 The control signals for a write operation.

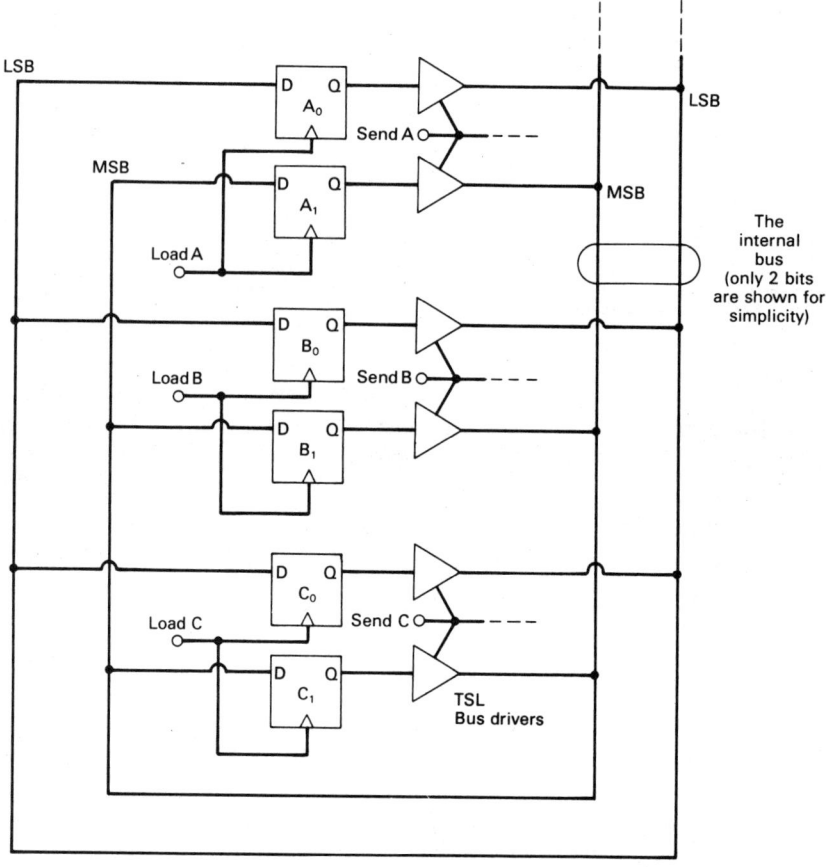

Figure 5.24 Register-to-register transfers on an internal bus.

the appropriate Send signal is activated, and the tri-state bus drivers will then "drive the bus lines" (make the appropriate voltages appear on the bus lines).

The control signals first activate the bus drivers and then delay a little bit to make sure that the logic voltages are properly established. Then one of the Load strobes will make a low-to-high transition. In this way, information can be sent from one register to any of the other registers that are tied to this bus.

The internal clocks. A microprocessor uses a relatively high-speed clock, such that a number of clock "ticks" can fit within one overall instruction fetch or execute cycle. An example of this is shown in Figure 5.25 in which seven sequential timing pulses are provided within the fetch and execute cycles. These timing signals control *when* the internal CPU

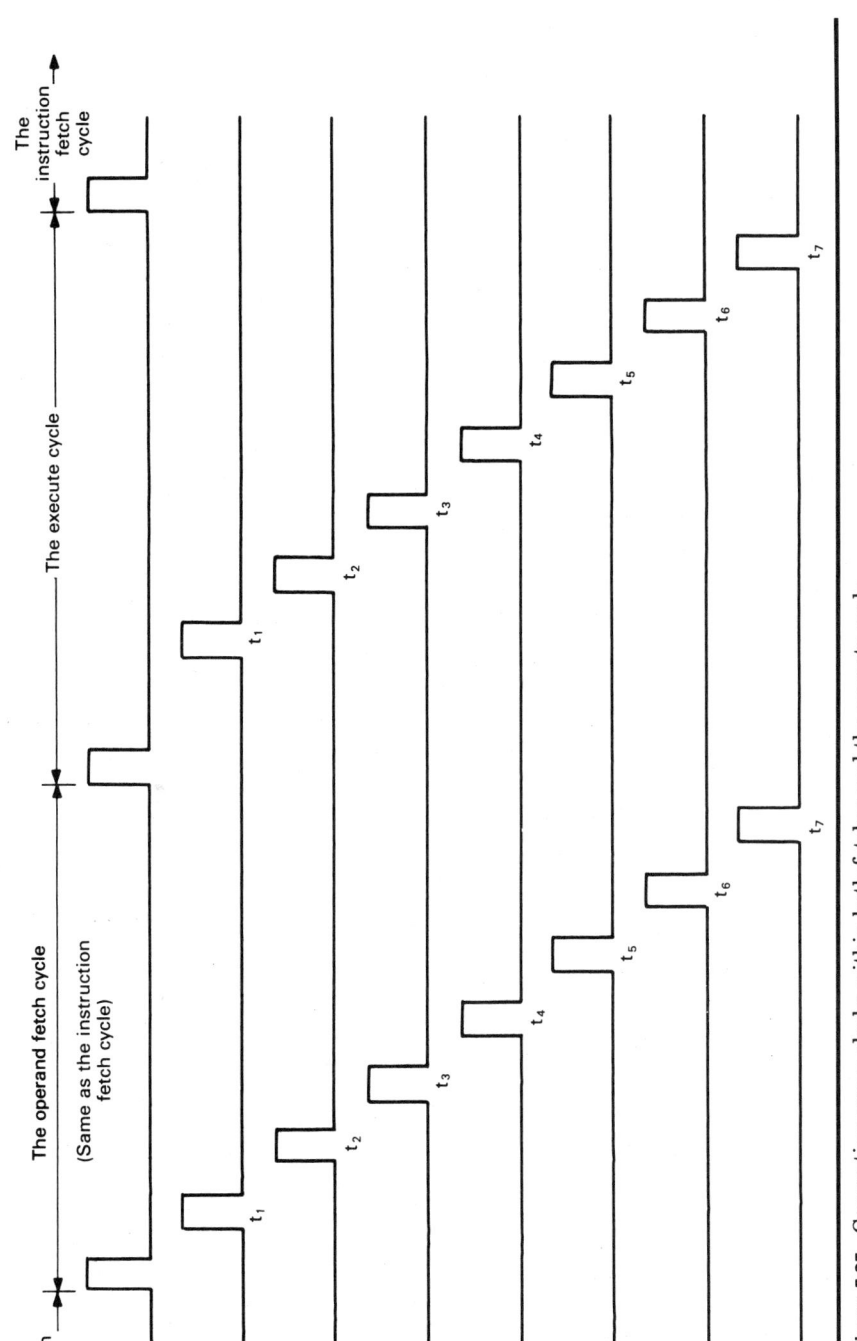

Figure 5.25 Generating seven clocks within both fetches and the execute cycle.

events happen, and control signals insure that the proper registers are activated to execute the current instruction.

Control. Internal control signals are derived by decoding the instruction word. An Instruction Decoder determines what operation is being requested by decoding the word in the instruction register.

An example of this is shown in Figure 5.26, where only a 3-bit instruction is used for simplicity. The instruction has been loaded into the instruction register and the 3 bits, IR_0, IR_1, and IR_2, are then passed over to a 1-of-8 Instruction Decoder. With 3 binary bits, eight codes are possible, such as HALT, AND, NOT, ADD, LOAD A, STORE A, JUMP, and NO OP. In a manner similar to this, an 8-bit instruction word can specify a maximum of 256 total instructions (although a smaller number is usually adequate).

Some typical instructions. An instruction set consists of internal scratchpad register instructions, an accumulator- (or one particular register) specific instructions, transfer of control instructions (jumps in the sequencing of the program execution), input/output instructions, and processor control instructions. Systems designers frequently select a microprocessor based on the particular set of instructions that has been provided, because certain instructions are more beneficial for a partic-

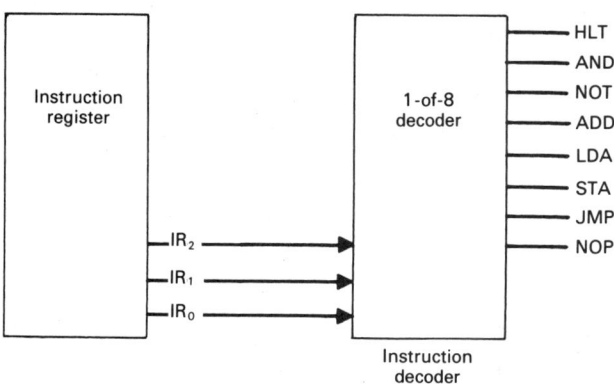

Note: This shows only 8 instructions as a simplified example (actual machines have many more). For example, the Z-80 microprocessor has 158 instructions.

Figure 5.26 Decoding the contents of the instruction register to determine control action.

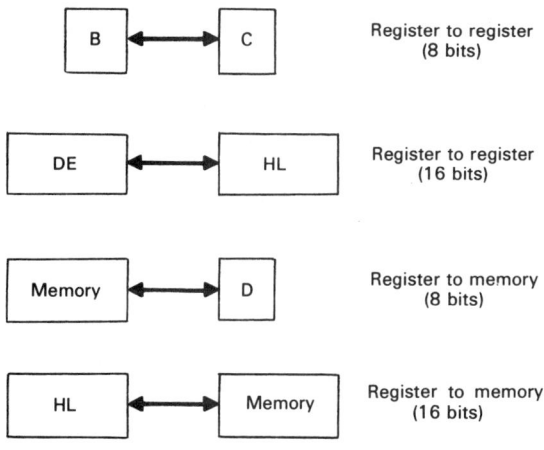

Figure 5.27 Load and exchange instructions.

ular application. If the particular instruction set is a good match for the application, more efficient programs can be written.

As an example of some of the categories of instructions that are provided by microprocessors, Figure 5.27 shows the Load and Exchange instructions. There are a number of these to allow such things as 8-bit register-to-register transfers, 16-bit register-to-register transfers, memory-to-register transfers, or register-to-memory transfers.

In Figure 5.28, the "block transfer" and "search" types of instructions are shown. The block transfer is simply an instruction that specifies a starting location in memory where a particular block of data is to be picked up and then moved to another location within memory.

The search instruction is shown in Figure 5.28b. This is a way to find the memory address that contains a particular byte of data. The

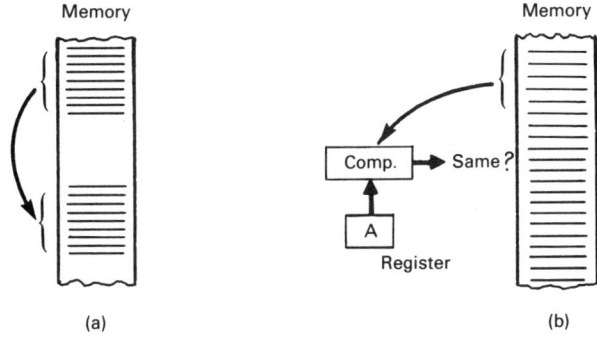

Figure 5.28 Block transfer and search instructions. (a) Block transfer and (b) search.

desired byte is loaded into the A register and successive memory locations are then read and compared to this reference byte. When the same byte is found, that memory address is stored in a register. These search operations can find the memory addresses of the successive letters that make up a searched-for word. An example of the use of this search algorithm is in a word processor program in which it is desired to find every instance where a particular word is used and to then either delete it or correct the spelling.

Some examples of arithmetic and logic instructions are given in Figure 5.29. These are the standard simple mathematics of add, subtract, increment (add 1), or decrement (subtract 1), plus the logical AND, OR, exclusive OR, and compare (is one number less than, greater than, or equal to another).

A whole group of instructions, called "bit manipulations," or "bit twiddling," are possible with some microprocessors. A particular register or memory location is specified and any one of the individual 8 bits within this register can then be accessed. This particular bit can be tested, set, or reset.

Subroutines. In writing programs, it is often convenient to use a given block of code more than one time. This one block of code is called a "subroutine." Program execution can jump to this subroutine whenever this identical sequence of operations must be performed. This not only prevents having to write out this same block of code every time it is used, but also the use of subroutines requires less space in program memory.

When a subroutine is "called," the program execution jumps to the particular place in memory that contains the subroutine. The computer executes this block of code, and then program execution jumps back to the next memory location from where it originally left. A "return" from a subroutine is the instruction that places the return address back into the Program Counter so the program execution will return to the proper segment of code.

Figure 5.30 shows the Jump, Call, and Return instructions which are used to force the program execution out of the standard flow. Jumps can be "unconditional," meaning "go start executing the code from this

Arithmetic	Logic
Add	XOR
Subtract	Compare
Increment	AND
Decrement	OR

Figure 5.29 Arithmetic and logic instructions.

Jump (unconditional)

Jump (conditional)

Call a subroutine

Return from a subroutine

Figure 5.30 Program transfer instructions.

new memory address." A "conditional" jump can depend on many conditions, a few of which are if an answer produces a negative sign (if there is a carry) or when a register is finally decremented to zero. This last jump condition allows an easy implementation of a program loop (a block of code that is repeatedly entered while a counter is decremented following each cycle, such as summing the numbers from 1 to 10). Program loops will continue cycling until a certain condition is reached (such as, has this loop been entered 10 times yet?), and then the program will jump out of that loop and continue with the main program.

I/O instructions. Typical I/O devices are printers, monitors, modems, and disk memories. Instructions that involve these input or output devices are called "I/O instructions." I/O instructions allow communication between the CPU and I/O devices.

Fetching and executing instructions

The operation of a digital computer is often characterized as simply "fetching" an instruction, fetching an operand, and then executing the instruction. The individual instructions are fetched from memory out of a sequence of instructions called a "program." This involves first fetching an instruction, then decoding that instruction (determining what is needed), incrementing the Program Counter, calculating the address for the operand (the data to be operated upon), fetching the operand, and finally executing the instruction. Once that instruction has been executed, the next instruction is fetched.

An instruction fetch cycle is shown in Figure 5.31. The time intervals t_1 through t_7 allow a number of separate things to be accomplished in order to fetch information from memory.

In the first time period (t_1) the control circuitry issues a Send command to the Program Counter. The Program Counter contains the address of the next instruction to be fetched from memory. The Send command moves the contents of the Program Counter into the Memory Address Register (MAR) and also into the A register. The memory

Intercycle time periods	Action provided by control circuit	Comments (what is happening)
t_1	"Send" PC — "Load" MAR & A	Copy PC to MAR and allow ABC to set up address bus signals. Also copy PC into A register of ALU.
t_2	"Send" 1 — "Load" B	Put 1 in B register of ALU.
t_3	"Send" SUM — "Load" PC	Increments PC to next sequential memory location.
t_4	Output $\overline{Rd}$ on control bus and input data bus to MBR	Output instruction from memory and load it from data bus to MBR.
t_5	"Send" MBR — "Load" IR	Copy the new instruction into IR and begin to decode it for next control sequence.
t_6	—	t_6 — not needed for an instruction fetch.*
t_7	Enter fetch operand mode	The instruction has been fetched — now fetch the operand.

*Note: These extra times can be used to immediately execute some simple instructions (called "one-cycle" instructions).

Figure 5.31 The instruction fetch cycle.

address is therefore moved into the buffering register (the MAR), and the control system will then output that address onto the address bus.

Loading the contents of the Program Counter into the A register is done to increment the memory address so it will "point" to the next sequential location in memory. Part of this incrementing operation is continued in the second time slot (t_2). The number 1 (the incrementing amount) is loaded into the B register. In the third time slot (t_3) the sum output (A plus B) of the ALU will be loaded back into the Program Counter. This increments the Program Counter; it has just been "bumped" (advanced by one count) and is now pointing to the address of the next instruction to be fetched.

In the next time slot (t_4), the Read strobe control is output to the memory and the resulting data that the memory places on the data bus is read into the Memory Buffer Register (MBR).

During t_5, the contents of the MBR are loaded into the Instruction Register. This instruction fetch is completed by the fifth time slot. Time slots t_6 and t_7 are not needed for this instruction fetch. The last time slot (t_7) will signal the control circuitry that the fetch operation has been completed and the operand fetch cycle should begin.

An example of how the control signals are generated to perform a fetch cycle is shown in Figure 5.32. This is a schematic diagram following the sequence of events that were charted in the previous figure to indicate the logic circuitry that is necessary to provide the internal control within a computer.

The lower control shown in this figure (the fetch/$\overline{\text{execute}}$ control), when in the 1 state, puts the computer system into a fetch cycle. This enables all of the AND gates shown in this diagram.

The events that take place to complete an execute cycle for an exclusive OR instruction (involving the Accumulator and the General-Purpose Register No. 1) are listed in Figure 5.33. In the first time period (t_1) the contents of the Accumulator are loaded into the A register of the ALU. This provides one input to the ALU for the exclusive OR operation. In the second time slot (t_2) the contents of the general-purpose register no. 1 (GP_1) are loaded into the B register of the ALU. During t_3, the exclusive OR output of the ALU is put on the Internal Bus and the Accumulator is instructed to receive this output. The exclusive OR instruction is therefore executed in three time slots.

In the last time slot (t_7) the internal Fetch and Execute flip-flop is triggered to transfer back into a fetch cycle to acquire the next instruction from memory. This toggling between fetch and execute is continually going on within a computer.

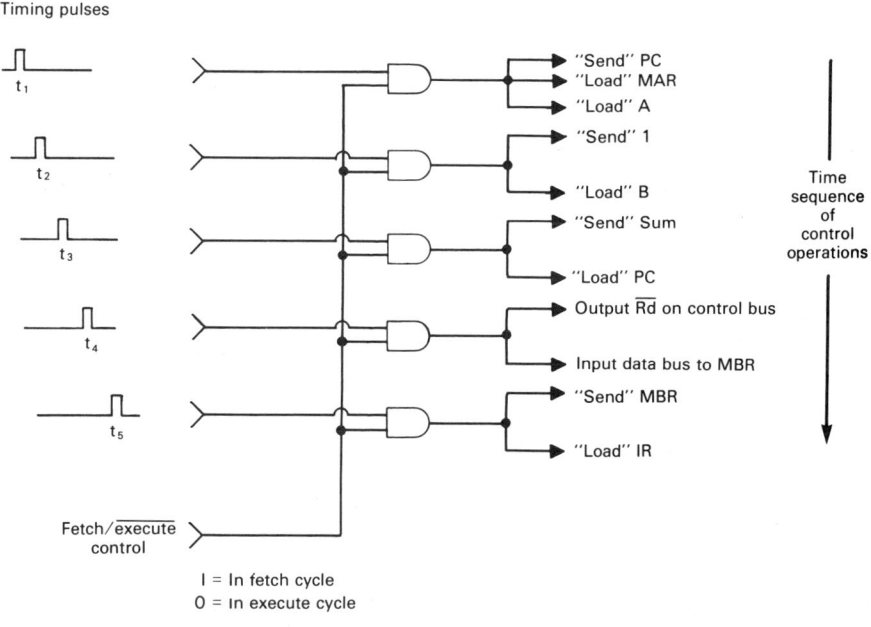

Figure 5.32 An example of some of the control circuitry for a fetch cycle.

Intercycle time periods	Action provided by control circuits	Comments (what is happening)
t_1	"Send" Acc — "Load" A	Load the contents of the accumulator into the A register of the ALU.
t_2	"Send" GP_1 — "Load" B	Load the contents of the general-purpose register no. 1 into the B register of the ALU.
t_3	"Send" XOR — "Load" Acc	Load the XOR output of the ALU into the accumulator.
t_4	—	($t_4 \rightarrow t_6$ provide room for executing more complex instructions.)
t_5	—	
t_6	—	
t_7	Enter instruction fetch cycle	Last instruction has been executed; therefore now enable the next instruction fetch cycle.

Figure 5.33 The execute cycle for an XOR of the accumulator and a general purpose resister.

Inputs and outputs (I/O)

In addition to communicating with memory, a computer system also communicates with particular input and output devices such as printers, disk memory, cathode ray tube (CRT) displays, and terminals.

Special I/O handling. In some microprocessors, special instructions are available to handle I/O devices. For example, the Z80 microprocessor chip has memory-read and memory-write strobes in addition to I/O-read and I/O-write strobes. For I/O instructions in the Z80, the 16-bit address bus is split and provides two identical 8-bit I/O addresses. This allows up to 256 I/O addresses or I/O devices, a very substantial number.

Some microprocessors even have special internal instructions that allow handling I/O routines such as taking a block of data from memory and outputting this data block to an I/O device. A starting memory address pointer and a byte counter are initialized, and an I/O address is specified so that this block move can be accomplished using only one instruction.

Memory mapping the I/O. In those microprocessors that do not provide special provisions for handling I/O, the input/output devices have to be addressed using part of the memory-address space. This is often called "memory-mapped I/O" because a part of the memory address space is used for the I/O devices.

Different-sized blocks of memory addresses can be allocated for I/O. In the previous example, with four 16K pages of memory, if only three of these pages of memory (48K of RAM) were needed in the application, an entire page of memory could be devoted to I/O. This means that one of the chip-select pulses coming out of the 1-of-4 decoder would indicate that an I/O device, rather than a memory device, is being addressed. In this example, 16K of memory is entirely devoted to I/O devices, even though only two or three I/O devices may be actually used in the application.

Interrupting the CPU. Interrupt instructions allow an I/O device to rapidly get the attention of the CPU. Certain rare events that are cumbersome to program but are important enough for immediate attention when they arise make use of interrupts (which are unexpected subroutine calls). An interrupt is very similar to a child in a classroom raising his or her hand to interrupt the teacher. This hand raising would be called "asserting an interrupt." Typically, the teacher will see that a hand has been raised and may just nod to the student. This "acknowledges" the interrupt. There will usually be a little delay because the teacher will finish whatever he or she was in the middle of and then will ask what is needed by the interrupting child. A computer works in a similar way.

If an I/O device does not make use of interrupts, it can be under "program control" and is called "programmed I/O." The CPU occasionally "polls" the I/O devices, asking them if they need attention.

The CPU, as soon as it finishes executing its current instruction, will address an interrupting I/O device to find out what is needed. If this is a printer, operating as an "interrupt-driven" I/O device, the interrupt might mean that the local buffer memory in the printer is empty and needs to be refilled with the next block of data to be printed.

Another typical example of an interrupt is to signal that the power-supply voltage is starting to fall. If special circuitry is in place that can detect this, the CPU can be interrupted and notified that a complete loss of power is just a few seconds away. The CPU, in the short time remaining, can then save any critical information by writing it out onto a floppy disk or some other nonvolatile memory. Therefore, valuable data will not be lost because of a power failure.

Interrupts can be "masked interrupts" or "nonmaskable interrupts." A masked interrupt can be turned on and off under program control. Interrupts can therefore be disabled while the CPU is operating in a certain section of the program in which disturbance by an interrupting device is not desired.

A nonmaskable interrupt (NMI) is a higher-priority interrupt. This would be used in the previous example to signal the approach of a power failure. Nonmaskable interrupts always have access to the CPU.

Real-time clocks. In many applications of computers, it is convenient to know the time of day and also the date and day of the week. This information is provided by continuously running clock circuitry that can be used to put dates and times on the printed output of a computer. This is a convenience for later determining when an output was generated. This special circuitry is called a "real-time clock." Real-time clocks are also useful for signaling special events such as birthdays, controlling the automatic transmission of data over the telephone lines to occur during the reduced rate times, or automatically turning on lights as a deterrent to burglary.

Computer Architectures

In the design of a computer system, there are many trade-offs that are typically made that are based on the intended application. Some of these trade offs involve the internal design and the operating modes that will be provided.

These internal details are called the "architecture" of the computer. Computer architecture has been defined as the attributes of a computer as seen by a machine-language programmer. This includes the instruction set, the instruction format, the operation codes (op codes, the two to four characters that are used to describe an instruction), the addressing modes, and all of the internal registers and memory locations that may be directly manipulated or tested by a machine-language programmer.

Harvard

Computer architectures have evolved steadily from the initial Harvard architecture that separated a mechanical type of external program memory from the internal electronic data memory. Even today, this separation of the program memory from the data memory is still referred to as a Harvard architecture.

Stored program

A big step forward in computer architecture came when John Von Neumann, one of the early computer scientists, picked up on an idea that was first conceived by Babbage nearly 150 years ago. This idea was to move away from the existing Harvard architecture and to recognize that the program can also be placed in internal memory, the "stored program" concept. Today, the "Von Neumann" (also known as a Princeton-class computer), stored-program architecture is very common. Only some of the smaller control-oriented processors still find advantages with the Harvard type of architecture.

Stacks

A "stack" is a number of internal registers or an external block of memory that is linked together in a manner like the stacks that are used in cafeterias to store trays. Trays are stacked on a spring-loaded table. As each tray is removed, the springs push up the next tray into position. As new trays are added at the top, the springs compress, making the top tray on the stack always available. This particular type of a stack is called a "last in, first out" (LIFO) stack.

Data or instructions can be similarily "pushed" onto a stack and then later "popped" off. As long as the order is remembered, a very simple and efficient program results. Stack architectures are very powerful and are used very frequently in modern computer systems.

A different type of a stack, a "first in, first out" (FIFO) stack, is also used as a data buffer in digital systems. This type of a stack is also called a "queue."

Multiple processors

Today the problem is to discover new ways of optimally using the hardware complexity that has been made available with very large-scale integrated circuits (VLSI). With all of the circuitry that can be placed on one chip, it now becomes possible to make use of larger quantities of hardware than were economically justifiable in the past. The challenge is to effectively use this low-cost hardware in ways that will provide increased functionality for a computer. One of the early ways of adding hardware to improve performance was to provide more than one processor, a multiprocessor computer.

A processor is a component that is capable of interrupting the execution of an active program in order to execute a sequence of its own operations. Processors include the control to obtain instructions from a memory and to also interpret these instructions as operations to be carried out. The central processor unit (CPU) handles the main tasks of the computer, and slave processors support the CPU by handling I/O and other tasks. This is known as "distributed processing." In contrast with this, "parallel processing" uses multiple processors executing blocks of code in parallel to achieve even higher levels of system performance.

There is an emphasis today on using multiple processors within the same computer system to handle more difficult problems and also to increase the computational speed. Multiprocessor computer systems can be any one of the following:

1. Processors sharing a common memory (tightly coupled processors)
2. Processors communicating via messages but cooperating on one task (loosely coupled, distributed, multiple processors)

3. Independent computer systems interconnected to share information (networks)

Whenever two or more independent computers (as in item 3, above) are linked by communication lines, a "network" is formed. Various network structures are shown in Figure 5.34. The communication paths are indicated by the arrows. "Gateways" are used to allow connections from one network to another.

Various operating protocols have been proposed for these network structures. When the computers are near each other, a local area network (LAN) can be set up.

There are various ways of communicating between computers in a network. The simplest is like a telephone connection (called "circuit switching") in which there is a succession of point-to-point links connecting the source of the information with the destination. This usually involves a slow rate of information flow and is not an efficient use of the communication channels. It also suffers when handling short messages because of the excessive time taken to set up the links.

To improve upon the utilization of the communication channels, "message switching" is used in which each message is bundled with extra bits to indicate the source and the destination. Complete individual messages can be stored, if necessary, before being forwarded to the final destination. This is referred to as "store and forward."

A more efficient technique is called "packet switching," in which each message is divided into many individual packets that each carry rout-

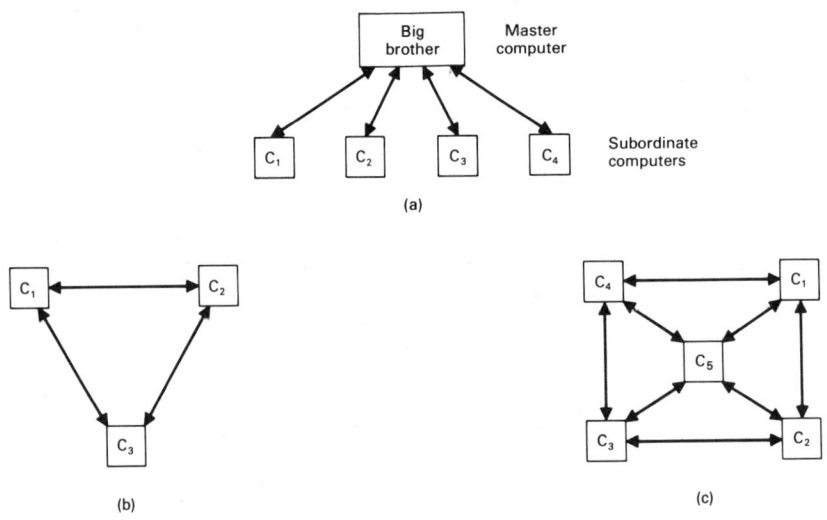

Figure 5.34 Network structures. (a) Hierarchical, (b) ring, and (c) star.

ing information. These packets can then be independently routed; a communication channel will not have to be continuously tied up for the transmission of the complete message.

Many schemes have been proposed to solve the dominant economic problem of communication now that many low-cost computer systems are available.

Programming: The Software Some Find Hard

Programming a digital computer is the craft that creates the sequence of instructions that a computer follows in order to provide a useful overall function. Programs are referred to as "software" (but when software is placed into a hardware ROM memory device, it is then called "firmware").

The generation of good software is very important. A major requirement in software is that it must be "user friendly"; that is, easy to work with, without "glitches" or tiresome procedures required of the user.

Many companies have come into existence to provide software as a service. Software can be purchased from these companies to do such operations as word processing, income tax preparation, accounts handling, and other business-related and games-related functions. Prepackaged software brings a computer system to life and allows it to perform useful functions without huge programming efforts on the part of each user.

Applications or systems

Software can be broken down into either "applications" or "systems" software. There are specialized groups of programmers working in both of these general areas of software generation.

Programs that allow a computer system to perform a useful function in a specific applications area are called applications software.

Systems software is concerned with making a computer more friendly to a user. This consists of programs for assemblers, translators, compilers (which will be discussed later), and other "utility" programs such as file handling systems, monitor systems, and other programs that make a computer more manageable or easier for people to work with.

As the number of these special programs grew and multiprogramming resource allocation problems appeared, these system programs were grouped into what is now called an "operating system." For example, an operating system manages the resources of a computer system, such as the memory space and the CPU time allocation, and also provides commonly used functions in ways that are easy for people to use.

Structured thought

In programming, the biggest requirement is to condition your thinking to be extremely logical and well organized in the approach to a problem. This helps provide programs with good structure.

The first act of programming is to understand the problem to be solved. Then a considerable amount of time is spent determining the most efficient ways to store and manipulate the data that are involved, considering the interfaces that are required with various users, deciding ways of inputting the data, and considering the best way to provide the required output from the computer.

In the earlier days of programming, flow charts were drawn to diagram the flow of the program. You still might hear of or see flow charts with symbols for decisions, inputs, and outputs. A special group of symbols was developed in support of flow charting. Today, because of the structured concept of the modern high-level computer languages, detailed flow charting has become almost obsolete.

Databases and nonnumeric processing

"Databases" and "database management programs" use a computer to process nonnumeric data. The basic difference between numeric processing and nonnumeric processing is that numeric processing deals with numbers and mathematical relations of these numbers. Nonnumeric processing deals with words, files of words, and symbols.

For example, a grouping of information about the people who are employed by an organization is called a personnel file. Within this file, the data about each employee may be listed on a card, as shown in Figure 5.35. This one card is called a "record." A "file" is therefore a collection of records. This same nomenclature is used in handling computer data.

In a large corporation, many different departments have requirements for data concerning the operation of the business. Data management programs are concerned with generating the records and also updating these records. Many different departments in large corporations keep many of the same types of records. This overlap in effort is a costly item for a company. Problems also exist because records are not updated with the same diligence by all departments.

All of this data (collectively called a database) is an asset of a corporation and represents a considerable investment of time and money. To reduce costs, data should be kept in one place and then everyone can access this common database. The expenses of maintaining the database can then be reduced because there is no longer duplication of effort. This is the idea behind databases and the software that is used to manage a database: the database management programs.

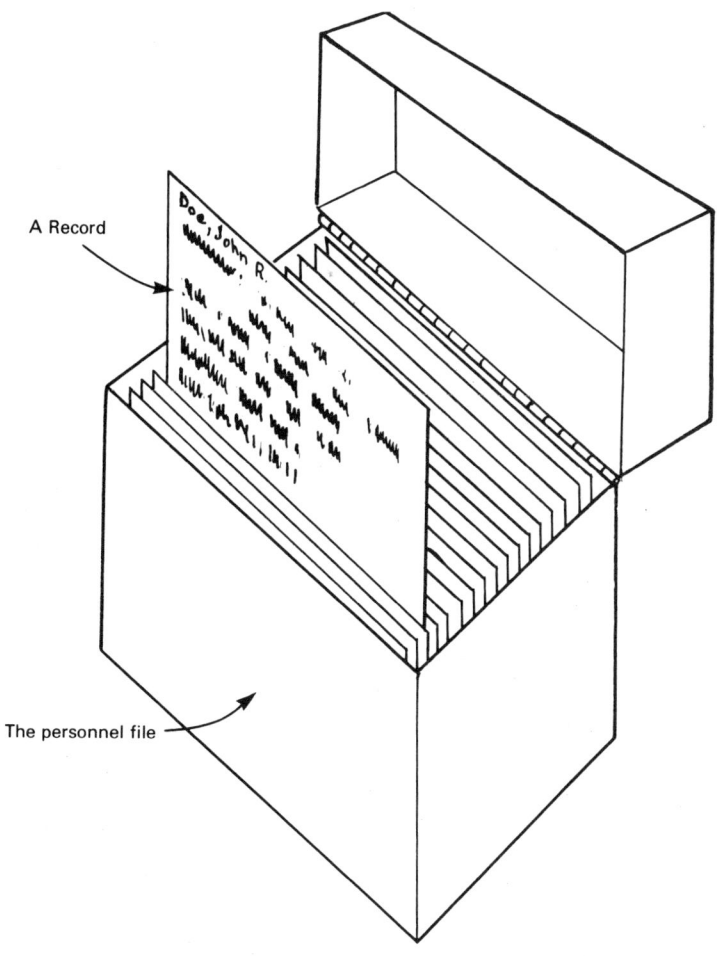

Figure 5.35 A 3 by 5 card file.

A good database management program allows information to be extracted relatively easily by the people who need to make use of the data. An additional goal of these programs is to provide a relatively simple programming language so that untrained people can easily ask questions about the data. The idea is to be able to derive information from the database in an easy manner without having to wait for an expert or a group of experts to write special programs.

Computer systems can maintain a file within memory in a manner similar to the example of a fixed-physical-location personnel file. This is diagrammed in a simplified way using locations on a wall, as shown in Figure 5.36. A block of sequential locations is shown that starts in the upper left-hand corner, proceeds vertically down the first column,

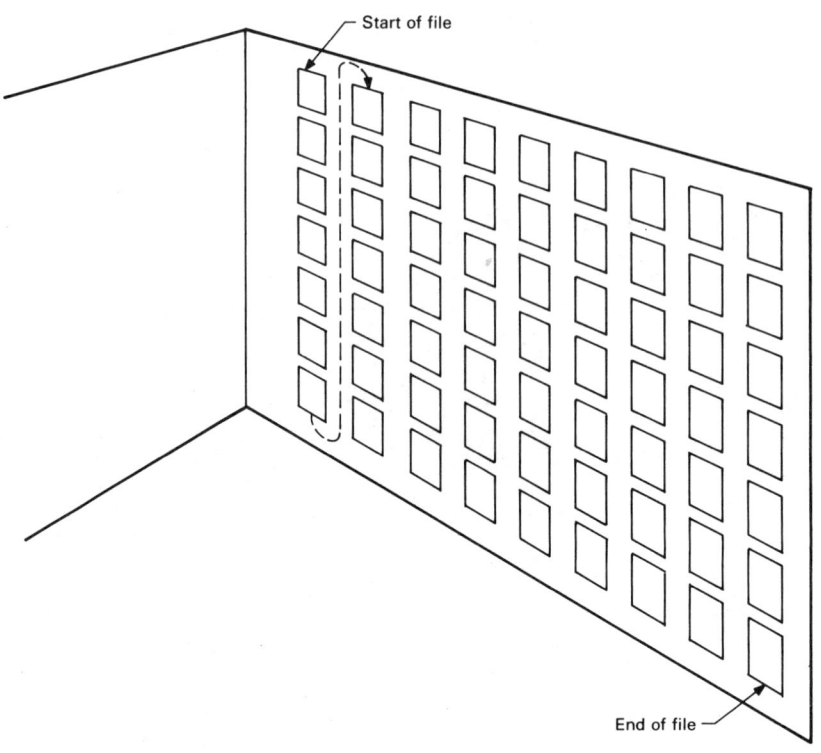

Figure 5.36 A fixed-physical-location file.

and then moves over and starts down the second column. The end of the file is indicated in the lower right-hand corner.

All of the problems of handling a 3 by 5 card file are also present when a computer stores a file. A file must be "opened" (transferred from secondary storage to primary storage, the computer RAM) and "closed" (returned, with updates, to secondary storage).

The operation of putting the records into an ordered sequence is called "sorting" and is shown in Figure 5.37. File maintenance involves sorting (after data has been added or deleted) to maintain the data in an orderly sequence. For example, one technique is that when new records are added, the first operation is to find the proper location for each of the new records, in turn, and then move all of the existing records to create a space for the new record.

The opposite problem of sorting is to find something when it is needed. This is the "searching" operation that is indicated in Figure 5.38.

As an example of searching for a word in the dictionary, your knowledge of the sequence of the alphabet allows you to open the dictionary at a place that is fairly close to the location of the word that you are

Figure 5.37 Sorting: putting records into an ordered sequence.

searching for. Then by seeing where you are after this first try, you know whether to go forward or backward in order to converge and find the exact word you are looking for. This same method of searching can be done by a computer to find a particular record out of a file.

There are a lot of software schemes available for sorting and searching. Many different techniques have been standardized and certain procedures are more efficient in particular applications. Part of the programmer's job is to be aware of the standard techniques and then to make use of an optimum one for each application.

What languages are spoken?

Computer programmers must communicate with a digital computer. They generate the instructions that the computer must follow in order to perform a useful overall function.

Whenever communication is involved, languages are needed. A basic problem is that the digital computer works with 1s and 0s, and people work with their native language. The goal of computer languages is to make it easy for human beings to create programs for a computer.

Figure 5.38 Searching: finding a particular record within a file.

High-level languages were developed because of the recognition of a basic problem of economics: programming and debugging costs were exceeding the cost of running a program. As computers became faster and cheaper, this economic imbalance became even worse.

We will now take a look at some of the popular computer languages and will start with the language that the computer operates with: "machine language."

The machine's code. The internal instructions for all digital computers are binary words that are decoded by the instruction register to provide the control functions that are necessary for the computer to execute that instruction. The problem is that there are a large number of these binary words that symbolize these instructions, and they are clumsy for human beings to work with. Early computers were programmed using this primitive machine language. This was cumbersome and difficult for the programmers.

A representation for the instructions that is closer to the English (or native) language is desired so that programmers will be less apt to make errors and also to reduce the amount of work that the programmers must do in creating programs.

A short course on foreign languages. Many computer languages have been developed. The reason for such a large number of languages is that computers are used in a wide range of applications. Business applications of computers are more easily programmed using a specific language that has been developed for business applications. Scientific uses of computers have languages that favor this specific application area. Special languages have also been developed to make other types of programs easier to generate.

Computer languages are constantly evolving. You may have heard of COBOL (COmmon Business-Oriented Language), which is predominantly used for business applications, and BASIC (Beginners' All-purpose Symbolic Instruction Code), which was developed as a vehicle to teach computer languages. BASIC has been extended and modified and is a popular language, especially in personal computers. Even some major computer manufacturers have adopted BASIC as their standard language.

More recently, Pascal (named for Blaise Pascal) was introduced and became popular because it is very structured and therefore tends to be "self-documenting." It is relatively easy for one programmer to quickly see what the originating programmer had in mind. Program documentation is a large problem. One programmer may originate a program, but as time goes on, the user will typically want a few additional features added or parts of the existing program may have to be modified. Programs have a tendency to grow with use, and it is therefore very important for the original author of a program to document the approach that was taken in an easily understood way so that the "maintenance programmer" can quickly see how to make any required revisions (this documentation problem will be discussed a little later on).

IBM's FORTRAN (FORmula TRANslation) was one of the early high-level languages, and it is still in use. There have been a number of modifications to it in the intervening years, and it also has become standardized.

The main reason for all programming languages is to provide an easy way for human beings to communicate with a computer. Therefore, languages more closely resembling human languages are desired.

Assembling, compiling, interpreting, and translating. A digital computer only understands the primitive machine-code representations for instructions. Therefore, when programmers work in a higher-level language, special utility programs have to be used to convert from these higher-level language statements to machine code. This is the job of the assemblers, compilers, and interpreters.

Chapter Five

"Assembly language" is the first step above machine language. Special acronyms are used for instructions rather than the binary words of machine language, for example, ADD (for addition), LD (for load), and JP (for jump). Assembly language is therefore more convenient to work with.

The rules for writing programs in assembly language are typically given in relatively large manuals, and, unfortunately, there are major differences from computer to computer. It is up to the programmer to precisely follow the details of these assembly-language statements so that a computer program called an "assembler" can "understand" what is written. The "syntax" (the exact details of each line of the code) has to be done correctly. If a mistake is made, a syntax error will be indicated to the programmer. This means that the programmer has left out a comma (or other required symbol), something is misspelled, or some other mistake has been made, and the computer has not been programmed to recognize this. Computers only understand what they have been programmed to understand. If the programmer makes a typing error, the computer will not find this misspelled statement within the list of "legal" (or allowed) statements, so the computer flags this as a syntax error.

People can more easily adapt to typographical errors, especially in textual material. This can cause a major problem with people unfamiliar with computers because they consider a computer to be much "smarter" than humans. This error-tolerance supremacy of a human is evident because even if every vowel is replaced with an "X," most people can still determine the meaning of: "XRX YXX HXVXNG XNY TRXXBLX RXXDXNG THXS SXNTXNCX?"

As mentioned earlier, assembly language programs are written using letter abbreviations for the operations to be performed. There are other benefits of using assembly language. For example, special symbols (called "labels") can be used to represent a particular line of code in a program so the programmer does not have to remember precisely where a specific section of the program exists. The programmer can simply give it a label and then let the computer take care of all of the details. In addition, labels can be used to represent data, such as constants. A label is simply assigned. This label can be an abbreviated form of the name of the constant. At the start of a program, the programmer states the values assigned to these labels. This makes it convenient because a programmer can deal with these simpler labels or even make changes in the numbers assigned to the labels, and the computer will sort out all of the details. Similarly, "symbolic addresses" can also be used to avoid concern for actual addresses during program generation.

Once a program is written in assembly language, an assembler program is used to convert the assembly language statements into the nitty-gritty details of machine language. The program, as it appears in assembly language, is called "source code." The conversion of this source code into machine language results in what is known as "object code." Object code consists of machine-language statements that can be executed by the computer system. If only the object code for a program exists, it is difficult to make modifications. But, if the source code exists, it is then relatively easy to understand what is taking place and to make major or minor changes to better suit a specific application.

Assembly language is a one-for-one substitution of a mnemonic language for the machine language, so it is still a relatively primitive language. Higher-level languages use single instructions that may require the execution of a relatively large number of machine-language instructions.

Higher-level languages, such as FORTRAN, Pascal, ALGOL, and COBOL, are therefore more difficult to convert into machine language. Special systems-level programs are available to do this conversion. These are called "compilers." It may not be obvious why the word compiler is used because to compile means to compose out of materials from other documents. This word originated because programmers would reuse short sequences of computer code that they had previously written. Today, this definition no longer applies for a compiler program, but programs written in high-level languages first must pass through a compiler to generate the object code.

"Interpreting" is very similar to the function that an interpreter performs among people who speak different languages. The interpreter has to be present when the conversation is taking place. Digital computers make use of special programs called "interpreters" that are resident in the machine while the higher-level language program is being executed. The technique, therefore, is that each line of code from the higher-level language is passed, in turn, to the interpreter program. The interpreter program then deciphers each line of code and converts it into machine language, which is then executed. When an interpreter is used, programs take longer to execute. Most of the computers that use BASIC make use of interpreters.

A major benefit of operating with an interpreter is that the program can be easily modified as it is being used. Changes can be made and the program can then be run again, because separate assembling or compiling operations are not required.

"Translators" are special systems programs that allow converting from one high-level language to another.

Getting the "bugs" out

If a programmer makes an error in a program, this error is called a "bug." When programs are first written (and tried out on a computer system), many times some errors have to be cleaned up. This operation is often referred to as "getting the bugs out of a program," or "debugging the program." Bugs can be relatively simple mistakes, or they can be major errors that require extensive changes. Debugging a program that was written by somebody else is often very difficult because it may not be clear what the original author had in mind. Much time has to be spent to understand what was originally intended before a problem can be found.

Tell me what you had in mind

Programs are very dynamic. It is rare that a program is written, put into service, and never changed. Almost every program has many changes within its operating life. Therefore, it becomes essential that the authors of the original program provide extensive documentation so that a maintenance programmer can rapidly understand the approach that has been taken. In order to modify or update a program, you first have to understand the original ideas involved to make sure that your changes will not create additional problems.

Documentation of programs is actually more costly than the original writing of the program. Today, there is a large emphasis on working with self-documenting programming languages because the flow of the problem solution is more evident. These are the structured languages, such as Pascal. These languages reduce the expensive documentation effort and also make work easier for maintenance programmers.

In the early days of programming, achieving a short computer run time was very important. Programmers went out of their way to be clever and to write programs in strange ways so that the program would execute faster. Today, computer time is not as important as programmers' time. The emphasis has therefore entirely changed to encouraging the use of longer programs, more memory, or whatever is necessary to make the program easier to write, easier to understand, and easier to maintain. This current trend is a major shift in the objectives and goals of programmers.

With a better understanding of computer technology, the obvious next question you may ask is, "Where is this all going?" We will now try to answer this with the final chapter, "A Look into the Future."

Chapter

6

A Look into the Future

The rapid development of integrated circuits has tremendously reduced the cost of all digital systems. Ever since the semiconductor era began with the transistor, there has been a continual utilization of these smaller, more energy-efficient, solid-state devices to allow producing complex digital systems. In general, digital systems require a larger number of transistors than is needed in a competing linear system. The large circuit-complexity advances of low-cost integrated circuits has allowed digital systems to be used in a wide range of applications. Some of these applications have previously used linear systems approaches.

In the future, expect to see a continuing emphasis on dense low-power digital circuitry. It is vital that the power drain of the digital circuitry be kept very small; this is the key that popularized CMOS processes and allows large chips for complex digital systems. Technologists are predicting a 1-billion-transistor chip by the year 2000.

Gate Arrays and Beyond

In the not too distant past, digital systems were built by assembling standard building-block ICs that were available from the semiconductor companies. Therefore, the digital engineers were somewhat limited in what they could build because of high cost and the limited set of building blocks that were provided for them to work with. There is a major shift away from this approach, because the digital systems designers are now taking complete responsibility for their systems.

One of the first ways to provide complex ICs for digital systems is known as "gate arrays." A gate array is a complex semiconductor product consisting of a very large number of transistors that have the capability of being custom wired (at the chip level) to provide a wide range of customer-specific logic functions.

The complexity of a gate array is measured in terms of the number of gates (transistor groupings) that are available. CMOS processes are predominantly used in the highest-complexity gate array products because of the low-power drain of CMOS logic circuits.

Gate arrays are somewhat limited because only a particular number of transistors are available on each standard chip size. Customization is accomplished by controlling the last three layers: the first layer of metal (that interconnects the individual transistors), an insulating layer over this first metal layer with holes (called "vias," used to contact between the metal layers), and a second layer of metal (for the overall interconnection that provides the desired logic function).

Beyond gate arrays are "cell arrays", which allow more freedom to the system designers. With gate arrays, the transistors cannot be relocated, but cell arrays allow the system designers to have almost a completely custom chip.

The day is rapidly approaching when very large complexities within digital systems can be provided at low cost by the semiconductor manufacturers. This is forcing the systems architects to come up with ways in which this increase in circuit complexity can provide significant benefits, such as improved testability and maintainability, simplified user interfacing (such as providing human speech, both synthesis and recognition), and higher processing speeds.

Interconnecting Computers

In the past, when computers were relatively expensive, a computer system would operate entirely on its own. Today, as computers are becoming very commonplace, it is becoming important to find ways of interconnecting computers so that computers (and people using computers) can communicate with each other. This has increased interest in "local area networks" (LANs) to provide communication between computers. Data is usually centralized within these networks and a "file server" is used to control the distribution and storage of data.

An example of this interconnection of computers is to have a number of relatively small computers (even personal computers) operating on individuals' desks. If a larger program or a larger database must be accessed, the interconnecting network will allow these smaller computers to communicate with a larger "host" computer, in which more complex processing can be accomplished in a shorter interval of time or a larger amount of data is available. In addition, one computer might communicate with another computer by operating under the control of a main host computer. You will hear of many ways of allowing multiple computers to exist within the same environment. You will also hear of "computer conferencing" in which people sit at terminals and converse with each other using their computers, without leaving their offices.

As more people use computers, there is a growing tendency to think of a computer as a companion, even a friend. This is expected to escalate when human speech synthesis and recognition are added as I/O devices.

The Electronic Office

Computers are solving many of the communication problems that exist within business offices. For example, "electronic mail" allows any member of an office to originate memos that are then automatically routed to particular members within the office. Electronic mail eliminates paper (and the delivering of paper) because messages are transmitted over an interconnecting network between the computers.

Typewriters are also rapidly becoming obsolete because computers (with word processor programs) can easily correct errors and provide many other benefits to a typist. For example, multiple letters or letters with slight modifications can be more efficiently produced.

Workstations

With continual computer support for workers, each worker will be provided a complete customized computer-based "workstation." These workstations will consist of the computer-type hardware that is most beneficial for each particular job. Rudimentary workstations got started with automatic testing in which electronic test equipment was automatically controlled by a computer using the "Hewlett-Packard interface bus" (HPIB, which was later standardized as IEEE-488). Even a PC can serve as the test controller to greatly assist the electrical testing problem.

A wide range of workstations will be available. For example, a workstation for a digital systems designer will provide the capability of "computer-aided engineering" (CAE), so that an optimum system design can be achieved. In addition, a relatively large screen will be available to display logic diagrams, time delays of critical paths, simulated functioning, and also any selected input and output voltage waveforms. Systems can be implemented with any desired mix of standard, custom, or semicustom ICs.

The ultimate for the system designers is what is known as "silicon compilation." This involves a high-level language that the designer uses to specify the block diagram and other high-level descriptions of the ICs' architecture, and then all the details of circuit design, performance simulation, and chip layout are handled by the computer. It is almost necessary for computer support to help the digital IC chip designers because the tremendous amount of detailed work that is involved is about at the limit of human patience and concentration.

Computers are similarly assisting the manufacturers with "computer-aided design" and "computer-aided manufacturing" (CAD/CAM). These sophisticated computer programs not only assist the mechanical engineers with computer-aided engineering (CAE), but they also automatically program the numerically controlled production machinery and even the robotic units that do the assembly. This spread of computers into the design, development, and production of both electrical and mechanical systems is moving to what is called "computer-aided integrated manufacturing" (CIM), in which artificial intelligence systems (the subject of a later section) are involved in all aspects of product development and production.

Graphics

Graphics is the output that provides complex displays for a human operator. A simple computer terminal typically presents typed characters that look like a page out of a typewriter. In addition, some of these systems can also provide a graphics option in which complex drawings are provided. The big move in graphics is to make use of large full-color screens with high resolution of the displayed images.

The Electronic Home

The widespread introduction of personal computers into homes initially satisfied everyone's curiosity about computers and also introduced computer games. Computers are now moving into a control phase. Homes can use computers as part of their burglar alarm system and as control for lighting, heating, and air conditioning. Once a computer system exists in a home, it has the capability to do many useful functions (because of the relatively small computer usage that is required by any of these control functions). Sprinkler systems for the yard and garden can be controlled, and a computer can be combined with a telephone to provide a very sophisticated communications system. Remembering dates and appointments can also be handled by a computer (instead of using appointment books and calendars). The tutoring of students is now also accomplished by use of special programs and computers.

A computer can use telephone lines to access large databases. You no longer have to go to a library to research material or call your broker to find out the latest stock quotations. A computer can interrogate a large database and provide any type of information that you may need. In fact, computers are being rapidly used in the telecom area and this is revolutionizing the former role of the telephone and adding many advances in the area of communication.

"Electronic shopping" has been introduced in which an at-home customer views selected merchandise that is shown on the display of his or her computer and then also uses the computer to place an order. There will be an increasing number of applications for computers in the home once computers become as common as television sets.

Artificial Intelligence

In the future, "artificial intelligence" is expected to dominate the field of computers. Artificial intelligence has been defined as the simulation of human skills and personality. Many researchers are working in this area. They are trying to determine the limits of computers. Can computers think? Can they compose original music? Can they invent? Can they do a lot of the mental functions that have been considered to be only possible with human beings?

Programs have been written to explore artificial intelligence (AI) that are self-adaptive, that learn from experience, that have exploratory routines, and that even have random functions built-in. The AI languages (LISP and PROLOG) can also write and/or modify programs that they execute. The programmer is therefore often surprised by the output produced by these programs. For true AI, a computer must think like a human, that is, plan, solve problems, actually *understand* a language, and finally it must be able to write a novel or compose music and to then realize that it has done this.

The computer complexity and the large memories that are available allow experimenting with complex programs, such as attempts to simulate the operation of a human brain. The human brain represents a large database that can be accessed in very strange ways. For example, an inventor working on a problem in one area, say, mechanical engineering, can think of something that he or she remembered from optics or hydraulics and can then make use of that same fundamental engineering principle to solve a problem in a different area. This ability of the human mind to rapidly cross back and forth, intermix data, perceive the essence, and invent new things is being studied to determine if there can be some way of programming this or at least lending more understanding to some of these mystical human processes. Much effort is being expended and the initial results are promising, but the power of the brain remains several orders of magnitude beyond even the most powerful computer of today.

Here Come the Robots

Whenever robots are mentioned, it is very common to think of a mechanical replacement for a complete human being: a mechanism that walks, has a head, arms and legs, and in many other ways replicates the human form and function. The name for a machine that closely resembles a human is an "android." Modern robots (that are used in manufacturing areas) are not based on this complete human replication. They consist of essentially the functioning of one arm with a simulated hand attached at the end. These computer-controlled mechanisms provide motion, and they can pick up and place (assemble) objects, position welders, operate tools, and in other ways replace rote human work on an assembly line.

Robots are being used in essentially all types of manufacturing areas. Robots are used by the automotive companies and are even at work in semiconductor fabrication lines.

A number of research teams are working on a computer-based walking biped. Walking is a very difficult function. Machines can now walk in a straight line or climb stairs, but walking over rough ground, turning around, and negotiating obstacles is still very difficult.

The age of robots is definitely here. This field is moving rapidly and represents the final evolution of the computer, from simply a device that *manipulates data* to a device that is exercising control and *manipulating things*. More of the tedious human tasks are becoming obsolete. We are well on our way toward automated factories and a new era for mankind in this escalation of the computer age.

Index

Access time, 183
Accumulator, 201, 210
Acknowledge an interrupt, 227
Acoustical coupling for a modem, 181
Active components, 16
Adaptive equalizers, 181
Address, symbolic, 238
Address bus, 209
Address bus control, 210
Addressing memory, 212–216
   extended addressing, 215
   immediate addressing, 214
   immediate, extended addressing, 214
   indexed addressing, 215
   register indirect addressing, 215
   relative addressing, 214
Algorithm, 120
Alternators, 27
Amperes, 56
Analog switch, 165
Analog-to-digital (A/D) converters, 142
AND gate, 124
Android, 246
Anode ("arrowhead"), 91
Application software, 231
Architecture of the computer, 228
   Harvard, 228
   stored-program (Von Neumann), 228
Arithmetic and logic unit (ALU), 205
Arithmetic shift, 207
Armature, 35
Artificial Intelligence (AI), 245
Assembler, 238
Assembly language, 238
Asserting an interrupt, 227
Asynchronous communication, 178
Attenuator (*see* Resistors, in voltage divider)

Baker clamp, 149
Base:
   of a number system, 116
   of a transistor, 101
BASIC (Beginner's All-Purpose Instruction Code), 237
Batteries, 22
   Ni-Cad, 22
   storage, 22
Baud rate, 181
Bell 103 standard, 181
Beta (β), 104
Binary addition, 119
Binary-coded decimal (BCD) code, 138
Binary digits (bits), 113
Binary number system, 113
Bistable circuit (*see* Flip-flops)
Boron, 93
"Bug," 239
Built-in electric field, 80
Built-in voltage, 80
Bus, 156
   address, 209
   data, 208, 216
   internal, 210, 217
Byte, 177

Cadmium-sulfide (Cd-S) photocell, 47–49
Capacitors, 67
   breakdown voltage of, 73
   dc leakage current of, 71
   disc ceramic, 70
   electrolytic, 69
   within an IC, 69
   made from common materials, 74
   in parallel (shunt), 70
   to provide voltage memory, 72
   as reservoirs, 81
   in series, 70

248 Index

Capacitors (*Cont.*):
  stray or parasitic, 84
  variable, 70
  voltage rating of, 73
Carbon, 5
Carries in addition, 116
Cathode, 91
Cathode-ray tube (CRT), 189
Cell arrays, 242
Cells, 22
  primary, 22
  secondary, 22
  solar, 28
Charge, 80
  fixed, 95
Chemical compounds, 2
Chemical reactions, 3
Circuit switching, 230
Clear input of a flip-flop, 169
Clock, 161, 168
  internal, 218
  real-time, 227
COBOL (Common Business-Oriented Language), 237
Codes, 137–142
  American Stancard Code for Information Interchange (ASCII), 141
  binary-coded decimal (BCD), 138
  hexadecimal, 139
  illegal, 138
  two's complement, 137
Collector of a transistor, 101
Combinational logic, 161
Communication:
  parallel, 182
  serial, 178
Compilers, 239
Complementary metal-oxide semiconductor (CMOS) transistor, 150
  D-type flip flop, 168, 172
  flow-through latch, 167
  logic inverter, 152
  NAND gate, 155
  NOR gate, 156
  transmission gate, 165
Computer-aided design/computer-aided manufacturing (CAD/CAM), 244
Computer-aided engineering (CAE), 243
Computer-aided integrated manufacturing (CIM), 244
Computer conferencing, 243
Concurrent operation, 195
Conductor, 6

Control and timing for microprocessor, 210
Control bus, 192
Control-oriented processors, 194
Cords:
  electrical, 41
  lamp, 41
  zip, 41
Coulomb, 56
Counter, "ripple," 174
Covalent bond, 3
Cross coupling, 107
Crystals, valence, 6
Current, 21, 25, 56
  alternating (ac), 39
  direct (dc), 39
  measuring directly, 58
  measuring indirectly, 60
Current gain of a transistor, 87

Data bus, 208, 216
Database, 232
Database management program, 232
Debouncing (switches), 164
Decoding, 144
  one-of-N decoders, 144
Decoding matrix, 144
Demodulation, 180
Diamond, 6
Dielectric, 67, 69
  Teflon, 88
Dielectric constant, 72
Digital-to-analog converter (DAC), 145
Diode(s), 10, 95–99
  AND gate, 92
  built-in voltage, 96
  collector-base, 102
  emitter-base, 102
  with forward voltage, 80
  germanium, 99
  light-emitting (LEDs), 191
  OR gate, 91
  PN, 3, 9, 79
  reverse current of, 99
  with reverse voltage, 80
  Schottky, 150
Displacement, 214
Displays, 189
  alphanumeric, 189
  cathode-ray tubes (CRTs), 189
  dot-matrix, 189
  liquid crystal (LCDs), 191
  segmental, 189

Displays (*Cont.*):
   vacuum fluorescent (VF), 192
Distributed processing, 229
Documentation of a program, 240
Doped silicon, 8
   N-type, 9
   P-type, 9
Drain of a FET, 151
Drop-in errors, 188
Drop-out errors, 188

Edge triggering, 168
Electric field, 73
Electrical energy, 65
Electronic circuit, 16
Electronic mail, 243
Electronic Project Kit, 17
Electronics, 1
Electrons, 2
  mobile, 7
  outermost, 3
  spare, 9
Elements, 1
Emitter, 101
Encoding, 137
   analog-to-digital (A/D) converters, 142
   RS-232C, 179
   self-clocking, 178
Equalizers, 181
   adaptive, 181
Ethane, 5
Executing instructions, 223
Exponent, 11
Exponential curve, 82

Fall time, 122
Fanout, 128
Farad, 69
Feature size in ICs, 187
Fetching from memory, 223
Field-effect transistors (FET), 99
   N-channel, 151
   P-channel, 152
Filament, 47
File, 232
File server, 242
Firmware, 231
Fixed-program computer, 207
Flip-flops, 161
  astable, 107
  bistable, 107
  carry (in serial adder), 198

Flip-flops (*Cont.*):
  clear input, 169
  cross coupling in, 107
  D-type (in CMOS), 168, 174
  JK, 174
  master-slave, 171
  monostable (one-shot), 109
  primitive RS, 106
  RS, 173
  T, 174
Flow chart, 232
FORTRAN (Formula Translation), 237
Forward bias, 96
Forward voltage, 96
Fragmentation in memory, 185
Full-scale range, 16
Functional logic diagrams, 131

Gate arrays, 241
Gates:
  AND, 124
  exclusive NOR, 127
  exclusive OR, 126
  of a FET, 151
  logic inverter (NOT), 123
    in CMOS, 152
  NAND, 125
    in CMOS, 155
  NOR, 126
    in CMOS, 156
  OR, 125
Gateways, 230
Germanium, 7
Germanium diodes, 99
Graphics, 244
Ground, 32

"Handshake," 178
Heat sink, 100
"Hermaphrodite" elements, 5
Hold time, 172
Hole, 9
"Hook connection," 110
Hydrogen atom, 2

Illegal state, 173
Immediate addressing, 214
Incandescent light, 41
  cold resistance of, 47
Indecision in a digital circuit, 123

Instruction(s):
  bit manipulations (bit "twiddling"), 222
  block transfer, 221
  call, 222
  conditional jump, 223
  decoding, 209
  exchange, 221
  executing, 223
  fetching, 223
  input/output (I/O), 223
  interrupt, 227
  jump, 222
  load, 221
  return, 222
  search, 221
  typical, 220
  unconditional jump, 222
Instruction location counter, 210
Instruction pointer, 210
Instruction register, 210
Interpreters, 239
Interrupt, 227
  masked, 227
  nonmaskable, 227
Interrupt-driven I/O device, 227
Inverter, 123

Kilo, 14
Kilowatthour, 65

Languages, 235
  machine, 236
Latch circuit, 161
  flow-through (CMOS), 167
  RS (using NAND gates), 162
  RS (using NOR gates), 162
Latch up, 110
Latency time, 187
Least-significant bits (LSBs), 142
Level triggering a flip-flop, 171
Levels of logic, 173
Light-emitting diodes (LEDs), 191
Lightning, 74
Line cords, 41
Liquid crystal displays (LCDs), 191
Load, 78
Load control for a register, 212
Local area networks (LANs), 242
Logic:
  0 state, 113
  1 state, 113

Logic (*Cont.*):
  CMOS circuits, 150
  combinational, 161
  levels of, 173
  negative, 121
  positive, 121
  right rotate, 206
  right shift, 205
  sequential, 162
  simplifying, 133
  tri-state (TSL), 157
  voltage levels of (in CMOS), 154
Logic diagrams:
  actual, 132
  functional, 131
Logic inverter (CMOS), 152

Magnetic tape, 188
Mainframe computers, 195
Major carry, 116
Mark, 179
Master-slave flip-flop, 171
Mega, 14
Memory, 182
  access time, 183
  addressing (*see* Addressing memory)
  associative, 186
  back-up, 182, 188
  cache, 185
  content addressable, 186
  contiguous, 185
  coordinate addressed, 186
  disk, 186
  dynamic RAM (DRAM), 183
  electrically erasable and programmable ROM (E^2PROM), 184
  erasable programmable ROM (EPROM), 184
  fetching from, 223
  flexible (floppy) disk, 186
  fragmentation in, 185
  integrated RAM (iRAM), 183
  magnetic tape, 188
  mapped I/O, 226
  nonvolatile, 184
  optical, 188
  page select, 212
  primary, 182
  programmable ROM (PROM), 184
  RAM (R/W), 183
  read only (ROM), 183
  rigid (hard) disk, 186
  R/W (RAM), 183

Memory (*Cont.*):
　secondary, 182, 186
　static RAM (SRAM), 183
　streamers, 188
　virtual, 185
　volatile, 184
Memory address register (MAR), 210, 223
Memory buffer register (MBR), 210, 224
Message switching, 230
Metric prefixes, 14
Micro, 15
Microcomputers, 194
Microfarad, 69
Microprocessors, 194, 208
Microprogrammable computer, 208
Milli, 14
Minterms, 133
Modem, 180
　acoustical coupling for a, 181
　Bell 103 Standard, 181
　direct connection interface, 181
Modulation, 180
Modulus of a counter, 175
Multiple processors, 229
Multiplicand, 201
Multiplication by successive addition, 201–205
　for binary numbers, 204
　for decimal numbers, 201
Multiplier, 201
Multiprocessing, 209
Multivibrator (*see* Flip-flops)

NAND gate, 125
　in CMOS, 155
Nano, 15
Nanofarad, 69
Negative logic, 121
Network, 230
Neutrons, 2
Nibble, 177
Nonvolatile storage (memory), 184
NOR gate, 126
　in CMOS, 155
　exclusive, 127
NOT gate, 123
　in CMOS, 152
Nucleus, 2

Object code, 239
Ohmmeter, 45

Ohm's law, 59
One's complement, 120
Operand, 214
Operating system, 231
OR gate, 125
　exclusive, 126
Oscillator (astable multivibrator), 107
Overflow in addition, 116
Overhead bits, 180
Oxygen, atom of, 3

Packet switching, 230
Page select in memory, 212
Parallel communication, 182
Parallel processing, 229
Parity:
　even, 179
　odd, 179
Parity bit, 179
Pascal, 237
Passive components, 16
Phosphorus, 93
Photocell, cadmimum-sulfide (Cd-S), 47–49
Photovoltaic effect, 28
Pico, 15
Picofarad, 69
Piezoelectric effect, 27, 89
Pixel, 191
Plotters, 193
PN junction, 10
　(*See also* Diode, PN)
Polling, 227
Popped off a stack, 229
Positional weighting, 115
Positive logic, 121
Potentiometer (*see* Resistors, potentiometer)
Power, 64
Power drain of home appliances, 67
Primary memory, 182
Printers, 192
　daisy wheel, 192
　dot-matrix, 192
　impact, 192
　ink jet, 193
　laser, 193
　thermal, 193
Program Counter (PC), 210
Programmed I/O, 227
Propagation delay, 123
Protocol, 178
Protons, 2

"Puff," 69
Pull-up resistor, 147
Push onto a stack, 229

Queue (*see* Stacks)

Race condition, 163
Raster scan, 189
Read strobe, 212
Record, 232
Refreshing a RAM, 183
Regeneration, 110, 159, 163
Registers:
    index, 215
    key, 196
    scratch pad, 185
    shift, 197
    working, 184
Relative addressing, 214
Relay, 34
Resistance, source, 62
Resistors, 39
    in an attenuator, 45
    color code, 44
    fixed, 39
    homemade carbon-film, 53
    in parallel (shunt), 49
    potentiometer, 37, 50, 55
    pull-up, 147
    rheostat, 39
    in series, 49
    temperature coefficient, 55
    temperature effects on, 55
    tolerance, 41
    in voltage divider, 49
Rheostat (variable resistor), 39
"Ripple" counter, 174
Rise time, 122
Robots, 246
RS-232C interface, 179

Saturation of a transistor, 149
Scaling factor, 11
Scheduler, 195
Schmitt trigger, 160
Schottky diode, 150
Scientific notation, 10
Searching, 234
Seek time, 187
Self-clocking in a code, 178
Self-time constant, 88

Semiconductors, 7
Send control for a register, 212
Sequential logic, 162
Serial adder, 198
Serial communication, 178
Serial-to-parallel converter, 198
Set-up time, 172
Shells of electrons, 2
Sign bit, 137
Silicon, 7
Silicon compilation, 243
Silicon-controlled rectifier (SCR), 110
Software, 231
    application, 231
    systems, 231
Solar cells, 28
Sorting, 234
Source of a FET, 151
Source code, 239
Source resistance, 62
Space, 179
Stacks, 229
    first in, first out (FIFO), 229
    last in, first out (LIFO), 229
Start bit, 180
Stop bit, 180
Storage (*see* Memory)
Store and forward, 230
Stored-program computer, 207
Streamers, 188
Strings, 141
Subroutines, 222
Symbolic addresses, 238
Synchronous communication, 178
Syntax, 238

Teflon dielectric, 88
Thunder, 74
Time constant, 82
    self-, 88
Time-delay circuit, 88
Timesharing of computers, 195
Toilet as a one-shot multivibrator, 110
Transistor(s), 99
    action of, 103
    bipolar, 99
    current gain (β) of, 104
    as an electronic switch, 105
    field-effect (FET), 99
    heat sinks for, 100
    leads of, 84
    N-channel, 151
    NPN, 101

Transistor(s) (*Cont.*):
  P-channel, 152
  packages for, 83
  PNP, 101
  (*See also* Complementary metal-oxide semiconductor transistor)
Transistor-transistor logic (T^{2}L), 146
Translators, 239
Transmission gate (CMOS), 165
Triac, 110
Triboelectricity, 27
Trigger voltage, 127
Triggering:
  edge, 168
  level, 171
Truth table, 123
Two's complement of a binary number, 120
Two's complement code, 137

User friendly programs, 231
Utility programs, 231

Valence crystals, 6
Vector scan, 190
Vias in IC layout, 242
Volatile storage (memory), 184
Voltage, 21
  built-in, 96
  forward, 96
  reverse, 96
  trigger (of a logic gate), 147
Voltage memory, 87
Voltage source, 62

Water molecule, 3
Water pressure, 25
Watt, 64
Winchester disk technology, 187
Word(s):
  long, 178
  quad, 178
Word size, 178
Workstations, 243
Write strobe, 212

ABOUT THE AUTHOR

Thomas M. Frederiksen, engineer, author, and seminar leader, founded his own company, Intuitive IC Seminars, to provide instruction to electronic design engineers and the many nonelectronically educated people who either work for, or with, a high-technology electronic company.

Upon earning his BSEE degree from California Polytechnic State University at San Luis Obispo, Frederiksen started his professional career as a development engineer with the Motorola Systems Development Laboratory. Subsequently he worked with the Microelectronics Group at Hughes Semiconductor Division and later became a senior project engineer at Motorola Semiconductor Products Division. Mr. Frederiksen then joined National Semiconductor Corporation, Santa Clara, California, where he developed custom ICs and standard single-supply building-block circuits for automotive and industrial applications. He designed the popular Quads: LM3900, LM324, and LM339. The LM324 is today's most popular operational amplifier. He has also been involved with analog-to-digital converters that will interface to microprocessors and other data acquisition circuits.

Mr. Frederiksen is the author of five books: *Intuitive IC Electronics*, *Intuitive CMOS Electronics*, and *Intuitive Op Amps* for engineers and technicians and *Intuitive Digital Computer Basics* and *Intuitive Analog Electronics*, which introduce the basics of electronics and also digital and analog circuits and systems, for nonelectronic professionals.

Mr. Frederiksen holds more than 40 patents on linear ICs and devices, has been a frequent contributor to the professional literature, and has given many major seminars on linear ICs for both Motorola and National Semiconductor within the United States and Canada and abroad. In 1977 he received the International Solid State Circuits Conference Best Paper Award.